ARI
and
NEW MEXICO
BIRDS

Kurt Radamaker
Cindy Radamaker
Gregory Kennedy

LONE
PINE

Lone Pine Publishing International

The Distributor: Lone Pine Publishing
1808 B Street NW, Suite 140
Auburn, WA, USA 98001

Website: www.lonepinepublishing.com

Library and Archives Canada Cataloguing in Publication

Radamaker, Kurt A. (Kurt Allan) 1960-
    Arizona and New Mexico birds / Kurt A. Radamaker, Cindy Radamaker, Gregory Kennedy

Includes bibliographical references and indexes.
ISBN-13: 978-976-8200-28-0
ISBN-10: 976-8200-28-6

    1. Birds--Arizona--Identification. 2. Birds—New Mexico--Identification.
I. Radamaker, Cindy II. Kennedy, Gregory, 1956- III. Title.

QL684.A6R33 2007   598.09791   C2007-901241-8

Cover Illustration: Western Meadowlark, by Gary Ross
Illustrations: Gary Ross, Ted Nordhagen, Ewa Pluciennik, Diane Hollingdale

PC:14

CONTENTS

DEDICATION

Dedicated to our parents H.H Biggers Jr., Carol Heuermann, Patricia Radamaker and Theodore Radamaker for nurturing our life long interest in birds.

— Kurt & Cindy Radamaker

ACKNOWLEDGMENTS

We thank Troy Corman for his invaluable assistance with the range maps.

—Kurt & Cindy Radamaker

Thanks are also extended to the growing family of ornithologists and dedicated birders who have offered their inspiration and expertise to help build Lone Pine's expanding library of field guides. Thanks also go to John Acorn, Chris Fisher, Andy Bezener and Eloise Pulos for their contributions to previous books in this series. In addition, thank you to Gary Ross, Ted Nordhagen, Ewa Pluciennik and Diane Hollingdale, whose skilled illustrations have brought each page to life.

Snow Goose
size 31 in • p. 20

Canada Goose
size 35 in • p. 21

American Wigeon
size 20 in • p. 22

Mallard
size 24 in • p. 23

Cinnamon Teal
size 16 in • p. 24

Northern Shoveler
size 19 in • p. 25

Northern Pintail
size 23 in • p. 26

Redhead
size 20 in • p. 27

Ring-necked Duck
size 16 in • p. 28

Common Merganser
size 25 in • p. 29

Ruddy Duck
size 15 in • p. 30

Blue Grouse
size 19 in • p. 31

Scaled Quail
size 11 in • p. 32

Gambel's Quail
size 10 in • p. 33

Montezuma Quail
size 8 in • p. 34

Pied-billed Grebe
size 13 in • p. 35

Eared Grebe
size 13 in • p. 36

Western Grebe
size 22 in • p. 37

American White Pelican
size 60 in • p. 38

Double-crested Cormorant
size 29 in • p. 39

Great Blue Heron
size 52 in • p. 40

Great Egret
size 39 in • p. 41

Green Heron
size 18 in • p. 42

Black-crowned Night-Heron
size 24 in • p. 43

White-faced Ibis
size 22 in • p. 44

Turkey Vulture
size 29 in • p. 45

Osprey
size 24 in • p. 46

Mississippi Kite
size 14 in • p. 47

Bald Eagle
size 37 in • p. 48

Northern Harrier
size 20 in • p. 49

Cooper's Hawk
size 17 in • p. 50

Common Black-Hawk
size 21 in • p. 51

Harris's Hawk
size 23 in • p. 52

Zone-tailed Hawk
size 19 in • p. 53

Red-tailed Hawk
size 21 in • p. 54

Golden Eagle
size 35 in • p. 55

American Kestrel
size 8 in • p. 56

Prairie Falcon
size 16 in • p. 57

Sora
size 9 in • p. 58

American Coot
size 14 in • p. 59

Sandhill Crane
size 45 in • p. 60

Killdeer
size 10 in • p. 61

Black-necked Stilt
size 14 in • p. 62

American Avocet
size 17 in • p. 63

Greater Yellowlegs
size 14 in • p. 64

Spotted Sandpiper
size 7 in • p. 65

Least Sandpiper
size 6 in • p. 66

Long-billed Dowitcher
size 12 in • p. 67

Ring-billed Gull
size 19 in • p. 68

DOVES & CUCKOOS

Band-tailed Pigeon
size 14 in • p. 69

White-winged Dove
size 12 in • p. 70

Mourning Dove
size 12 in • p. 71

Greater Roadrunner
size 23 in • p. 72

OWLS

Barn Owl
size 15 in • p. 73

Great Horned Owl
size 22 in • p. 74

Burrowing Owl
size 8 in • p. 75

NIGHTHAWKS, & HUMMINGBRIDS

Common Nighthawk
size 9 in • p. 76

Broad-tailed Hummingbird
size 4 in • p. 77

Elegant Trogon
size 12 in • p. 78

Belted Kingfisher
size 12 in • p. 79

WOODPECKERS

Lewis's Woodpecker
size 11 in • p. 80

Acorn Woodpecker
size 9 in • p. 81

Gila Woodpecker
size 9 in • p. 82

Ladder-backed Woodpecker
size 7 in • p. 83

Downy Woodpecker
size 6 in • p. 84

Northern Flicker
size 13 in • p. 85

FLYCATCHERS

Western Wood-Pewee
size 6 in • p. 86

Gray Flycatcher
size 6 in • p. 87

Cordilleran Flycatcher
size 7 in • p. 88

Black Phoebe
size 6 in • p. 89

Say's Phoebe
size 7 in • p. 90

Vermillion Flycatcher
size 6 in • p. 91

Ash-throated Flycatcher
size 7 in • p. 92

Sulphur-bellied Flycatcher
size 8 in • p. 93

Thick-billed Kingbird
size 9 in • p. 94

Western Kingbird
size 8 in • p. 95

Loggerhead Shrike
size 9 in • p. 96

Gray Jay
size 11 in • p. 97

Stellar's Jay
size 11 in • p. 98

Western Scrub-Jay
size 11 in • p. 99

Mexican Jay
size 11 in • p. 100

Pinyon Jay
size 11 in • p. 101

Clark's Nutcracker
size 12 in • p. 102

Black-billed Magpie
size 18 in • p. 103

American Crow
size 19 in • p. 104

Common Raven
size 24 in • p. 105

Purple Martin
size 8 in • p. 106

Tree Swallow
size 6 in • p. 107

Northern Rough-winged Swallow
size 6 in • p. 108

Cliff Swallow
size 5 in • p. 109

Mountain Chickadee
size 5 in • p. 110

Bridled Titmouse
size 4 in • p. 111

Juniper Titmouse
size 6 in • p. 112

Verdin
size 4 in • p. 113

Bushtit
size 4 in • p. 114

White-breasted Nuthatch
size 6 in • p. 115

Brown Creeper
size 5 in • p. 116

Cactus Wren
size 9 in • p. 117

CHICKADEES, NUTHATCHES & WRENS

Rock Wren
size 6 in • p. 118

Bewick's Wren
size 5 in • p. 119

American Dipper
size 8 in • p. 120

KINGLETS, BLUEBIRDS & THRUSHES

Ruby-crowned Kinglet
size 4 in • p. 121

Blue-gray Gnatcatcher
size 5 in • p. 122

Western Bluebird
size 7 in • p. 123

Hermit Thrush
size 7 in • p. 124

American Robin
size 10 in • p. 125

Northern Mockinbird
size 10 in • p. 126

MIMICS & WAXWINGS

Curve-billed Thrasher
size 10 in • p. 127

Cedar Waxwing
size 7 in • p. 128

Phainopepla
size 8 in • p. 129

WOOD-WARBLERS & TANAGERS

Olive Warbler
size 5 in • p. 130

Yellow Warbler
size 5 in • p. 131

Yellow-rumped Warbler
size 6 in • p. 132

Black-throated Gray Warbler
size 5 in • p. 133

Townsend's Warbler
size 5 in • p. 134

Red-faced Warbler
size 6 in • p. 135

Painted Redstart
size 6 in • p. 136

Yellow-breasted Chat
size 7 in • p. 137

Hepatic Tanager
size 7 in • p. 138

Western Tanager
size 7 in • p. 139

Green-tailed Towhee
size 7 in • p. 140

Spotted Towhee
size 8 in • p. 141

Canyon Towhee
size 7 in • p. 142

Chipping Sparrow
size 6 in • p. 143

Lark Sparrow
size 7 in • p. 144

Black-throated Sparrow
size 5 in • p. 145

White-crowned Sparrow
size 7 in • p. 146

Dark-eyed Junco
size 6 in • p. 147

Northern Cardinal
size 8 in • p. 148

Pyrrhuloxia
size 8 in • p. 149

Black-headed Grosbeak
size 8 in • p. 150

Blue Grosbeak
size 7 in • p. 151

Lazuli Bunting
size 6 in • p. 152

Red-winged Blackbird
size 8 in • p. 153

Western Meadowlark
size 9 in • p. 154

Yellow-headed Blackbird
size 10 in • p. 155

Great-tailed Grackle
size 16 in • p. 156

Brown-headed Cowbird
size 7 in • p. 157

Bullock's Oriole
size 8 in • p. 158

Scott's Oriole
size 9 in • p. 159

Gray-crowned Rosy-Finch
size 6 in • p. 160

House Finch
size 6 in • p. 161

Lesser Goldfinch
size 4 in • p. 162

American Goldfinch
size 5 in • p. 163

House Sparrow
size 6 in • p. 164

INTRODUCTION

In recent decades, birding has evolved from an eccentric pursuit practiced by a few dedicated individuals to a continent-wide phenomenon that boasts millions of professional and amateur participants. There are many good reasons why birding has become such a popular activity. Many people find it simple and relaxing, while others enjoy the outdoor exercise it affords. Some see it as a rewarding learning experience, an opportunity to socialize with like-minded people and a way to monitor the health of the local environment.

Whether you are just beginning to take an interest in birds or have already learned to identify many species, this field guide has something for you. We've selected 145 of the state's most common and noteworthy birds. Some live in specialized habitats, but most are common species that you have a good chance of encountering.

BIRDING IN ARIZONA AND NEW MEXICO

Whether you are looking out your back window or walking a secluded trail, you will find that there are always birds close by. Many birds, such as doves, sparrows and finches, are our neighbors year-round, while other birds only visit Arizona and New Mexico in spring and summer to take advantage of the abundance of food available and raise their young. Included in this category are many montane birds, hummingbirds and songbirds. Yet other birds only pass through Arizona and New Mexico briefly each spring and fall on their way to more northern and southern locales. Still, many winter here, taking advantage of our mild climate.

Some of the birds featured in this book are so familiar that you probably encounter them on a regular basis. Others are more shy and secretive or are restricted to certain habitats, so seeing them may be a noteworthy event. Likewise, some species are easily identified; if you see a Greater Roadrunner, you are not likely to confuse it with any other bird. Flycatchers, on the other hand, and many songbirds and raptors, can be more challenging to correctly identify.

Arizona and New Mexico have a long tradition of friendly birding. In general, birders here are willing to help beginners, share their knowledge and involve novices in their projects. Christmas bird counts, breeding bird surveys, nest box programs, migration monitoring studies, feeder watch programs and birding lectures and workshops all provide a chance for birders of all levels to interact and share their appreciation for birds. So, whatever your level of knowledge, there is ample opportunity for you to learn more and get involved.

Broad-tailed Hummingbird

TOP 50 SITES

Arizona

1. Bill Williams Delta, Colorado River
2. Hassayampa River Preserve, Wickenberg
3. Red Rock SP, Sedona
4. Oak Creek Canyon, Sedona
5. Needle Rock, Verde River
6. Desert Botanical Garden, Phoenix
7. Sycamore Creek and Mt. Ord, Sunflower
8. Roosevelt Lake, Roosevelt
9. Boyce Thompson Arboretum SP
10. Winkleman-Dudleyville, Dudleyville
11. Peppersauce Canyon, Santa Catalina Mts
12. Mt. Lemmon, Santa Catalina Mts
13. Sweetwater Wetlands, Tucson
14. Organ Pipe, Cactus National Monument
15. California Gulch, Pajarito Mts
16. Sycamore Canyon, Pajarito Mts
17. Madera Canyon
18. San Rafael Grasslands
19. Patagonia Lake SP, Patagonia
20. Patagonia-Sonoita Creek Preserve
21. Ramsay Canyon
22. Kino Springs, Nogales
23. Miller Canyon, Huachuca Mts
24. Whitewater Draw Wildlife Area, Cochise
25. Cave Creek, Chiracahuas Mts
26. Willcox Playa, Willcox
27. San Pedro Riparian National Conservation Area
29. Sunrise Lake and Sunrise Campground, White Mts
28. French Joe Canyon, Whetstone Mts
30. South Fork Little Colorado River, White Mts

New Mexico

31. Gila River, Red Rock
32. Gila National Forest
33. Animas Valley
34. Guadalupe Canyon
35. The Old Refuge, Las Cruces
36. Percha Dam SP
37. San Mateo Mts
38. Bosque del Apache NWR
39. Pinos Altos Mts
40. Rio Grande Nature Center
41. Sandia Crest
42. Pecos Wilderness
43. Sangre de Cristo Mts
44. Maxwell NWR
45. Las Vegas NWR
46. Conchas Lake SP
47. Tucumcari Lake
48. Bitter Lake NWR
49. Carlsbad Caverns NP
50. Rattlesnake Springs Preserve

NP =	National Park
NWR =	National Wildlife Refuge
SP =	State Park

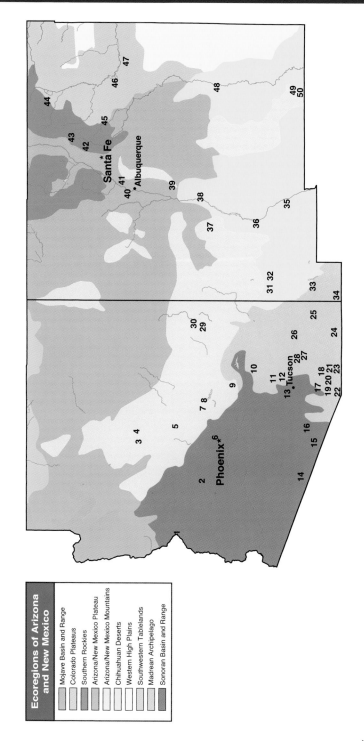

Ecoregions of Arizona and New Mexico

- Mojave Basin and Range
- Colorado Plateaus
- Southern Rockies
- Arizona/New Mexico Plateau
- Arizona/New Mexico Mountains
- Chihuahuan Deserts
- Western High Plains
- Southwestern Tablelands
- Madrean Archipelago
- Sonoran Basin and Range

ARIZONA AND NEW MEXICO'S TOP 10 BIRDING SITES

Arizona and New Mexico are as diverse as they are large. From the Colorado River Valley and arid Yuma Desert at an elevation of 70 feet, to the snow-capped Wheeler Peak at over 13,000 feet, the region covers a wide variety of habitats ranging from riparian river bottom, pristine grassland and desert scrub to pine-oak woodland, fir forest and alpine meadow. Because of this diversity, it has a lot to offer birds (and humans!).

There are hundreds of good birding areas throughout the state. The following areas have been selected to represent a broad range of bird communities and habitats, with an emphasis on diversity and accessibility.

Madera Canyon, AZ

Madera Canyon, a cool retreat from the surrounding desert, is nestled in the picturesque Santa Rita Mountains, just 30 minutes south of Tucson. This canyon, the name of which means "lumber" or "wood" in Spanish, boasts big trees, a perennial creek and stunning views of the surrounding Santa Rita Mountains. This beautiful canyon offers world-class birding, with more than 240 species of birds recorded within this peaceful haven. Because of its varied habitats, perennial stream and proximity to Mexico, over the years the canyon has hosted an impressive number of rare species normally found only south of the American border. It is most famous for the summering and breeding Elegant Trogons and lays claim to an impressive list of hummingbirds, including the spectacular Magnificent Hummingbird.

Ramsey Canyon Preserve, AZ

About 90 miles south of Tucson in the magnificent Huachuca Mountains, the 380-acre Ramsey Canyon Preserve owned by the Nature conservancy is a must-see destination for birders of all levels. From mixed conifer forests of the higher reaches of the Huachuca Mountains to the semi-desert grasslands at the canyon entrance, the lush riparian woodland of maples, sycamores, cottonwoods, willows and ash along Ramsey Creek supports a tremendous diversity of birds. Ramsey

Black-headed
Grosbeak

Canyon is best known for its hummingbirds; 14 species have been recorded at the Ramsey Canyon Preserve. In summer, park personnel and volunteers maintain a number of hummingbird feeders, providing relaxed and easy viewing. In season, preserve naturalists offer a variety of nature and natural history walks.

Boyce Thompson Arboretum State Park, AZ

Just 60 miles east of Greater Phoenix, Boyce Thompson Arboretum offers an excellent opportunity to see a variety of birds and most of the species characteristic of the Sonoran Desert. This 320-acre park is located in the shadow of historic Picket Post Mountain, which was used by the U.S. Army in the 1800s to communicate with other outposts, sending Morse code by flashes of reflected sunlight (a heliograph station). The park has an abundant network of well-constructed trails that take you through a variety of desert habitats. To enhance your visit, the trails offer interpretive displays describing the environment and the hundreds of plant and cactus species found here. The friendly and knowledgeable park staff and volunteers offer guided bird and nature walks and educational programs throughout most of the year.

Patagonia-Sonoita Creek Preserve, AZ

A verdant floodplain valley between the Patagonia and Santa Rita mountains of southeastern Arizona, the Patagonia-Sonoita Creek Preserve includes more than 850 acres owned and managed by The Nature Conservancy, with another 500 acres protected through conservation easements and landowner agreements. This preserve protects a magnificent area of cottonwood-willow riparian forest. Some of these trees are among the largest (over 100 feet tall) and oldest (130 years old) Fremont cottonwood trees in this country. This is one of the few remaining sites in Arizona where this once-common forest type still persists.

Downy
Woodpecker

Approximately 60 miles southeast of Tucson, the Patagonia-Sonoita Creek Preserve is best known for the 300 bird species observed here. Several unusual, rare or unique species such as the Gray Hawk, Green Kingfisher, Thick-billed Kingbird, Northern Beardless-Tyrannulet, Violet-crowned Hummingbird and Rose-throated Becard attract birders from around the world.

San Pedro Riparian National Conservation Area, AZ

Flowing northward from Mexico into the Gila River, the San Pedro River is the largest river in the Southwest that has not been dammed, and it is a biological gem. The approximately 58,000-acre area, run by the Bureau of Land Management, is 1–3 miles wide and stretches for 36 miles from the Mexican border to near St. David. This conservation area is one of the most important wildlife corridors in the United States and is a principal recovery area for the endangered jaguar. The area attracts birders from all over the world each year with its 100 species of breeding birds, and with its over 250 species of migrant and wintering birds. Thirty-six species of raptors are also found here, including the Gray Hawk, Mississippi Kite and Crested Caracara. Other sought-after birds include the Green Kingfisher, Northern Beardless-Tyrannulet and Yellow-billed Cuckoo.

Rattlesnake Springs Preserve, NM

A short distance from Carlsbad Caverns National Park along Hwy 62/180, Rattlesnake Springs Preserve is a mecca for devoted New Mexico birders. This 13-acre riparian oasis consists of a ½-mile wetland and a small stream, creating a magnet for migrating birds. Because of its isolation and small size, it tends to concentrate the birds and it is not uncommon, in a morning of birding during migration, to see 70 species or more. Although it is off the beaten path, the National Park Service maintains an adjacent picnic area with running water, picnic tables and restrooms. A visit here can easily be combined with a trip to the must-see Carlsbad Caverns.

Bosque del Apache National Wildlife Refuge, NM

Bosque del Apache, Spanish for "woods of the Apache," and named for the Native Americans that once camped beside the river, is located along the Rio Grande, 15 miles south of Socorro, New Mexico. One of the premier wildlife refuges in the Southwest, Bosque del Apache is the winter home to tens of thousands of migratory waterfowl, including Sandhill Cranes, Canada Geese and Snow Geese. Birding can be good to excellent at any time of the year.

The refuge consists of 57,191 acres located at the northern edge of the Chihuahuan desert spanning the Rio Grande, where water is diverted to create extensive wetlands, farmlands and riparian forests. Hiking trails crisscross parts of the refuge, allowing incredible views of birds and other wildlife. You can even bird from your car because Bosque has a series of loops through various habitats. Numerous viewing decks extend out into the marshes, providing for more up-close viewing and great opportunities for photographs.

American
Robin

Sandia Crest, NM

An excellent area to escape the hustle and bustle of the city, Sandia Crest is located a short distance from Albuquerque and soars 1 mile above the metropolitan city, allowing for spectacular views of the city and the Rio Grande River. Providing excellent montane birding at elevations between 6500 and 10,678 feet along NM 536, Sandia Crest is renowned as being one of the most accessible locations in the United States to find all three species of Rosy-Finches—Black, Brown-capped and Gray-crowned—which can be seen from November through early April. Summer birding highlights include the Broad-tailed Hummingbird, Steller's Jay, Clark's Nutcracker, Western Tanager and Mountain Chickadee.

Rio Grande Nature Center, NM

Nestled within the city limits of Albuquerque, the Rio Grande Nature Center is a winter home to Canada Geese, Sandhill Cranes and various species of ducks and other waterfowl. Located on the central Rio Grande flyway, this *bosque*, or cottonwood-covered river bottom, features 2 miles of nature trails, which wind through partially wooded areas to open sand flats along the river. Many migratory birds take advantage of this peaceful stopover. Spring and fall migrations add additional species such as warblers, flycatchers and vireos.

Percha Dam State Park, NM

Percha Dam State Park may be one of the best hidden treasures for birding in New Mexico. Relatively unknown, it is a quiet and serene getaway under the deep shade of towering cottonwoods and velvet ash trees. At an elevation of 4100 feet, this rich riparian area covers 80 acres of land and 11,500 acres of lake.

Western
Bluebird

Along the east side of the park flanking the river, a thick growth of willow and cottonwood bosque provides some of the best warbler-watching in the valley during the migration of May, August and September. Birding is excellent at any time of the year, and this area should not be missed if possible as it is one of the best sites for landbirds along the entire length of the Rio Grande. Because other activities in this grass-covered park include hiking, swimming, camping and fishing, you may want to arrive early. Percha Dam State Park is 21 miles south of Truth or Consequences via I-25, exit 59.

About the Species Accounts

This book gives detailed accounts of 145 bird species regularly found in Arizona and New Mexico. The majority of the species included are the most common and easily detected, but a few less common species, such as Greater Roadrunner and Elegant Trogon, were chosen because they are distinctive to the region, are well-known or are "specialty birds" frequently sought after by birders. The order of the birds and their common and scientific names follow the American Ornithologists' Union's *Check-list of North American Birds* (7th edition, July 1998 and *The Forty-fifth Supplement, 2004*).

One of the challenges of birding is that many species look different in spring and summer than they do in fall and winter. Many birds have breeding and non-breeding plumages, and immature birds often look different from their parents. This book does not try to describe or illustrate all the different plumages of a species; instead, it focuses on the plumages that are most likely to be seen in our area. As well as discussing the identifying features of each bird, the species accounts also attempt to bring the birds to life by describing their various character traits.

ID: It is difficult to describe the features of a bird without being able to visualize it, so this section is best used in combination with the illustrations. Where appropriate, the description is subdivided to highlight the differences between male and female, breeding and nonbreeding and immature and adult. The descriptions use as few technical terms as possible, and favor easily understood language. Birds may not have eyebrows or chins, but these and other terms are easily understood by all readers, in spite of their scientific inaccuracy. Some of the most common features of birds are pointed out in the Glossary illustration (p. 165).

Size: The average length of the bird's body from bill to tail, as well as its wingspan, give an approximate measurement of the bird as it is seen in nature. The size of larger birds is often given as a range, because there is variation among individuals. Please note that birds with long tails often have large measurements that do not necessarily reflect "body" size.

Status: A general comment, such as "common," "uncommon" or "rare" is usually sufficient to describe the relative abundance of a species. Wherever possible, we have also indicated status at different times of the year. Situations are bound to vary somewhat because migratory pulses, seasonal changes and centers of activity tend to concentrate or disperse birds.

Habitat: The habitats we have listed describe where each species is most commonly found. In most cases, it is a generalized description, but if a bird is restricted to a specific habitat, the habitat is described precisely.

Nesting: In each species account, nest location and structure, clutch size, incubation period and parental duties are discussed. Remember that birding ethics discourage the disturbance of active bird nests. The nesting behavior of birds that do not nest in our region is not described.

Feeding: Birds spend a great deal of time foraging for food. If you know what a bird eats and where the food is found, you will have a good chance of finding that bird. Birds are frequently encountered while they are foraging.

Voice: You will hear many birds, particularly songbirds, which may remain hidden from view. Easily remembered paraphrases of distinctive sounds will aid you in identifying a species by ear. Please note that these paraphrases may only loosely resemble the call, song or sound produced by the bird. Should one of our paraphrases not work for you, feel free to make up your own.

Similar Species: Easily confused species are discussed briefly. If you concentrate on the most relevant field marks, the subtle differences between species can be reduced to easily identifiable traits. You might find it useful to consult this section when finalizing your identification; knowing the most relevant field marks will speed up the identification process. Even experienced birders can mistake one species for another.

Best Sites: If you are looking for a particular bird, you will have more luck in some locations than in others, even within the range shown on the range map. We have listed places that, besides providing a good chance of seeing a species, are easily accessible. As a result, many nature centers, national wildlife refuges and state parks are mentioned.

Range Maps: The range map for each species represents the overall range of the species in an average year. Most birds will confine their annual movements to this range, although each year some birds wander beyond their traditional boundaries. These small maps do not show differences in abundance within the range. They also cannot show small pockets within the range where the species may actually be absent, or how the range may change from year to year.

Unlike most other field guides, we have attempted to show migratory pathways—areas of the region where birds may appear while en route to nesting or winter habitats. The representations of the pathways do not distinguish high-use migration corridors from areas that are seldom used.

Range Map Symbols

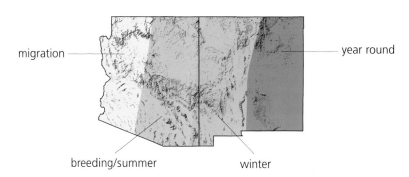

migration — — year round

breeding/summer   winter

19

SNOW GOOSE

Chen caerulescens

Watch for oscillating, wavy lines of Snow Geese in the morning and evening, when flocks fly from lakes and wetlands to feed in agricultural fields. These geese breed in the High Arctic from western Siberia and Alaska to Greenland, and they winter in the southern United States and Mexico. In recent years, Snow Goose populations have increased dramatically in North America, taking advantage of human-induced changes to the landscape and food supply. • Snow Geese can fly at speeds of up to 20 miles per hour. They are also strong walkers, and mothers have been known to lead their goslings up to 45 miles on foot in search of suitable habitat. • Snow Geese occur in two color morphs—white and blue—the blue morph being uncommon in our region. The two morphs were considered different species until 1983. • The similar looking Ross's Goose *(C. Rossi)* is often found among large flocks of Snow Geese, especially along the lower Colorado River in Arizona, and at Bosque del Apache National Wildlife Refuge in New Mexico.

blue morph

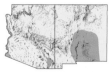

ID: stocky body; pink legs; pink bill with dark "grinning patch." *White morph:* all white except for black primaries. *Blue morph:* white head and upper neck; dark blue-gray body. *Immature:* gray or dusty white plumage; dark bill and feet.
Size: *L* 28–33 in; *W* 4½–5 ft.
Status: locally abundant at wildlife refuges and agricultural areas throughout the region from October to April.

Habitat: shallow marshes, lakes, agricultural fields and suburban areas.
Nesting: does not nest in Arizona or New Mexico.
Feeding: grazes on aquatic vegetation, grasses, sedges and roots; also takes grain in agricultural fields.
Voice: loud, nasal, constant *houk-houk* in flight.
Similar Species: *Ross's Goose:* smaller; smaller, rounded head; stubby bill lacks black "grinning patch"; shorter neck.
Best Sites: *AZ:* Cibola NWF. *NM:* Bitter Lake NWR; Bosque del Apache NWR.

CANADA GOOSE

Branta canadensis

When you think of migration, you may visualize a steady stream of geese flying overhead in a V-formation, with a distinctive and resonant honking as they pass by. The Canada Goose, one of the most recognized of waterfowl, has often been considered the harbinger of fall and winter as flocks make their way south to warmer climates. • Canada Geese have increased noticeably in our region in recent times owing to widespread agriculture and increases in urban wildlife habitats. They are now familiar visitors to many urban lakes and golf courses throughout the region. • Canada Geese mate for life and are devoted parents. Unlike most birds, the family stays together for nearly a year, which increases the survival rate of the young. • The Canada Goose was split into two species in 2004. The larger subspecies, which breed in the central U.S., are known as Canada Geese, while the smaller, arctic-breeding subspecies have been renamed Cackling Geese *(B. hutchinsii)*.

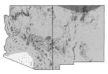

ID: brown body, paler below; long, black neck; white "chin strap"; black bill, legs and feet; white undertail coverts; short, black tail.
Size: *L* 30–48 in; *W* 3½–5 ft.
Status: fairly common to common migrant and winter visitor, and uncommon and local in summer throughout the region.
Habitat: ponds and lakes, farmland, residential areas and city parks.
Nesting: on an island or shoreline; usually on the ground; female builds a nest of plant materials and lines it with down;

female incubates 3–8 white eggs for 25–28 days while the male stands guard.
Feeding: grazes on new sprouts, aquatic vegetation, grass and roots; tips up for aquatic roots and tubers.
Voice: loud, familiar *ah-honk.*
Similar Species: *Cackling Goose:* smaller; shorter neck; smaller, stubby bill. *Greater White-fronted Goose:* brown neck and head; no white "chin strap"; orange legs; white around base of bill; dark speckling on belly.
Best Sites: most major wildlife refuges and large lakes. *AZ:* Cibola NWF. *NM:* Bitter Lake NWR; Bosque del Apache NWR.

AMERICAN WIGEON

Anas americana

American Wigeons and other members of the *Anas* genus, the dabbling ducks, feed by tipping up their tails and dunking their heads underwater. They have small feet situated near the center of their bodies. Other ducks, including Redheads and Ruddy Ducks, dive underwater to feed and are propelled by large feet set farther back on their bodies. • Wigeons favor the succulent stems and leaves of aquatic bottom plants. Some of these plants grow too deep to reach, so wigeons often pirate from accomplished divers. Unlike other ducks, American Wigeons are also good walkers and are commonly observed grazing on shore. • During winter, American Wigeons are often found with Gadwalls *(A. strepera)* and American Coots.

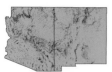

ID: rounded head; pale bluish gray bill with black tip; large, white upperwing patch. *Male:* rusty breast and sides; gray head with white forehead and crown; wide, iridescent, green cheek patch; white belly; black undertail coverts. *Female:* grayish head; brown underparts; dusky undertail coverts.
Size: *L* 18–22½ in; *W* 32 in.
Status: common to abundant migrant and winter visitor from September to April.
AZ: rare breeder in White Mts. **NM:** rare breeder in northernmost regions.
Habitat: shallow wetlands, lakes and ponds.

Nesting: always on dry ground, often far from water; nest is well concealed in tall vegetation and is built with grass, leaves and down; female incubates 8–11 white eggs for 23–25 days.
Feeding: dabbles and tips up for the leaves and stems of pondweeds and other aquatic plants; also grazes on land; may eat some invertebrates.
Voice: *Male:* nasal, frequently repeated whistle. *Female:* soft, seldom heard quack.
Similar Species: male's head pattern is distinctive. *Gadwall:* white speculum; no white wing patch; male lacks green cheek patch; female has orange swipes on bill.
Best Sites: rivers, lakes and golf course ponds regionwide.

MALLARD

Anas platyrhynchos

The male Mallard, with his iridescent, green head and chestnut brown breast, is the classic wild duck. The female's loud *QUACK quack quack* is the quintessential and most familiar of the duck calls. Mallards can be seen year-round, often in flocks and always near open water. • A nesting hen generates enough body heat to make the grasses around her nest grow faster. She uses the tall grasses to further conceal her nest. • After breeding, male ducks lose their elaborate plumage, helping them stay camouflaged during their flightless period. In early fall, they molt back into breeding colors. • The Mexican form of the Mallard, the "Mexican Duck," once considered a separate species, can be found in Southeastern Arizona and Southwestern New Mexico. Both sexes closely resemble the female Mallard.

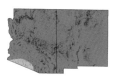

ID: *Male:* "dirty white" upperparts and paler underparts; glossy, green head separated from chestnut breast by bold white ring; yellow bill; black central tail feathers curl upward. *Female:* mottled brown overall with finely streaked, grayish brown head; orange bill spattered with black. *In flight:* dark blue speculum bordered with white.
Size: *L* 20–27½ in; *W* 35 in.
Status: common to abundant resident and less common and widespread in summer throughout the region.

Habitat: ponds, lakes, marshes, residential areas and city parks.
Nesting: in tall vegetation or under a bush, often near water; female builds nest of grass and other plant material and lines it with down; female incubates 7–10 light green to white eggs for 26–30 days.
Feeding: tips up and dabbles in shallows for the seeds of aquatic vegetation; may take some aquatic invertebrates; commonly accepts handouts of bread.
Voice: *Male:* deep, quiet quacks.
Female: loud quacks; very vocal.
Similar Species: *Northern Shoveler* (p. 25): much larger bill; green speculum bordered by white; breeding male has white breast, chestnut flanks and dark back.
Best Sites: widespread.

CINNAMON TEAL

Anas cyanoptera

If the Stetson is "the hat of the West," the Cinnamon Teal is "the duck of the West." The principal distribution of both the hat and the bird define that great reach of arid country where the presence of water is dramatic and important. You will instantly recognize the intense reddish brown plumage of the male Cinnamon Teal, accented by its ruby red eyes. The drab female and eclipse plumage, however, are nearly identical to the female Blue-winged Teal *(A. discors)* and are difficult to differentiate in the field. Both species have broad, flat bills, pale blue forewings and green speculums. The Cinnamon Teal is a common summer resident throughout much of our region, but the Blue-winged Teal is an uncommon transient. Small numbers of both species overwinter in central AZ and along the lower Colorado and Rio Grande river valleys. • A third teal, the small, colorful Green-winged Teal *(A. crecca)*, winters in our region. Males have a chestnut head with a green cheek stripe and a white vertical shoulder slash.

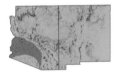

ID: large bill. *Male:* intense cinnamon red head, neck and underparts; red eyes. *Female:* mottled warm brown overall; dark eyes. *In flight:* conspicuous pale blue forewing patch; green speculum.

Size: L 15–17 in; W 22 in.

Status: common migrant and winter resident and fairly common but local breeding resident throughout the region.

Habitat: freshwater ponds, marshes, sloughs and flooded swales with surface-growing or submergent aquatic vegetation.

Nesting: in tall vegetation, occasionally far from water; female places nest of grass and down in a concealed hollow; female incubates 7–12 white to buff eggs for 21–25 days.

Feeding: gleans the water's surface for grass and sedge seeds, pondweed, duckweed and aquatic invertebrates.

Voice: not often heard; male utters a whistled *peep;* female gives a rough *karr, karr, karr.*

Similar Species: *Ruddy Duck* (p. 30): male has white cheek, blue bill and stiff, upward-angled tail. *Green-winged Teal:* small bill; no forewing patch. *Blue-winged Teal:* male has white crescent in front of eye.

Best Sites: *AZ:* Sweetwater Wetlands; Wilcox Playa; Kino Springs. *NM:* Bosque del Apache NWR; Bitter Lake NWR.

NORTHERN SHOVELER

Anas clypeata

An extra large, spoonlike bill allows the Northern Shoveler to strain small invertebrates from the water and from the bottom of ponds. This strangely handsome duck eats much smaller organisms than do most other waterfowl, and its intestines are elongated to prolong the digestion of these hard-bodied invertebrates. The shoveler's specialized feeding strategy means that it is rarely seen tipping up, and is more likely to be found in the shallows of ponds and marshes where the mucky bottom is easiest to access. • The scientific name *clypeata*, Latin for "furnished with a shield," possibly refers to the chestnut patches on the flanks of the male. This species was once placed in its own genus, *Spatula,* the meaning of which needs no explanation.

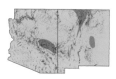

ID: large, spatulate bill; blue forewing patch; green speculum. *Male:* green head; yellow eyes; black bill; white breast; chestnut flanks. *Female:* mottled brown overall; orange-tinged bill.
Size: *L* 18–20 in; *W* 30 in.
Status: common to abundant migrant and winter visitor from October to April throughout the region; local and uncommon in summer, primarily in the north.
Habitat: ponds, lakes and shallow marshes.
Nesting: in a shallow hollow on dry ground, usually within 170 ft of water; female builds

a nest of dry grass and down; female incubates 10–12 pale buff olive eggs for 21–28 days.
Feeding: dabbles in shallow water; strains out plant and animal matter, especially aquatic crustaceans, insect larvae and seeds; also takes small fish.
Voice: generally silent; raspy chuckles or quacks given during courtship.
Similar Species: spatulate bill is distinctive. *Mallard* (p. 23): blue speculum bordered by white; no blue forewing patch; male has chestnut brown breast and white flanks. *Blue-winged Teal:* smaller overall; much smaller bill; male has white crescent on face; spotted breast and sides.
Best Sites: *AZ:* Bill Williams Delta; Roosevelt L.; Willcox Playa. *NM:* Bosque del Apache NWR; Bitter Lake NWR.

NORTHERN PINTAIL

Anas acuta

The elegant Northern Pintail's trademark long, tapering tail feathers are easily seen in flight and point skyward when this duck dabbles. The rich brown color of the male's head flows gracefully down the back of his neck, accentuating the stark white on his neck and chest. • Though the Northern Pintail was once one of the most numerous ducks in North America, populations have declined steadily in recent decades owing to drought, wetland drainage and loss of grassland habitat. This species is also especially susceptible to lead poisoning, often mistaking the lead shot left behind by hunters for hard seeds. One ingested pellet contains enough lead to poison a bird. Fortunately, lead shot has been banned in most states.

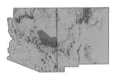

ID: long, slender neck; slim, gray bill. *Male:* grayish upper and under-parts; white neck extends onto hindneck as narrow wedge; brown head; long, tapering, black tail feathers. *Female:* mottled light brown overall; head paler and plain. *In flight:* slender body; brownish speculum with white trailing edge.
Size: *L* 21–25 in; *W* 34 in.
Status: uncommon to abundant migrant and winter visitor from September to April throughout the region; rare to uncommon in summer, predominantly in the north.
Habitat: impoundments, marshes, lakes and ponds.

Nesting: in a small depression in vegetation, usually near water; female builds a nest of grass, leaves and moss and lines it with down; female incubates 6–9 eggs for up to 24 days.
Feeding: tips up and dabbles in shallows for the seeds of grasses and sedges; also eats aquatic invertebrates.
Voice: generally silent in our region. *Male:* soft, whistling call. *Female:* rough quack.
Similar Species: male is distinctive. *Mallard* (p. 23) and *Gadwall:* females are chunkier, usually have dark or 2-tone bills and lack tapering tail and long, slender neck.
Best Sites: *AZ:* Bill Williams Delta; Roosevelt L.; Willcox Playa. *NM:* Bosque del Apache NWR; Bitter Lake NWR.

REDHEAD

Aythya americana

The striking Redhead, with contrasting colors of red, black and gray, is one of the few diving ducks that can be found breeding in our region. In fall, its numbers increase, and small groups may be found on the ponds and lakes of southern Arizona and southern New Mexico. • Redheads share similar plumage and habitat preferences with Canvasbacks *(A. valisineria)*. The best way to separate the two species is by head shape. The Redhead has a round head that meets the bill at an angle, whereas its close cousin, the Canvasback, has a sloping head that seems to merge with the bill. In males, the most obvious difference is the color of their backs—white in Canvasbacks, gray in Redheads.

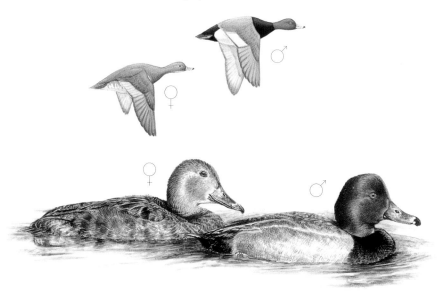

ID: rounded head; black-tipped, blue-gray bill. *Male:* red head; yellow eyes; black breast and hindquarters; gray back and sides. *Female:* dark brown overall; lighter chin and cheek patch.
Size: *L* 18–22 in; *W* 29 in.
Status: fairly common migrant, common winter resident and fairly common, with reduced numbers, in summer in both states.
Habitat: marshes or lakes.
Nesting: suspended over water at the base of emergent vegetation; female builds a deep basket nest of reeds and grass and lines it with white down; female incubates 9–14 eggs for 23–29 days; female may lay eggs in other ducks' nests.

Feeding: dives to depths of 10 ft; eats primarily aquatic vegetation, especially ditchgrass, sedges and water lilies; occasionally eats aquatic invertebrates.
Voice: generally quiet in our region. *Male:* catlike meow in courtship. *Female:* rolling *kurr-kurr-kurr; squak* when alarmed.
Similar Species: *Canvasback:* clean white back; bill slopes onto forehead. *Ring-necked Duck* (p. 28): female has more prominent white eye ring, white ring on bill and peaked head. *Lesser Scaup* and *Greater Scaup:* males have dark head and whiter sides; females have white at base of bill.
Best Sites: *AZ:* Roosevelt L.; Bill Williams Delta. *NM:* Bosque del Apache NWR; Bitter Lake NWR.

RING-NECKED DUCK

Aythya collaris

The Ring-necked Duck's characteristic tricolored bill, yellow eye and black back are field marks that immediately strike an observer. Many birders wonder why this bird was not named the "Ring-billed Duck." The name originated with an ornithologist looking at an indistinct cinnamon "collar" on a museum specimen, not a birder looking at a live duck through binoculars. • Ring-necked Ducks are diving ducks, but they prefer to feed in shallower shoreline waters, frequently tipping up for food like a dabbler. They ride high on the water and tend to carry their tails clear of the water's surface. Ring-necks are generalized feeders, which allows them to capitalize on the low resources found in the subarctic and boreal settings where they commonly nest.

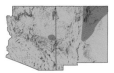

ID: tricolored bill; peaked crown. *Male:* black upperparts; dark purple head; yellow eyes; black breast and hindquarters separated by gray sides; white shoulder slash. *Female:* brown overall; paler head; whitish face; white eye ring extends behind eye as a narrow line.
Size: *L* 14–18 in; *W* 25 in.
Status: locally common migrant and winter visitor from October to March and rare and local in summer throughout the region. *AZ:* rare breeder in the White Mts.

Habitat: ponds vegetated with lily pads and other surface vegetation; swamps, marshes and lakes.
Nesting: rarely nests in Arizona or New Mexico; on a floating island or hummock; bulky nest of grass and moss is lined with down; female incubates 8–10 olive eggs for 25–29 days.
Feeding: dives for aquatic vegetation, rarely eats aquatic invertebrates and mollusks.
Voice: generally silent in our region. *Male:* low-pitched, hissing whistle. *Female:* growling *churr*.
Similar Species: *Lesser Scaup* and *Greater Scaup:* gray back; white sides; lack tricolored bill; females have broad, clearly defined, white face patch around base of bill.
Best Sites: widespread.

COMMON MERGANSER

Mergus merganser

Lumbering like a jumbo jet, the Common Merganser must run along the surface of the water, beating its heavy wings to gain sufficient lift to take off. Once up and away, this large duck flies arrow straight and low over the water, making broad, sweeping turns to follow the meandering shorelines of rivers and lakes. • Common Mergansers are highly social and often gather in large groups during migration. In winter, any source of open water with a fish-filled shoal will support good numbers of these skilled divers. • The similar looking Red-breasted Merganser *(M. serrator)* is more typical of saline habitats but occurs in small numbers in winter and migration in our region, especially along the Colorado River in Arizona and the Rio Grande Valley of New Mexico. • "Merganser" is derived from the Latin for "diving goose."

ID: large, elongated body; long, slender, red bill. *Male:* glossy green head with no crest; red feet; white body plumage; black spinal stripe; large, white patch on upper forewing. *Female:* rusty head; clean white neck and throat; gray body. *In flight:* shallow wingbeats; body is compressed and arrowlike; white speculum.
Size: *L* 22–27 in; *W* 34 in.
Status: uncommon to abundant migrant and winter visitor in both states from October to April; uncommon and local in summer, mainly in the north.

Habitat: large, often fast-flowing rivers and deep lakes; may also use estuaries and coastal lagoons.
Nesting: does not nest in Arizona or New Mexico.
Feeding: dives underwater (up to 30 ft) for small fish, usually trout, carp, suckers, perch and catfish; may also eat shrimp, salamanders and mussels; young eat aquatic invertebrates.
Voice: generally silent in winter.
Male: utters a harsh *uig-a,* like a guitar twang. *Female:* harsh *karr karr.*
Similar Species: *Red-breasted Merganser:* shaggy crest; male has spotted, red breast; female lacks cleanly defined white throat. *Mallard* (p. 23): male has chestnut breast.
Best Sites: *AZ:* Roosevelt L.; Bill Williams Delta. *NM:* Conchas Lake SP; Bitter Lake NWR.

RUDDY DUCK

Oxyura jamaicensis

Small, stiff-tailed Ruddy Ducks occur in most of our wetland areas and occasionally breed on our smaller ponds and lakes, where cattails and emergent vegetation can be used for cover. They have flattened, somewhat elongated heads, short necks and short tails, which are often held up at an angle. • In March, the male molts into his resplendent breeding plumage and sports a bright, rusty body and bright azure bill. During his energetic courtship display, the male puffs out his chest by inflating his neck sacs, tilts his head backward and emits a series of notes. • Although the Ruddy is one of our smallest ducks, the female lays enormous eggs—her eggs are bigger than those of a Mallard, even though the Mallard is twice the size of a Ruddy Duck!

breeding

nonbreeding

Habitat: *Breeding:* shallow marshes with dense emergent vegetation and muddy bottoms. *Winter:* large lakes.

Nesting: in cattails, bulrushes or other emergent vegetation; female suspends a woven platform nest over water; female incubates 5–10 rough, whitish eggs for 23–26 days.

Feeding: dives for aquatic vegetation and lesser amounts of crustaceans and insects.

Voice: generally silent in our region. *Male:* chuck-chuck-chuck-chur-r-r-r during courtship display.

Similar Species: *Cinnamon Teal* (p. 24): lacks white cheek and blue bill. *Other diving ducks* (pp. 27–29): females lack long, stiff tail and dark facial stripe.

Best Sites: *AZ:* Roosevelt L.; Bill Williams Delta. *NM:* Bosque del Apache NWR; Bitter Lake NWR.

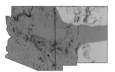

ID: small, pudgy body; large head; short neck; short tail, often held upraised. *Breeding male:* bright, rusty body; bright azure bill; black crown and nape. *Nonbreeding male:* dull grayish brown body, darker above; blackish crown and nape; large, white cheek patch; grayish bill. *Female:* similar to nonbreeding male, but cheek is marked with wide, dark, horizontal stripe.

Size: *L* 15–16 in; *W* 18½ in.

Status: locally common to abundant migrant and winter visitor and uncommon to rare breeder throughout the region.

DUSKY GROUSE

Dendragapus obscurus

The biggest of our mountain grouse, the Dusky Grouse is well adapted to living at the timberline. In winter, additional scales grow around each toe, widening the specialized feet into "snowshoes." • Prior to breeding, Dusky Grouse migrate to lower elevations, where the male's deep courting notes signal the arrival of spring. The male's owl-like hoots are so deep that the human ear can detect only a fraction of the sounds produced. • Newly hatched broods frequent forest edges and grassy clearings where food is abundant. Their mottled brown plumage blends in so well with their surroundings that these birds often freeze when threatened — a habit that has earned them the name "Fool's Hen."

ID: mottled, brownish gray overall; long neck; white undertail coverts; feathered legs; long, unbarred tail. *Male:* orangish comb above eye; blue-gray crown, nape, upper back and tail feathers; dark gray breast; when displaying, shows inflated yellow-orange throat patches surrounded by white feathers. *Female:* blue-gray lower breast and belly; faint yellow comb. *In flight:* tail nearly all dark, or with faint gray subterminal band.
Size: *L* 17–22 in; *W* 24–28 in. Male is larger than female.

Status: uncommon and local resident of high mountain forests above 8000 ft in both states.
Habitat: coniferous forests of higher foothills and mountains; often in burns or other forest clearings.
Nesting: often near fallen log or under shrub; scrape nest is lined with vegetation; female incubates 7–10 brown-speckled, pale pink or buff eggs for 25–28 days.
Feeding: mainly plants, berries, seeds and insects; takes conifer needles and buds in winter; young birds eat insects.
Voice: 5–8 extremely deep, ventriloquial hoots, the first or second hoot loudest, then trailing off.
Similar Species: none.
Best Sites: *AZ:* Mt. Baldy Trail (White Mts.). *NM:* Hyde SP.

SCALED QUAIL

Callipepla sqamata

The Scaled Quail, also called "Cottontop" or "Blue Quail," is a stocky bird with a bushy, white crest and black feather edgings that give a "scaly" appearance. A favorite of both hunters and birdwatchers, this quirky little bird can be found hiding beneath farm equipment or mesquite bushes in arid scrubland habitat. • These birds are swift on the ground and prefer to run rather than fly. They require pockets of cover for escape, roosting, nesting and hiding, ranging from small grasses to shrubs and brush piles. Overgrazing and land management often destroy suitable cover, allowing the more adaptable Gambel's Quail to encroach. • Seeds make up a large part of the Scaled Quail's diet, but insects are also an important source of nutrition and water. During winter, this bird's gut morphology changes to collect more energy from lower-quality foods such as tumbleweed seeds.

ID: stocky body; pale bluish gray and brown overall; "scaly" neck and upperparts; white tuft on head (largest on male); white horizontal stripes along sides; 1 white wing bar; gray-tipped tail.
Size: *L:* 10–12 in; *W* 14 in.
Status: *AZ:* uncommon resident of the Chihuahuan Desert and adjacent desert grasslands. *NM:* uncommon resident in desert grasslands statewide.
Habitat: arid scrub and grasslands; may be found in coveys around log piles or farm equipment; usually close to water.
Nesting: on the ground; in a small depression under thick vegetation; female incubates 12–14 white eggs, with brown speckling, for 22–23 days as male defends nesting territory; may raise two broods.
Feeding: feeds in groups at dawn and dusk; eats seeds, insects and vegetation.
Voice: throaty *chip-Chuk!* when separated; various clicks and trills. *Male:* gives a loud *sheesh!*
Similar Species: *Gambel's Quail* (p. 33): female has chestnut sides, buffy chest and thin, black plume on her head. *Montezuma Quail* (p. 34): plump; short tail; male has round crest, black and white facial markings, mottled upperparts and dark sides with white spots.
Best Sites: *AZ:* Portal; Willcox Playa; Sierra Vista. *NM:* Las Cruces area.

GAMBEL'S QUAIL

Callipepla gambelii

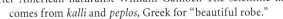

Gambel's Quails are plump, robin-sized birds with a half-curled forehead plume and a head-bobbing gait. They are found mainly in the warm deserts of the Southwest, especially Arizona, and often occur near water in brush and thorn habitats. • Coveys of up to 40 birds travel together for most of the year, then break into breeding pairs in March or April. Courting males display on top of shrubs or rocks, throwing back their heads and uttering boisterous *chi-ca-go-go* calls. • To survive the hot, arid climate, desert quails feed mainly during dawn and dusk. They are also able to derive water from the food they eat. • This bird is named after American naturalist William Gambel. The scientific name *callipepla* comes from *kalli* and *peplos*, Greek for "beautiful robe."

ID: *Male:* black teardrop-shaped plume; black face and forehead bordered by white; rusty crown; gray breast and upperparts; chestnut sides with white streaking; buffy belly with black inner patch. *Female:* resembles male but has brownish head and lacks black belly patch. *Immature:* mottled gray and tan plumage; brown forecrown and wings.
Size: *L* 11 in; *W* 15 in.
Status: *AZ:* common resident throughout Mogollon Rim. *NM:* resident in southwestern New Mexico, north through the Rio Grande valley to Espanola.
Habitat: mesquite thickets, desert scrublands, canyons and brushy open country, especially near sources of water; occasionally visits suburban bird feeders.

Nesting: usually nests on the ground under a shrub or rock; occasionally in a tree; scrape nest is lined with vegetation; female incubates 10–12 brown marked, dull white eggs for 21–23 days.
Feeding: in groups at dawn or dusk; eats seeds, fruit and occasionally insects.
Voice: calls include a loud 4-note *chi-ca-go-go*, a sorrowful *qua-al* and a variety of grunting and clucking noises.
Similar Species: *Scaled Quail* (p. 32): white head tuft; "scaly" neck and upperparts. *Montezuma Quail* (p. 34): lacks plume; male has brown, rounded crest, black and white facial pattern, black sides with white dots, and mottled black and brown upperparts; female is brownish overall.
Best Sites: *AZ:* most desert parks around Phoenix and Tucson. *NM:* Rio Grande Valley north to Albuquerque.

MONTEZUMA QUAIL

Cyrtonyx montezumae

Found mainly in Mexico's Sierra Madre mountains, the Montezuma Quail reaches the northern limit of its range in southern Arizona and New Mexico. This mountain quail is typically found in the oak savanna and oak-pine woodlands between 3280 and 9840 feet. • Montezuma Quails freeze when approached and can be extremely difficult to spot unless they are flushed. These quails rarely fly but elude predators and birdwatchers alike by running swiftly to the closest cover, where they crouch, motionless. In fact, the Arizona Game and Fish Department uses hunting dogs to detect these cryptic quails during bird surveys. • The scientific name *Cyrtonyx* is Greek for "curved claw" and refers to this bird's long claws, used for digging up tubers and bulbs. Montezuma was the Aztec ruler during the Spanish conquest; the name means "angry chief."

ID: round body; short tail and bill; patterned wings. *Male:* buffy, rounded crest; black and white facial pattern; black sides with white dots; mottled black and brown upperparts. *Female:* brown patterned body and head. **Size:** *L* 8–9 in; *W* 15–16 in. **Status:** *AZ:* uncommon and local resident in eastern Arizona from the White Mts south to the Mexican border. *NM:* rare and local resident in southwestern NM from the Mogollon Mts. south to the Animas Mts. **Habitat:** grassy floor of oak savanna or oak-pine forests; usually found on dry, cool, north-facing hillsides.

Nesting: on the ground; depression is lined and domed with grass; female incubates 6–14 white or creamy white eggs for 25 days. **Voice:** gives a loud, descending whinny during breeding. **Feeding:** *Winter:* scrapes out tubers and roots. *Summer and dry season:* eats acorns and insects. *Fall:* eats seeds. **Similar Species:** male is distinctive. *Gambel's Quail* (p. 33): female has gray upperparts, chestnut sides, thin, black head plume and buffy chest. *Scaled Quail* (p. 32): white head tuft; "scaly" neck and upperparts. **Best Sites:** *AZ:* Ruby Road in Nogales. *NM:* Peloncillos Mts.; Animas Mts.

PIED-BILLED GREBE

Podilymbus podiceps

Relatively solid bones and the ability to partially deflate its air sac allow the Pied-billed Grebe to sink below the surface of the water like a tiny submarine. This inconspicuous grebe can float low in the water or submerge with only its nostrils and eyes showing above the surface. It tends to stick to the shallow waters of quiet freshwater ponds and rivers. • This grebe builds its floating nest among sparse vegetation so it can see its numerous predators — including Great Blue Herons, small turtles and water snakes — approaching from far away. When frightened by an intruder, it covers its eggs and slides underwater, leaving a nest that looks like nothing more than a mat of debris. • The scientific name *podiceps* means "rump foot" because this bird's feet are located toward the back of its body.

nonbreeding

ID: stocky body; short neck; stocky bill. *Breeding:* brown body; black ring on pale bill; black throat; pale belly. *Nonbreeding:* no black ring on bill; white chin and throat; brownish crown.
Size: *L* 12–15 in; *W* 16 in.
Status: uncommon and local resident of lakes and ponds regionwide; less numerous in summer.
Habitat: ponds, marshes, impoundments and backwaters; flooded agricultural lands.
Nesting: in a pond or marsh; floating platform of plant material anchored to or placed among emergent vegetation; pair incubates 4–5 white to buff eggs for about

23 days; pair raises the striped young together.
Feeding: dives shallowly and gleans the water's surface for aquatic invertebrates, small fish and amphibians; occasionally eats aquatic plants.
Voice: loud, variable whooping song begins quickly then slows down: *kuk-kuk-kuk cow cow cow cowp cowp cowp.*
Similar Species: *Eared Grebe* (p. 36): black and white plumage during winter; short, thin bill; red eyes. *Least Grebe:* extremely rare; smaller; thin bill; yellowish eyes. *American Coot* (p. 59): wholly black body; white bill extends onto forehead.
Best Sites: small lakes and ponds statewide.

EARED GREBE

Podiceps nigricollis

The Eared Grebe is flightless for nine to ten months over the period of a year—longer than any other flying bird. During the cyclical flightless periods, the Eared Grebe's internal organs and pectoral muscles shrink or swell, depending on whether or not the birds need to migrate. • Grebes eat feathers, which pack the digestive tract and may protect the stomach lining and intestines from sharp fish bones or parasites, or perhaps slow the passage of food, allowing more time for complete digestion. • The Eared Grebe inhabits parts of Europe, Asia, Central Africa and South America, making it the most abundant grebe not only in North America, but also in the world. • The scientific name *nigricollis* means "black neck," a characteristic of this bird's breeding plumage.

nonbreeding

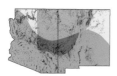

ID: *Breeding:* black neck, cheek, forehead and back; red flanks; fanned-out, golden "ear" tufts; white underparts; thin, straight bill; red eyes; slightly raised crown. *Nonbreeding:* dark cheek and upperparts; light underparts; dusky upper foreneck and flanks. *In flight:* wings beat constantly; appears hunchbacked; legs trail behind tail.
Size: *L* 11½–14 in; *W* 16 in.
Status: common to uncommon winter visitor to lakes and ponds regionwide; rare to uncommon and local in summer in the north.
Habitat: freshwater wetlands, larger lakes and sewage disposal ponds.

Nesting: in shallow bodies of water with sparse emergent vegetation; pair places lake bottom material among a foundation of bent over reeds; pair incubates 2–3 white to buff eggs for about 21 days; parents raise young together.
Feeding: makes shallow dives and gleans the water's surface for aquatic insects, crustaceans, mollusks, small fish and larval and adult amphibians.
Voice: usually quiet outside the breeding season.
Similar Species: *Pied-billed Grebe* (p. 35): thicker, stubbier bill; mostly brown body. *Least Grebe:* extremely rare; smaller; slender bill; yellow eye; grayish plumage.
Best Sites: *AZ:* Roosevelt L.; San Carlos L.; Willcox L. *NM:* Bosque del Apache NWR; Bitterlake NWR.

WESTERN GREBE

Aechmophorus occidentalis

Elegant Western Grebes are famous for their elaborate courtship rituals, in which pairs caress each other with aquatic vegetation and sprint side by side, literally running on water. The grebes stand high, feet paddling furiously, with their wings stretched back and heads and necks held rigid, until the race ends with the pair breaking the water's surface in a graceful dive. • Breeding attempts may fail when changing water levels flood or strand the floating nests before eggs have hatched. • The Clark's Grebe *(A. clarkii)*, which until 1985 was thought to be a color phase of the Western Grebe rather than a distinct species, looks and acts like the Western Grebe and the two are most often found together. Overlapping ranges and similar habitat preferences add to the challenge of separating the two species. Black surrounds the eye of the breeding Western Grebe, while the Clark's Grebe's eye is surrounded by white. Nonbreeding birds are more difficult to tell apart.

breeding

ID: long, slender neck; black upperparts from base of bill to tail; long, thin, yellow bill; white cheek; white underparts from chin to belly. *Breeding:* black on face extends below red eyes.
Size: *L* 25 in; *W* 24 in.
Status: *AZ:* locally common resident of larger lakes and reservoirs. *NM:* uncommon to locally abundant migrant and winter visitor to larger lakes and reservoirs statewide; local in summer.
Habitat: large, deep lakes.
Nesting: usually in colonies; floating nest of fresh and decaying vegetation is anchored or placed among emergent vegetation; pair incubates 2–7 bluish green to buffy eggs (becoming stained brown) for about 23 days.
Feeding: gleans the water's surface and dives for small fish, some amphibians and aquatic invertebrates.
Voice: high-pitched, double-note *crreeet-crreeet;* repeated call sounds like a squeaky wheel.
Similar Species: *Clark's Grebe:* white on face extends above eyes; orange-yellow bill; single-note call. *Double-crested Cormorant* (p. 39): immature has thicker, crooked neck, longer tail and yellow-orange throat patch.
Best Sites: *AZ:* Roosevelt L.; San Carlos L. *NM:* Elephant Butte L.

AMERICAN WHITE PELICAN
Pelecanus erythrorhynchos

Pelicans are a majestic wetland presence with a wingspan only a foot shy of the height of a basketball hoop. Their porous, bucketlike bills are dramatically adapted for feeding. One of only a few bird species that feeds cooperatively, a group of foraging pelicans will paddle with their feet to herd fish into schools, then dip their bills and scoop up the prey. As the pelican lifts its bill from the water, the fish are held within its flexible pouch while the water drains out. In a single scoop, a pelican can hold over 3 gallons of water and fish, which is about two to three times as much as its stomach can hold. This impressive feat confirms Dixon Lanier Merritt's quotation: "A wonderful bird is a pelican, His bill will hold more than his belican!" • The pelican's black wing tips contain a pigment called melanin, which makes the feathers stronger and more resistant to wear.

nonbreeding

nonbreeding

ID: stocky body; white plumage; long, orange bill and pouch; black flight feathers; short tail.
Breeding: plate develops on upper mandible.
Size: *L* 4½–6 ft; *W* 9 ft.
Status: rare to locally common migrant and winter visitor regionwide; rare in summer.
Habitat: freshwater lakes and flooded agricultural fields; migratory flocks may be seen over any habitat.

Nesting: does not breed in Arizona or New Mexico.
Feeding: forages cooperatively; pelicans swim side-by-side to "herd" fish into shallows, then dip their bills into the water to scoop up prey.
Voice: generally quiet; adults rarely issue piglike grunts.
Similar Species: no other large, white bird has long bill with pouch.
Best Sites: *AZ:* Lower Colorado R.; Roosevelt L.; San Carlos L. *NM:* Bosque del Apache NWR; Elephant Butte L.

DOUBLE-CRESTED CORMORANT

Phalacrocorax auritus

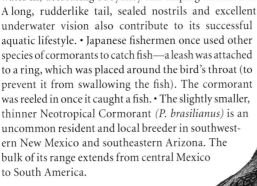

Double-crested Cormorants are commonly seen in large, V-shaped or single-file flocks flying between foraging and roosting areas or perched with their wings partially spread to dry their feathers. Most water birds have water-proof feathers, but the structure of the Double-crested Cormorant's feathers allows water in, decreasing buoyancy and helping this bird dive. A long, rudderlike tail, sealed nostrils and excellent underwater vision also contribute to its successful aquatic lifestyle. • Japanese fishermen once used other species of cormorants to catch fish—a leash was attached to a ring, which was placed around the bird's throat (to prevent it from swallowing the fish). The cormorant was reeled in once it caught a fish. • The slightly smaller, thinner Neotropical Cormorant *(P. brasilianus)* is an uncommon resident and local breeder in southwestern New Mexico and southeastern Arizona. The bulk of its range extends from central Mexico to South America.

juvenile

breeding

ID: black plumage; stocky neck; orange throat patch; dark bill, hooked at tip; blue eyes.
Juvenile: brown upperparts; pale throat and breast; yellowish throat patch.
In flight: strong, direct flight on rapid wingbeats; kinked neck.
Size: *L* 26–32 in; *W* 4½ ft.
Status: common transient and winter visitor regionwide; uncommon and local in summer.
Habitat: large lakes and reservoirs; roosts and nests in trees or shrubs.

Nesting: colonial; in a shrub or tree, usually on an island or in a swamp; nest is built of sticks; pair incubates 3–4 bluish white eggs for 25–29 days; pair feeds young by regurgitation.
Feeding: dives to depths of 30 ft or more for fish; surfaces to swallow prey.
Voice: generally quiet away from breeding colonies; occasional grunts or croaks.
Similar Species: *Neotropic Cormorant:* smaller, slender body; thinner bill; breeding birds have white plume, white outline on bill and yellow throat patch.
Best Sites: *AZ:* Roosevelt L.; San Carlos L., Willcox L. *NM:* Bosque del Apache NWR; Bitterlake NWR.

GREAT BLUE HERON

Ardea herodias

The long-legged Great Blue Heron has a stealthy, often motionless hunting strategy. It waits for a fish or frog to approach, spears the prey with its bill, then flips its catch into the air and swallows it whole. This heron usually hunts near water, but it also stalks fields and meadows in search of rodents. Anglers occasionally catch a fish with distinctive triangular scars—evidence that it once survived a heron attack. • Colonies of herons—known as rookeries—are usually located on isolated islands or in wooded swamps to avoid terrestrial predators such as raccoons. Colonies are sensitive to human disturbance, so be careful to observe the birds' behavior from a distance. • Great Blue Herons use a wide variety of freshwater and saltwater habitats throughout their range. They may turn up at virtually any water body that supports fish, from small riparian creeks to large reservoirs.

breeding

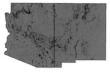

breeding

ID: long legs; curved neck; blue-gray back and wing coverts; large, straight, yellow bill; chestnut thighs. *Breeding:* richer colors; plumes on crown and throat. *In flight:* slow, steady wingbeats.
Size: *L* 4–4½ ft; *W* 6 ft.
Status: uncommon to common resident of wetland habitats throughout the region.
Habitat: forages along the edges of various types of wetlands; also stalks fields or yards.
Nesting: colonial; in a tree, snag, tall bush or marsh vegetation; flimsy to elaborate stick and twig platform can be up to 4 ft in diameter; pair incubates 3–5 pale blue-green eggs for 25–29 days.
Feeding: patient stand-and-wait predator; spears fish, snakes, amphibians and even rodents, then swallows prey whole.
Voice: a deep *frahnk-frahnk-frahnk* when startled.
Similar Species: *Black-crowned Night-Heron* (p. 43): much smaller and stockier; short neck; black crown and back. *Sandhill Crane* (p. 60): unfeathered red crown; flies with neck outstretched. *Little Blue Heron:* rare; is smaller and darker; greenish legs; bicolored dark bill.
Best Sites: most wetland habitats.
AZ: Roosevelt L.; San Carlos L.; Willcox L.
NM: Bosque del Apache NWR; Bitterlake NWR.

GREAT EGRET

Ardea alba

The plumes of the Great Egret and Snowy Egret *(Egretta thula)* were widely used to decorate hats in the early 20th century. An ounce of egret feathers cost as much as $32—more than an ounce of gold at that time—and, as a result, egret populations began to disappear. Some of the first conservation legislation in North America was enacted to outlaw the hunting of Great Egrets, and the nation's first National Wildlife Refuge, Pelican Island, Florida, was established in 1903. The Great Egret is also the symbol for the National Audubon Society, one of the oldest conservation organizations in the United States. • Egrets are named after the silky breeding plumes (called aigrettes) that most species produce during courtship. The plumes of a Great Egret can grow up to 4½ feet long! • Great, Snowy and Cattle egrets are permanent residents along the Gila River and Colorado River in Arizona and the Rio Grande in New Mexico. Cattle Egrets *(Bubulcus ibis)* are found primarily in overgrown fields and pastures, whereas other egrets are usually found near water.

breeding

nonbreeding

ID: white plumage; black legs; yellow bill. *Breeding:* white plumes trail from lower back; green lores. *In flight:* slow wingbeats; neck folds back over shoulders; legs extend backward.
Size: *L* 3–3½ ft; *W* 4 ft.
Status: *AZ:* common resident of rivers and marshland along the Lower Colorado R. and Gila R.; sparse winter visitor south of the Mogollon Rim. *NM:* rare to uncommon migrant and summer resident statewide; rare in winter along the southern Rio Grande.
Habitat: edges of marshes, lakes and ponds; flooded agricultural fields.

Nesting: colonial; in a tree or tall shrub; pair builds a platform of sticks and incubates 3–5 pale blue-green eggs for 23–26 days.
Feeding: patient stand-and-wait predator; occasionally stalks slowly; feeds primarily on fish and aquatic invertebrates.
Voice: generally silent away from colonies.
Similar Species: *Snowy Egret:* much smaller; black bill; yellow feet on black legs. *Cattle Egret:* not found in water; breeding bird has yellow-orange legs and bill and a buff orange throat, rump and crown.
Best Sites: *AZ:* Roosevelt L.; Lower Colorado R.; Tres Rios Wetlands. *NM:* Bosque del Apache NWR; Percha Dam SP; Rio Grande Nature Center.

GREEN HERON

Butorides virescens

Sentinel of mangroves and marshes, the ever-vigilant Green Heron sits hunched on a shaded branch at the water's edge. In summer, this crow-sized heron is widely distributed throughout our region and can show up at just about any watering hole, from a drainage ditch to a large lake. It often perches just above the water's surface along wooded streams, waiting to stab frogs and small fish with its daggerlike bill. This bird has also been observed dropping feathers, leaves or other small debris into the water to attract fish, which are then captured and eaten. The Green Heron is therefore one of the few birds in North America known to use tools. • The scientific name *virescens* is Latin for "growing or becoming green," and refers to this bird's transition from a streaky brown juvenile to a greenish adult.

nonbreeding

nonbreeding

ID: stocky body; slight crest; greenish black crown; chestnut face and neck; white foreneck and belly; blue-gray back and wings with greenish iridescence; short tail; yellow-green legs. *Breeding:* bright orange legs. *Juvenile:* heavy streaking along neck and underparts; dark brown upperparts.
Size: *L* 15–22 in; *W* 26 in.
Status: *AZ:* rare to uncommon migrant statewide; rare to uncommon resident and local breeder along the Colorado R. through central and southern Arizona.
NM: rare to uncommon local migrant and summer visitor statewide.
Habitat: marshes, lakes and canals.

Nesting: nests singly or in small, loose groups; male begins and female completes construction of a stick platform in a tree or shrub, usually very close to water; pair incubates 3–5 pale blue-green to green eggs for 19–21 days; young are fed by regurgitation.
Feeding: stabs prey with its bill after slowly stalking or standing and waiting; eats mostly small fish.
Voice: generally silent; alarm call is a loud *skow*.
Similar Species: *Yellow-crowned Night-Heron* and *Black-crowned Night-Heron* (p. 43): juveniles are much larger with brownish plumage and white streaks or spots on upperparts. *Least Bittern:* buffy yellow shoulder patch, sides and flanks.
Best Sites: *AZ:* Roosevelt L.; Lower Colorado R.; Tres Rios Wetlands. *NM:* Bosque del Apache NWR; Percha Dam SP; Rio Grande Nature Center.

BLACK-CROWNED NIGHT-HERON

Nycticorax nycticorax

When dusk's long shadows shroud the marshes, Black-crowned Night-Herons arrive to hunt in the marshy waters. These herons crouch motionless, using their large, light-sensitive eyes to spot prey lurking in the shallows. They remain alongside water until morning, when they flap off to treetop roosts. • The Black-crowned Night-Heron breeds throughout much of the United States and is the most abundant heron in the world, occurring virtually worldwide. • Watch for these birds in summer, between dawn and dusk, as they fly from nesting colonies to feeding areas and back. • *Nycticorax*, meaning "night raven," refers to this bird's loud call: a single *quock!* that is often heard as it flies between roosting and feeding areas.

immature

breeding

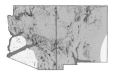

ID: stocky body; black crown and back; white cheek, foreneck, and underparts; gray neck and wings; stout, black bill; red eyes.
Breeding: two white plumes on crown.
Juvenile: lightly streaked underparts; brown upperparts with white flecking; yellowish bill. *In flight:* only tips of feet project beyond tail.
Size: *L* 23–26 in; *W* 3½ ft.
Status: uncommon to common migrant and summer resident regionwide; locally uncommon in winter.
Habitat: uses a variety of wetlands.

Nesting: colonial; in a tree or shrub; male gathers nest material for female to build a platform of twigs and line it with finer materials; pair incubates 3–4 pale green eggs for 21–26 days.
Feeding: often at dusk; patient stand-and-wait predator; stabs for fish, crustaceans, amphibians, and other aquatic prey.
Voice: deep, guttural *quock!*
Similar Species: *American Bittern:* rarely seen in the open and never in flocks; similar to juvenile but is larger; black "mustache" streak.
Best Sites: *AZ:* Roosevelt L.; Lower Colorado R.; Tres Rios Wetlands. *NM:* Bosque del Apache NWR; Percha Dam SP; Rio Grande Nature Center.

WHITE-FACED IBIS

Plegadis chihi

Ibises are slender, long-legged, highly social wading birds revered in many parts of the world. The White-faced Ibis is an elegant bird of western North America's larger wetlands and occupies the same habitats as the Glossy Ibis *(P. falcinellus)* of eastern North America. The White-faced Ibis prefers flooded croplands and the expansive reedbeds or muddy shallows of federal wildlife refuges. It flies rapidly, easily traversing the miles between secluded nesting colonies and outlying feeding locations. • Seen at any distance in flight or on the ground, White-faced Ibises look entirely dark brown because light must reflect off the feather's barbules at just the right angle to produce iridescence. When these ibises stand in front of the light source, their glistening color disappears.

breeding

breeding

ID: slender body; dark chestnut overall; long, downcurved bill; dark red eyes; long, dark legs; narrow strip of white feathers borders naked facial patch; iridescent greenish lower back and wing coverts. *Breeding:* rich red legs and facial patch. *In flight:* gangly-looking but graceful, with outstretched neck and long, downcurved bill visible at long range; intersperses rapid wingbeats with brief periods of gliding on stiffly bowed wings.

Size: *L* 19–26 in; *W* 36 in.

Status: uncommon to common migrant around agricultural areas and wetlands regionwide; rare and local in summer.

Habitat: marshes, lake edges, mudflats, wet pastures and irrigation ditches.

Nesting: colonial; in bulrushes or other emergent vegetation; deep cup nest of coarse materials is lined with fine plant matter; pair incubates 3–4 bluish green eggs for about 22 days.

Feeding: probes and gleans soil and shallow water for aquatic invertebrates, amphibians and other small vertebrates.

Voice: generally quiet; occasionally gives a series of low, ducklike quacks.

Similar Species: *herons and egrets* (p. *40–43*): all lack thick-based, downcurved bill. *Long-billed Curlew:* rich buffy brown with cinnamon underwing linings; uniformly thin bill.

Best Sites: *AZ:* Arlington Valley; Gila Bend; Lower Colorado R.; Tres Rios Wetlands.

NM: Bosque del Apache NWR; Percha Dam SP; Rio Grande Valley.

TURKEY VULTURE

Cathartes aura

Vultures are intelligent, playful and social birds. Groups live and sleep together in large trees or roosts. Some roost sites are over a century old and have been used by the same family of vultures for several generations. Two vulture species occur in our region: the more common Turkey Vulture and the rare Black Vulture *(Coragyps atratus)*, which is found in southern Arizona but not in New Mexico. • Turkey Vultures are unmatched at using updrafts and thermals—they can tease lift from the slightest pocket of rising air. Pilots have reported seeing these vultures soaring at 20,000 feet. • Perhaps the Turkey Vulture's most unique feature is a highly developed sense of smell. In the United States, these birds were once used to locate gas leaks. A scented substance, similar to a chemical emitted from carrion, was pumped through the pipelines, then engineers watched to see where Turkey Vultures gathered. • A threatened Turkey Vulture will throw up. The odor of its vomit repulses attackers, much like the odor of a skunk's spray does.

ID: black body with paler flight feathers; unfeathered head; longish, slender tail. *Adult:* red head. *Juvenile:* gray head. *In flight:* head appears small; wings held in a shallow "V"; rocks from side to side when soaring.
Size: *L* 26–32 in; *W* 5½–6 ft.
Status: common to abundant summer resident and migrant regionwide; small numbers winter in extreme southwestern AZ.
Habitat: forages over open country, but roosts and nests in forested areas.
Nesting: on the ground, often under saw palmettos; no nest is built; pair incubates 2 white eggs, blotched with reddish brown, for 38–41 days.

Feeding: solely on carrion, often road-killed mammals, especially Nine-banded Armadillos.
Voice: generally silent; an occasional hiss or grunt if threatened.
Similar Species: *Black Vulture:* gray head; shorter, rounded wings with bold silver tips; short, rounded tail; holds wings horizontally in flight; does not soar, flaps and glides. *Golden Eagle* (p. 55) and *Bald Eagle* (p. 48): lack silvery gray wing linings; wings are held flat and do not rock when soaring; head is more visible in flight.
Best Sites: widespread in summer. *AZ:* Boyce Thompson Arboretum. *NM:* Bosque del Apache NWR.

OSPREY

Pandion haliaetus

The Osprey is one of the most widely distributed birds and occurs on all continents except for Antarctica. It feeds nearly exclusively on fish and is often called "fish hawk." • The large and powerful Osprey is almost always found near water. This bird often hovers while hunting for fish, it's dark eye line blocking the glare of the sun off the water. Once it spots a fish, the Osprey folds its wings and hurls itself downward in a dramatic headfirst dive toward its target. An instant before striking the water, the Osprey simultaneously flips upright and thrusts its feet forward, often striking the water with a tremendous splash. The Osprey has specialized feet for gripping slippery prey—two toes point forward, two point backward and all are covered with sharp spines.

ID: dark brown upperparts; white underparts; yellow eyes; white face with brown crown, nape and eye line; indistinct "necklace" across upper breast (may be absent on male). *In flight:* dark "wrist" marks on underwings; wings held in a shallow "M."

Size: *L* 22–25 in; *W* 4½–6 ft.

Status: uncommon migrant and localized breeding resident around larger bodies of water regionwide.

Habitat: forages in all open-water habitats except shallow marshes.

Nesting: in a tree (usually a snag), atop a telephone pole or on other human-made structures; massive stick nest is reused over many years; pair incubates 2–4 yellowish eggs, blotched with reddish brown, for 32–33 days.

Feeding: dramatic, feet-first dives into the water; fish, averaging 2 lbs., make up almost all of the diet.

Voice: series of melodious ascending whistles: *chewk-chewk-chewk;* also an often heard *kip-kip-kip.*

Similar Species: *Bald Eagle* (p. 48): immature is larger, always has some black in its plumage, has yellow legs and larger bill with yellow base and holds its wings flatter.

Best Sites: *AZ:* Colorado River Valley; White Mts.; Roosevelt L. *NM:* Bosque del Apache NWR; Percha Dam SP; Heron Lake SP.

MISSISSIPPI KITE

Ictinia mississippiensis

Most often seen in flight, the Mississippi Kite floats buoyantly above rich riparian cottonwood habitats, flapping lazily but rarely gliding. This bird feeds on flying insects such as dragonflies, cicadas and grasshoppers, which it plucks out of the air with its feet and eats while in flight. Occasional acrobatic aerial pursuits end in the successful capture of larger vertebrates, including bats, swallows and swifts. • Mississippi Kites were traditionally restricted to the southern states, but their breeding range seems to be expanding northward, with spring or summer sightings now occurring to southern New England. • The graceful White-tailed Kite *(Elanus leucurus)* also occurs locally in southeastern Arizona and, rarely, in the Sandia Mountains of New Mexico. Populations exhibit swings in abundance, fluctuating along with the rodent population. In the 1900s, the White-tail was nearly extirpated from the United States. It has recently made a strong comeback, perhaps partially owing to the introduction of the house mouse, a readily available food source.

Habitat: deciduous or mixed woodlands, swamps and riparian areas.

Nesting: in a tall tree; pair constructs a flimsy stick platform and lines it with leaves; pair incubates 2 bluish white eggs for 30–32 days.

ID: long wings and tail; dark gray back and wings; pale head; dark gray underparts; black tail; chestnut at base of primaries (often inconspicuous). *Juvenile:* dark brownish upperparts; underparts heavily marked with rufous; banded tail. *In flight:* distinctive short outermost primary feathers.

Size: *L* 14½ in; *W* 3 ft.

Status: *AZ:* uncommon and local summer resident along riparian corridors in the southeast. *NM:* locally common in the southeastern plains.

Feeding: plucks flying insects out of the air, or small vertebrates from foliage.

Voice: generally silent; alarm call: *kee-kew, kew-kew*; call of fledgling an emphatic *three-beers*.

Similar Species: *White-tailed Kite:* little habitat/regional overlap; pale gray wings with black shoulders; white underparts including tail; black "wrist" patches on underwings. *Northern Harrier* (p. 49): little seasonal/habitat overlap; male has white on rump not uppertail and does not hover.

Best Sites: *AZ:* Dudleyville; St. David. *NM:* Roswell; Clovis; Tucumari.

BALD EAGLE

Haliaeetus leucocephalus

The Bald Eagle, a symbol of freedom, longevity and strength, became the emblem of the United States in 1872. One of the most magnificent birds in our region, the Bald Eagle is a species that no birder ever tires of seeing. • This majestic bird hunts mostly fish and is often found near water. While soaring hundreds of feet high in the air, an eagle can spot fish swimming underwater and small rodents scurrying through the grass. • Populations of eagles and other fish-eating species suffered dramatic declines beginning in the late 1940s, which were linked to DDT poisoning. Banning of DDT in the 1970s allowed eagle populations to recover. • Bald Eagles do not molt into adult plumage until their fourth year, only then acquiring their characteristic white head and tail.

immature

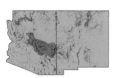

ID: white head and tail; dark brown body; yellow bill and feet. *Immature:* mostly dark bill; variable amounts of white mottling on upperparts, underwings and undertail; acquires adult plumage in fourth year. *In flight:* soars on broad, flat wings.
Size: *L* 30–43 in; *W* 5½–8 ft.
Status: threatened. *AZ:* uncommon migrant; local summer resident and winter visitor. *NM:* uncommon migrant and winter visitor to larger bodies of water statewide.

Habitat: forages over large water bodies.
Nesting: does not breed in Arizona or New Mexico.
Feeding: feeds primarily on fish and waterbirds such as American Coot; frequently pirates fish from Ospreys; scavenges carrion.
Voice: thin, weak squeal or gull-like cackle.
Similar Species: adult distinctive. *Golden Eagle* (p. 55): dark overall, except for golden nape; immature has prominent white patches on wings and base of tail.
Best Sites: *AZ:* Verde R; Salt R.; Roosevelt L. *NM:* Bosque del Apache NWR; Percha Dam SP; Navajo Reservoir.

NORTHERN HARRIER

Circus cyaneus

With its prominent white rump and distinctive, slightly upturned wings, the Northern Harrier may be the easiest raptor to identify in flight. Unlike other midsized birds, it often flies close to the ground, cruising low over fields, meadows and marshes, relying on sudden surprise attacks to capture prey. Owl-like, parabolic facial discs allow the Northern Harrier to hunt by sound when prey is hidden in the vegetation.

• The Northern Harrier was once known as "Marsh Hawk" in North America, and it is still called "Hen Harrier" in Europe. Britain's Royal Air Force was so impressed by this bird's maneuverability that it named its Harrier aircraft after this bird.

• The North American population of harriers has declined in recent years, owing to the loss of wetland habitat.

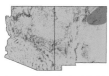

ID: long wings and tail. *Male:* gray upperparts; white underparts with faint rusty streaking; tail banded with black. *Female:* dark brown upperparts; buff underparts streaked with dark brown. *Juvenile:* rich brown upperparts; head and upper breast streaked with brown. *In flight:* flies low over marshes; conspicuous white rump; black wing tips.
Size: *L* 16–24 in; *W* 3½–4 ft.
Status: common migrant and winter visitor statewide; rare in summer.
Habitat: open habitats such as fields, pastures and marshes.
Nesting: rare breeder in Arizona or New Mexico; occasionally nests locally in our

northern regions; on the ground, usually in tall vegetation or on a raised mound; shallow depression is lined with grass, sticks and cattails; female incubates 4–6 bluish white eggs for 30–32 days.
Feeding: flies low, often skimming the top of vegetation; feeds on rats, small rabbits, snakes and birds such as Red-winged Blackbirds.
Voice: generally silent; high-pitched *ke-ke-ke-ke-ke-ke* near the nest.
Similar Species: *Red-tailed Hawk* (p. 54): lacks white rump and long, narrow tail. *Harris's Hawk:* also has white rump but has dark underparts.
Best Sites: *AZ:* Sulphur Springs Valley; Arlington Valley. *NM:* Rio Grande River Valley.

COOPER'S HAWK

Accipiter cooperii

The Cooper's Hawk is a member of the *Accipiter* genus, or woodland hawks, and it preys almost exclusively on small birds. Its short, rounded wings, long, rudderlike tail and flap-and-glide flight allow it to maneuver through the forest at high speed, using surprise and speed to snatch its prey from midair. The female can seize and decapitate birds as large as chickens, which has earned it the name "chicken hawk." • Distinguishing the slightly larger and heavier Cooper's Hawk from the Sharp-shinned Hawk *(A. striatus)* is challenging. In flight, the Cooper's has a longer, more rounded tail with a broader, white tail tip, whereas the Sharpie has a shorter, square tail. • Sharp-shinned Hawks are uncommon permanent residents in northern Arizona and New Mexico and uncommon to common residents in the south.

Habitat: forages over any wooded or semi-wooded habitat, even suburban yards.
Nesting: in the fork of a tree; may reuse an abandoned squirrel nest, or male builds nest of sticks and twigs; female incubates 4–5 bluish white eggs for 30–36 days.
Feeding: chases or dives at medium-sized landbirds.
Voice: silent except around nest; a fast *cac-cac-cac.*
Similar Species: *Sharp-shinned Hawk:* smaller; square tail tip; dark nape. *American Kestrel* (p. 56): long, pointed wings; 2 black facial stripes; typically seen in open country, often perched on power lines. *Merlin:* rapid wingbeats on pointed wings; single dark facial stripe; brown streaking on buff underparts; dark eyes.
Best Sites: *AZ:* Patagonia Sonoita Creek Sanctuary; White Mts.; Flagstaff. *NM:* Sandia Mts.; Santa Fe; Taos.

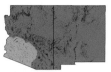

ID: blue-gray upperparts; pale face with dark crown; pale nape; red eyes; white underparts heavily barred with orange. *Juvenile:* brown upperparts; yellow eyes; white underparts streaked with brown. *In flight:* short rounded wings; long round-tipped tail; flap-and-glide flight.
Size: *Male: L* 15–17 in; *W* 27–32 in. *Female: L* 17–19 in; *W* 32–37 in.
Status: uncommon migrant and winter visitor regionwide; widespread and local in summer in mountain canyons and riparian woodlands.

COMMON BLACK-HAWK

Buteogallus anthracinus

An undisturbed, mature gallery of cottonwood and sycamore next to a gently flowing stream is paradise for a Common Black-Hawk. Unfortunately for this summer visitor, these two requirements are becoming increasingly scarce in the southwestern U.S. • These raptors arrive in March to begin courtship, soaring and diving with their legs drooping beneath them. When nest construction begins, males plunge from the air to snap off large sticks to bring to the building females. If disturbed too often, Common Black-Hawks will abandon their nest and relocate to another area. • These resourceful raptors may perch above the water, waiting to snatch up prey with their talons. They also wade through shallow water, dipping in their wing tips to scare prey to the surface.
• *Buteogallus anthracinus* is Latin for "chicken hawk that is as black as coal."

ID: stout, black body; thick, white tail band; yellowish bill has dark tip; long, yellow legs; pale gray wingtips (primaries). *Juvenile:* heavily streaked plumage; chest and undertail buffy with black streaks; leg feathers and tail streaked black and white; back and nape mostly brown with buffy streaks; buffy face.
Size: *L* 20–23 in; *W* 46–50 in.
Status: *AZ:* fairly common summer resident along permanent streams in canyons of southeastern and central regions.
NM: uncommon and local summer resident in the southwest in riparian and wooded canyons with perennial stream.
Habitat: undisturbed, streamside, mature woods, especially sycamore and cottonwood.
Nesting: 30–100 ft high, in a crook of a large sycamore or cottonwood; male brings

large sticks to female, who builds a platform nest and lines it with green leaves; mainly the female incubates 1–2 eggs for 34 days.
Feeding: often hunts near streams; captures large insects, amphibians, lizards, fish and small birds.
Voice: generally silent; a sharp, whistled *keer!..keer!..keer!* near nest.
Similar Species: *Zone-tailed Hawk* (p. 53): narrower wings held higher above body while soaring; 3 white tail bands; outer wings gray with black stripes.
Best Sites: *AZ:* Aravaipa Canyon; Camp Creek; Sycamore Creek at Sunflower.
NM: Redrock Springs; Mangas Springs; Glenwood Fish Hatchery.

51

HARRIS'S HAWK

Parabuteo unicinctus

Harris's Hawks are highly sophisticated, cooperative feeders that use different hunting strategies for specific prey. Before each hunt, up to five birds assemble for a hunting "ceremony," and perch together, sometimes sharing the same branch. Depending on the type of prey, the birds may all converge at the same time, or one may flush the animal while the others ambush from other directions. On long chases, birds switch off as lead chaser, until the exhausted prey is caught. After a successful hunt, the prey is shared among the group. • These hawks breed in a social unit made up of two to seven hawks, including adults and juveniles. Whether groups are monogamous, polygynous or, rarely, polyandrous seems to vary with geographic location. • This raptor is named after Edward Harris, a friend and benefactor of John James Audubon. *Unicinctus* is Latin for "once girdled," referring to the large, black band around the hawk's tail.

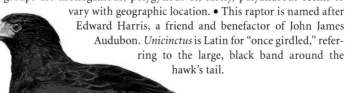

from Phoenix to Tucson. **NM:** uncommon resident of deserts in the southeast and southwest.

Habitat: desert savanna with saguaro and dead trees appropriately spaced for perch-and-fly hunting; proximity to water very important.

Nesting: on saguaro or stable perch; large platform of branches is lined with cactus pieces and leaves; female, sometimes relieved by male, incubates 1–4 eggs for 33–36 days; may have 2 broods; "helpers" defend nest and feed young.

Feeding: may hunt singly or cooperatively using a variety of techniques but mainly sit-and-wait; eats small birds and mammals.

Voice: 1 long, harsh note; a defensive *kah-kah-kah-kah*.

Similar Species: dark plumage, chestnut wing coverts, white rump and tail band are distinctive.

Best Sites: AZ: Arthur Pack Park; Sweetwater Wetlands area; McDowell Mountain Regional Park. **NM:** San Simon Cienega; Anima Valley; Laguna Grande area.

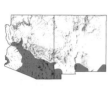

ID: dark brown body; chestnut shoulders and thighs; white rump and under-tail; thick, black tail band; white terminal tail band; yellow legs and beak. *Juvenile:* white and brown vertically streaked belly. *In flight:* appears black; broad wings.

Size: *L* 17–24 in; *W* 3½ ft

Status: AZ: locally common resident in palo verde-saguaro deserts in central Arizona

ZONE-TAILED HAWK

Buteo albonotatus

The Zone-tailed Hawk lazily soars and tilts among thermal updrafts, holding its wings in a "V." This hawk's flight pattern, slightly translucent flight feathers and dark underwing linings resemble a Turkey Vulture's, and these two raptors are often found soaring together. To distinguish the two, watch for the Zone-tailed Hawk's blackish, feathered head, thinly barred flight feathers and black and white tail barring. Feeding strategies can also lend a clue to identity. Zone-tailed Hawks swoop down to prey on small animals while vultures scavenge for their prey.

ID: dark gray to slate black overall; light underwing flight feathers with thin, dark barring; alternating black and grayish white tail bands; bright yellow legs; black-tipped, yellow bill. *In flight:* wings held in a "V"; often tilts side to side.

Size: *L* 18½–21½ in; *W* 47–53 in.

Status: *AZ:* common summer resident in riparian woodlands in foothills and mountains of the southeast, north across the Mogollon Rim. *NM:* uncommon and local resident of wooded canyons primarily in the southwest.

Habitat: open country habitats including chaparral, desert scrub and grassland, desert mountains, canyons and streamside woodlands.

Nesting: only 1 nesting record for our region; bulky stick platform built high above the ground in a tall tree (often cottonwood or pine) near a cliff or stream; female incubates 1–3 white to pale bluish white eggs, with gray or tan spots, for about 35 days.

Feeding: seasonally available small mammals, reptiles, amphibians and birds are taken from the ground in a swooping attack; hunts from a high perch or from the air; may eat carrion.

Voice: alarm call is a long, screaming whistle.

Similar Species: *Turkey Vulture* (p. 45): very similar in flight, but lacks whitish tail bands. *Black Vulture:* lacks barring in wings and tail. *Common Black-Hawk* (p. 51): rare; shorter, broader wings and tail; 1 wide, white tail band. *Golden Eagle* (p. 55): much larger; lacks barring in flight feathers and tail; immatures have white at base of tail.

Best Sites: *AZ:* Camp Creek; Sycamore Creek at Sunflower; Catalina Mts.; Huachuca Mts. *NM:* Guadalupe Mts.; Animas Mts.

RED-TAILED HAWK

Buteo jamaicensis

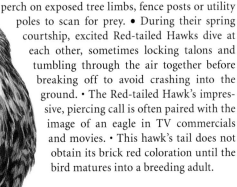

R ed-tailed Hawks are the most common hawks throughout North America and can often be seen using thermals and updrafts to soar. The pockets of rising air provide substantial lift, which allows migrating hawks to fly for almost 2 miles without flapping their wings. On cooler days, resident Red-tails perch on exposed tree limbs, fence posts or utility poles to scan for prey. • During their spring courtship, excited Red-tailed Hawks dive at each other, sometimes locking talons and tumbling through the air together before breaking off to avoid crashing into the ground. • The Red-tailed Hawk's impressive, piercing call is often paired with the image of an eagle in TV commercials and movies. • This hawk's tail does not obtain its brick red coloration until the bird matures into a breeding adult.

Harlan's Hawk

ID: mottled brown wings and back; brown head; white throat; white or pale buff underparts with a brown belly band; orange tail. *Juvenile:* brown tail has dark bands. *In flight:* white or buffy underwing linings; dark leading edge on pale, faintly barred underwings.
Size: *Male: L* 18–23 in; *W* 3½–4½ ft. *Female: L* 20–25 in; *W* 4–5 ft.
Status: common and widespread resident throughout the region.
Habitat: open country with scattered trees.

Nesting: in open pinewoods or at the edge of woodlands; often in a pine; bulky stick nest is usually added to each year; pair incubates 2–4 brown-blotched, whitish eggs for 28–35 days; male brings food to the female and nestlings.
Feeding: forages by scanning the ground from a tall perch and then captures prey after a short flight; feeds primarily on rodents, but takes a variety of animal prey.
Voice: powerful, descending scream; *keeeearrr.*
Similar Species: *Swainson's Hawk:* all-dark back; dark flight feathers, pale wing linings and more pointed wing tips in flight; holds wings in shallow "V." *Rough-legged Hawk:* white tail base; dark "wrist" patches on underwings; broad, dark, terminal tail band.
Best Sites: widespread.

GOLDEN EAGLE

Aquila chrysaetos

For many centuries, the Golden Eagle has embodied the wonder and wildness of the North American landscape. Unfortunately, beginning in the late 1800s, this regal bird was perceived as a threat to livestock, and shooting and poisoning was encouraged. Today, as are all other migratory birds, the Golden Eagle is protected under the Migratory Bird Act. • The Golden Eagle is actually more closely related to the *Buteo* hawks than it is to the Bald Eagle. Unlike the Bald Eagle, the Golden Eagle is an active, impressive predator, taking prey as large as foxes, cranes and geese. It can soar high above mountain passes for hours, sometimes stooping at great speeds—150–200 miles per hour—for prey or for fun. • Few people ever forget the sight of a Golden Eagle soaring overhead—the average wingspan of an adult exceeds 6 feet! • This eagle was previously thought to be nonmigratory, but it's migration route along the Rocky Mountains was discovered in 1992.

immature

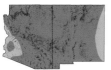

ID: brown overall with golden tint to neck and head; brown eyes; dark bill; brown tail has grayish white bands; yellow feet; fully feathered legs. *Immature:* white tail base; white patch at base of underwing primary feathers. *In flight:* relatively short neck; long tail; long, large, rectangular wings. **Size:** *L* 30–40 in; *W* 6½–7½ ft. **Status:** uncommon migrant and winter visitor throughout the region; locally fairly common summer resident in mountainous regions area wide. **Habitat:** semi-open woodlands and fields. **Nesting:** usually in a tree in open habitats; huge stick nest is reused for many years;

pair incubates 1–2 white eggs for 43–45 days; pair feeds the young. **Feeding:** swoops on prey from a soaring flight; eats hares, grouse, rodents, foxes and, occasionally, young ungulates; often eats carrion. **Voice:** generally quiet in winter; thin, weak squeal or gull-like cackle: *kleek-kik-kik-kik* or *kah-kah-kah*. **Similar Species:** *Bald Eagle* (p. 48): longer neck; shorter tail; immature lacks distinct, white underwing patches and tail base. *Turkey Vulture* (p. 45): naked, pink head; pale flight feathers; dark wing linings. **Best Sites:** *AZ:* widespread. Boyce Thompson Arboretum; Sulphur Springs Valley; San Rafael Grasslands; Tanto National Forest. *NM:* widespread.

AMERICAN KESTREL

Falco sparverius

The colorful American Kestrel, formerly known as "Sparrow Hawk," is a common and widespread falcon, not shy of human activity and adaptable to habitat change. This small falcon has benefited from the grassy rights-of-way created by interstate highways, which provide habitat for grasshoppers and other small prey. Watch for this robin-sized bird along rural roadways, perched on poles and telephone wires or hovering over agricultural fields, foraging for insects and small mammals. It often repeatedly lifts its tail while perched to scout below for prey. • Another small falcon, the Merlin *(F. columbarius),* is an uncommon winter resident in woodlands, hedgerows and savanna throughout our region. Unlike American Kestrels, Merlins seldom perch on power lines; they usually hunt from a snag or other conspicuous perch and feed mostly on birds, some as large as doves.

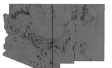

ID: black barring on rufous back; multi-colored head; gray crown with rusty centre; white face; buffy nape with black patch; 2 black facial stripes; whitish underparts; rufous tail. *Male:* blue wings; black-spotted underparts; bold, black subterminal tail band. *Female:* rufous wings; underparts streaked with rufous; rufous-and-black-banded tail. *In flight:* frequently hovers.
Size: *L* 7½–8 in; *W* 20–24 in.
Status: common migrant and resident in a wide variety of habitats throughout the region; numbers augmented in winter by arrivals from the north.

Habitat: virtually any open or semi-wooded area.
Nesting: in a tree cavity; may use a nest box; mostly the female incubates 4–6 finely speckled, white to pale brown eggs for 29–30 days; both parents raise the young.
Feeding: swoops from a perch or hovers overhead; eats primarily insects (especially *F. s. paulus*) and small vertebrates.
Voice: shrill *killy-killy-killy.*
Similar Species: *Merlin:* larger; lacks rufous on back, wings and tail; only 1 facial stripe; does not hover. *Sharp-shinned Hawk:* lacks rufous on back, wings and tail; no facial stripes; flap-and-glide flight; does not hover.
Best Sites: widespread.

PRAIRIE FALCON

Falco mexicanus

This western raptor of arid, open landscapes is best identified by its brown plumage and dark "armpits." • In spring and summer, Prairie Falcons often concentrate their hunting efforts on ground squirrel colonies, swooping over windswept grass to pick off naive youngsters. As summer fades to fall, large flocks of migrating songbirds often capture the attention of these pallid "ghosts of the plains." • Freshly fledged, inexperienced falcons risk serious injury or death when pushing the limits in early hunting forays. Swooping falcons can easily misjudge their flight speed or their ability to pull out of a dive. • Another large falcon, the Peregrine Falcon *(F. peregrinus)* is a permanent resident throughout much of our region. Peregrines are darker overall and occur in a wide variety of habitats, most often near water.

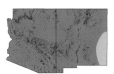

ID: brown upperparts; pale face with dark brown, narrow "mustache" stripe; white underparts with brown spotting. *In flight:* diagnostic dark "wing pits"; pointed wings; long, narrow, banded tail; quick wingbeats and direct flight.
Size: *Male: L* 14–15 in; *W* 37–39 in. *Female: L* 17–18 in; *W* 41–43 in.
Status: rare to uncommon resident in deserts and plains throughout the region; numbers increase in fall and in winter in the southern deserts and grasslands in response to availability of food.
Habitat: *Breeding:* river canyons, cliffs, rimrocks or rocky promontories in arid, open lowlands or high intermontane valleys. *In migration and winter:* open, treeless country, such as fields, pastures and sagebrush flats.

Nesting: on cliff ledges, in crevices or on rocky promontories; rarely in abandoned nests of other raptors or crows; nest is usually unlined; mainly the female incubates 3–5 whitish eggs, spotted with brown, for 29–30 days; male brings food to the female and young.
Feeding: high-speed strike-and-kill by diving swoops, low flights or chases on the wing; eats small mammals, birds and some lizards and large insects; females consume more mammalian prey than do males.
Voice: generally silent; alarm call near nest is a rapid, shrill *kik-kik-kik-kik.*
Similar Species: diagnostic dark wing pits. *Peregrine Falcon:* dark distinctive "helmet." *Merlin:* much smaller. *American Kestrel* (p. 56): smaller and much more colorful; 2 bold facial stripes; often hovers.
Best Sites: widespread.

SORA

Porzana carolina

Soras have small bodies and large, chickenlike feet for walking on aquatic vegetation. Even without webbed feet, these unique creatures swim quite well over short distances. • Two rising *or-Ah or-Ah* whistles followed by a strange, descending whinny indicate that a Sora is nearby. Although the Sora is the most common and widespread rail species in North America, it is seldom seen. This secretive bird prefers to remain hidden in dense marshland, but it will occasionally venture into the shallows to search for aquatic insects and mollusks. • Though it appears to be a weak and reluctant flier, the Sora migrates hundreds of miles each year between breeding grounds in Canada and the central United States to wintering wetlands in Central and South America. • The species name *carolina* means "of Carolina" and this bird is also known as "Carolina Rail."

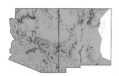

ID: short, yellow bill; black upperparts streaked with brown and white; brown nape and crown; black face; gray head, neck and breast; underparts barred black, brown and white; yellow legs and feet.
Size: *L* 8–10 in; *W* 14 in.
Status: rare to uncommon migrant and summer visitor to cattail marshes throughout the region; rare and local in winter.
Habitat: wetlands with abundant emergent cattails, bulrushes, sedges and grasses.
Nesting: usually over water or in a wet meadow; well-built basket nest, made of grass and aquatic vegetation, often includes an entrance ramp and overhead canopy; pair incubates 10–12 darkly speckled, buff or olive buff eggs for 18–20 days.
Feeding: gleans and probes for seeds, plants, aquatic insects and mollusks.
Voice: several calls, among them a simple *peep*, a *kerwee* and a "whinny" consisting of a rolling, descending jumble of notes that last about three seconds.
Similar Species: *Virginia Rail:* larger; long, downcurved bill; chestnut brown wing patch; rufous breast.
Best Sites: *AZ:* Salt R.; Verde R.; Granite Reef; Tres Rios Wetlands. *NM:* Bosque del Apache NWR; Rio Grande Nature Center.

AMERICAN COOT

Fulica americana

American Coots resemble ducks but are actually more closely related to rails and gallinules. They are also the only birds in our region with white bills, which stand out against their dark bodies. Coots squabble constantly during the breeding season and can often be seen running along the surface of the water, splashing and charging at intruders. Outside of breeding season, they gather amicably in large groups. • Coots are strong swimmers and can use their lobed toes and their wings to paddle quickly through the water. They are capable of completely submerging to avoid predators, though the young often fall victim to pike or other fish. • Along the Rio Grande River and the Colorado River and in southeastern Arizona, the American Coot shares its wetland habitat with the similar looking, but more elusive, Common Moorhen *(Gallinula choropus)*.

ID: chunky, black body; white frontal shield; white bill with dark band near tip; red eyes; pale yellow legs and lobed toes. *Juvenile*: paler underparts; no frontal shield.
Size: *L* 13–16 in; *W* 24 in.
Status: common to abundant migrant and winter visitor to wetland habitats throughout the region; less common and widespread in summer.
Habitat: shallow marshes, ponds and wetlands with open water and emergent vegetation; also sewage lagoons.
Nesting: in emergent vegetation; pair builds a floating nest of cattails and grass

in emergent vegetation; pair incubates 6–11 brown-spotted, buffy white eggs for 21–25 days.
Feeding: feeds primarily on plant material obtained from grazing on land, gleaning from the water's surface or diving to depths of up to 25 feet.
Voice: a variety of cackles, grunts and whistles.
Similar Species: *Ducks* (p. 22–30): lack chickenlike, white bill and uniformly black body. *Grebes* (p. 35–37): lack white forehead shield and all-dark plumage. *Common Moorhen:* reddish forehead shield; yellow-tipped bill; white streak on flanks.
Best Sites: almost anywhere near rivers, lakes and golf courses. *AZ:* Roosevelt L. *NM:* Bosque del Apache NWR.

SANDHILL CRANE

Grus canadensis

Deep, resonant, rattling calls announce the approach of a flock of Sandhill Cranes long before it passes overhead. The coiling of the birds' trachea adds harmonies to the notes of their calls, allowing them to call louder and farther. • To differentiate these birds in flight from similar long-necked birds, look for the crane's snapping upstroke and slower downstroke. • Sandhill Cranes mate for life, reinforcing pair bonds each spring with an elaborate courtship dance. Successful pairs usually produce one or two young—called colts—each year. • With a lifespan of more than two decades, these cranes are among the longest-living birds, but continuing development increasingly threatens populations.

ID: grayish overall; unfeathered red crown; "shaggy" tail; blackish bill, legs and feet. *In flight:* flies with neck and legs extended; large migrant flocks often soar.
Size: L 3½–4 ft; W 6–7 ft.
Status: locally abundant winter resident.
Habitat: upland areas, pastures, shallow marshes and agricultural fields.

Nesting: does not nest in Arizona or New Mexico.
Feeding: probes and gleans the ground for plant tubers; takes invertebrates and small vertebrates on occasion.
Voice: call is a loud, resonant, rattling call audible for great distances.
Similar Species: *Great Blue Heron* (p. 40): lacks red forehead patch; neck is folded back over shoulders in flight.
Best Sites: *AZ:* Willcox Playa; Sulpur Springs Valley; Cibola NWR; Havasu NWR.
NM: Bosque del Apache NWR; Bitter Lake NWR.

KILLDEER

Charadrius vociferus

Plovers are part of the shorebird family, a highly diverse and conspicuous—and increasingly threatened—order of birds. These small- to medium-sized, chunky shorebirds have large, rounded heads, large eyes, short, thin bills and shortish legs. • The ubiquitous Killdeer is often the first shorebird a birder learns to identify. It has adapted well to urbanization, and it finds golf courses, farms, fields and abandoned industrial areas as much to its liking as shorelines. • The Killdeer is a gifted actor, well known for its "broken wing" distraction display. When an intruder wanders too close to its nest, the Killdeer greets the interloper with piteous cries while dragging a wing and stumbling about as if injured. Most predators take the bait and follow, and once the Killdeer has lured the predator far away from its nest, it "recovers" from the injury and flies off with a loud call. • The scientific name *vociferus* aptly describes this vocal bird, but double-check all calls in spring, when the Killdeer is often imitated by European Starlings *(Sturnus vulgaris).*

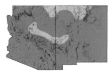

ID: brown upperparts, often with rusty wings; white neck ring; brown crown, nape and ear patch; white eyebrow and throat; 2 black breast bands; orange rump and tail; dull pinkish legs and feet.
Size: *L* 9–11 in; *W* 24 in.
Status: *AZ:* common resident in a variety of open habitats near water. *NM:* common migrant and summer resident in a variety of open habitats near water; uncommon and local in winter in the south.

Habitat: most open or grassy habitats; even found in urban and suburban areas.
Nesting: on open ground; in a shallow, usually unlined, depression; pair incubates 4 darkly blotched, pale buff eggs for 24–28 days; occasionally raises 2 broods.
Feeding: run-and-stop foraging technique; eats mostly insects; also takes spiders, snails, earthworms and crayfish.
Voice: distinctive onomatopoeic calls include *kill-dee, dee-dee-dee,* and *deer-deer.*
Similar Species: *Semipalmated Plover:* smaller; only 1 breast band.
Best Sites: widespread in open agricultural areas, lakes and reservoirs.

BLACK-NECKED STILT

Himantopus mexicanus

Stilts are uniquely shaped shorebirds, with long slender necks and—as is suggested by their name—extremely long legs. The sole species that occurs regularly in North America is the Black-necked Stilt, which is found from the United States through central South America and in the West Indies. • Black-necked Stilts are found in a variety of freshwater wetlands such as impoundments, marshes and flooded agricultural fields. When nesting, Black-necked Stilt parents are easily provoked; the birds circle low over their nest site while incessantly uttering loud *kip* notes. • On hot summer days, adult Black-necked Stilts routinely take turns sheltering their eggs from the warmth of the sun. Adults repeatedly wet their belly feathers to cool off their eggs and young during incubation.

ID: extremely long, red legs; white tail and rump forms inverted "V" on back; black upperparts; white face with black eye patch merges with nape; long, thin, black bill; white underparts. *In flight:* black wings.
Size: *L* 14–15 in; *W* 29 in.
Status: *AZ:* locally fairly common to common migrant and summer resident in southern and central Arizona. *NM:* locally fairly common migrant and summer resident nearly statewide.
Habitat: marshes and lakeshores; also forages in flooded agricultural fields, impoundments and salt evaporation ponds.

Nesting: in a shallow depression on slightly raised ground near water; nest is lined with shells, pebbles or vegetative debris; pair incubates 4 darkly blotched, buff eggs for about 25 days; both adults tend the precocial young.
Feeding: gleans prey from the water's surface or from the bottom substrate; feeds on small fish, crustaceans, mollusks and aquatic insects.
Voice: loud, sharp *kip* notes repeated continuously, often while in flight.
Similar Species: black and white plumage and long, red legs unique. *American Avocet* (p. 63): upturned bill; no black on head.
Best Sites: *AZ:* Lower Colorado R.; Tres Rios Wetlands; Willcox L. *NM:* Bosque del Apache NWR; Bitterlake NWR; Percha Dam SP.

AMERICAN AVOCET

Recurvirostra americana

An American Avocet in full breeding plumage is a sight to remember. Its peachy head, needlelike bill and bold, black and white body paint an elegant picture against the uniform mudflats. Often by August, its peach-colored hood has been replaced by more subdued winter grays, which this bird will wear for the greater part of the year. It is the only avocet in the world that undergoes a yearly color change. • Avocets nest on the shorelines of low elevation, alkaline lakes and wetlands, including Willcox Playa and Bosque del Apache NWR. Females have been known to parasatize the nests of other avocets and perhaps other species. Conversely, avocets have incubated Common Tern *(Sterna hirundo)* and Black-necked Stilt eggs, raising the stilt chicks along with their own young. • The American Avocet can issue a specialized, rising alarm call that simulates the Doppler effect and gives the impression of quickly moving closer.

nonbreeding

ID: bold, black and white wing pattern; long, slender, delicately upturned black bill; white under-parts; long, dull, gray legs and feet. *Breeding:* peachy head and neck. *Nonbreeding:* pale gray head and neck. **Size:** *L* 17–18 in; *W* 31 in. **Status:** *AZ:* locally fairly common to common migrant statewide; locally common summer resident in southern and central Arizona. *NM:* locally fairly common migrant and summer resident nearly statewide. **Habitat:** marshy lakeshores or flooded fields.

Nesting: semi-colonial; in a shallow depression along a dried mudflat, exposed shoreline or open area, always near water; pair builds a shallow scrape or a mound of vegetation and lines it with pebbles or other debris; pair incubates 4 darkly blotched eggs for 23–25 days. **Feeding:** sweeps its bill from side to side along the water's surface, picking up minute aquatic vegetation and invertebrates and occasionally seeds; occasionally tips up like a dabbling duck. **Voice:** generally silent; alarm call is harsh, shrill *pleek*, often repeated. **Similar Species:** bold black and white wing pattern and thin, upturned bill unique. *Black-necked Stilt* (p. 62): straight bill; mostly black head; red legs. **Best Sites:** *AZ:* Lower Colorado R.; Tres Rios Wetlands; Willcox Playa. *NM:* Bosque del Apache NWR; Bitterlake NWR; Percha Dam SP.

GREATER YELLOWLEGS

Tringa melanoleuca

The Greater Yellowlegs and Lesser Yellowlegs *(T. flavipes)* are medium-sized sandpipers with very similar plumages. Both species differ subtly, and a solitary yellowlegs is difficult to identify until it flushes and utters its distinctive call (the Greater Yellowlegs peeps three times, whereas the Lesser peeps twice). As its name suggests, the Greater Yellowlegs is the larger species and has a longer, slightly upturned bill that is about 1½ times the width of its head. • Greater Yellowlegs often perform a lookout role among mixed flocks of shorebirds. At the first sign of danger, these large sandpipers bob their heads and call incessantly. If forced to, they will usually retreat into deeper water, becoming airborne only as a last resort.

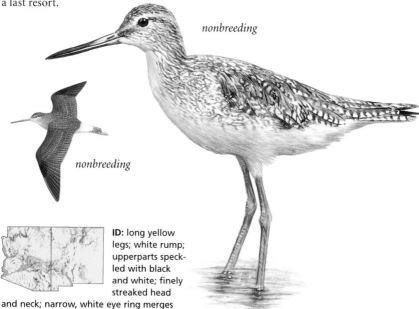

nonbreeding

nonbreeding

ID: long yellow legs; white rump; upperparts speckled with black and white; finely streaked head and neck; narrow, white eye ring merges with eye line; bill is longer than length of head, is slightly upturned and may have gray base; finely barred tail. *Breeding*: streaked breast; flanks barred with black. *Nonbreeding*: upperparts less marked; dusky breast; pale underparts.
Size: *L* 13–15 in; *W* 28 in.
Status: common migrant to shores and muddy flats regionwide. *AZ:* fairly common winter resident in the south, particularly the lower Colorado R. and Phoenix regions. *NM:* uncommon and local in the south in winter.
Habitat: almost all wetlands, including lakeshores, marshes, flooded fields and river shorelines; salt and freshwater ponds.
Nesting: does not nest in Arizona or New Mexico.

Feeding: picks up prey from the surface of the water or mud, or sweeps its bill back and forth; feeds on small fish, crustaceans, tadpoles and aquatic insects.
Voice: quick, whistled series of *tew-tew-tew*, usually 3 notes.
Similar Species: *Lesser Yellowlegs:* smaller; straight bill is shorter (roughly equal to length of head); call is quieter and one or two notes. *Stilt Sandpiper:* downcurved bill; nonbreeding has unbarred tail. *Willet:* black and white wings; heavier, straighter bill; dark, greenish legs.
Best Sites: *AZ:* Lower Colorado R.; Gila R.; Tres Rios Wetlands; Willcox L. *NM:* Bosque del Apache NWR; Bitterlake NWR; Percha Dam SP.

SPOTTED SANDPIPER

Actitis macularius

Even though its breast spots are not noticeable from a distance, the Spotted Sandpiper is easily recognizable by its stiff-winged, quivering flight pattern and its tendency to burst from the shore. This bird is also known for its continuous "teetering" behavior as it forages. • The female Spotted Sandpiper, unlike most other female birds, lays her eggs and leaves the male to tend the clutch. She diligently defends her territory and may mate with several different males. Only about one percent of birds display this unusual breeding strategy known as "polyandry." Each summer, the female can lay up to four clutches and is capable of producing 20 eggs. As the season progresses, available males become harder to find. Come August, there may be seven females for every available male. • The scientific name *macularia* is Latin for "spot," referring to the spots on this bird's underparts in breeding plumage.

nonbreeding

nonbreeding

ID: short legs; plain brown upperparts, including tail and rump; pale yellow or pink legs and feet; bobs hind end almost continuously. *Breeding:* unique; white underparts with bold, black spotting. *Nonbreeding:* brown head with short, white eyebrow and black eye line; whitish throat; brown "spur" on sides of breast.
Size: *L* 7–8 in; *W* 15 in.
Status: *AZ:* fairly common migrant and winter resident in the south, particularly the lower Colorado R. and Phoenix regions; local summer resident above the Mogollon Rim. *NM:* fairly common migrant statewide; uncommon and local in summer east of the plains; uncommon and local in winter in the far south.
Habitat: along lake or pond edges and flooded agricultural fields.

Nesting: usually near water; sheltered by vegetation; shallow scrape is lined with grass; male incubates 4 darkly blotched, creamy buff eggs for 20–24 days.
Feeding: gleans prey from the surface of the water or ground; feeds mostly on insects but also takes small fish, crustaceans, mollusks and worms.
Voice: call is a sharp *peet-weet*.
Similar Species: *Solitary Sandpiper:* spotted upperparts; dusky face with white eye ring; olive legs and feet; plain wings in flight. *"Peep" sandpipers* (p. 66): usually in flocks; do not bob their hind end; lack combination of pale legs and feet and pale bill; all lack spotted underparts in breeding plumage.
Best Sites: *AZ:* White Mts.; Lower Colorado R.; Tres Rios Wetlands; Willcox L. *NM:* Bosque del Apache NWR; Bitterlake NWR; Percha Dam SP.

LEAST SANDPIPER

Calidris minutilla

The distinction of being the world's smallest shorebird doesn't make the Least Sandpiper any easier to identify. The Least Sandpiper falls into a confusing category of small, similar looking sandpipers known collectively as "peeps" because of the similarity in their high-pitched calls. • Like most other "peeps," Least Sandpipers migrate almost the entire length of the globe twice each year, from the Arctic to the southern tip of South America and back. To optimize their breeding efforts during the brief Arctic summer, female Least Sandpipers begin to develop their eggs as they migrate north. When the female nests, her entire clutch may weigh more than half of her body weight! The young hatch in an advanced state of development and have only a few weeks to grow strong enough to endure their long migration southward.

nonbreeding

nonbreeding

ID: yellow legs and feet; short, black, slightly downcurved bill; upperparts streaked with brown. *Breeding:* rusty wash to back and wings; breast more finely streaked. *Nonbreeding:* faint pale eyebrow; brown streaked breast contrasts with white underparts. *In flight:* narrow, white wing stripe; black line through white tail; white underwings.
Size: *L* 5–6½ in; *W* 13 in.
Status: common migrant to shores and mudflats throughout the region; locally common in winter in the south in both states.

Habitat: sewage lagoons, mudflats, lakeshores, ditches and wetland edges.
Nesting: does not nest in Arizona or New Mexico.
Feeding: probes or gleans mud or sand for prey; feeds on aquatic insects, small mollusks, crustaceans and worms.
Voice: call is a high-pitched *kree*.
Similar Species: *other peeps:* in nonbreeding plumage, all are larger with black legs; also note the Least Sandpiper's short, slightly downcurved bill and streaked breast.
Best Sites: *AZ:* Lower Colorado R.; Tres Rios Wetlands; Willcox L. *NM:* Bosque del Apache NWR; Bitterlake NWR; Percha Dam SP.

LONG-BILLED DOWITCHER

Limnodromus scolopaceus

Each winter, mudflats and marshes host small numbers of enthusiastic Long-billed Dowitchers. These chunky, sword-billed shorebirds forage up and down through shallow water and mud in a quest for invertebrates. A diet of insects and shellfish provides migrating or overwintering Long-bills with plenty of fuel for flight and essential calcium for bone development. • Dowitchers have shorter wings than most shorebirds so they often take flight from shallow water, where a series of hops helps them become airborne. • Mixed flocks of shorebirds demonstrate a variety of foraging styles: some species probe deeply, while others pick at the water's surface or glean the shorelines. Different feeding strategies and specialized diets probably allow large numbers of shorebird species to coexist without exhausting the food supply.

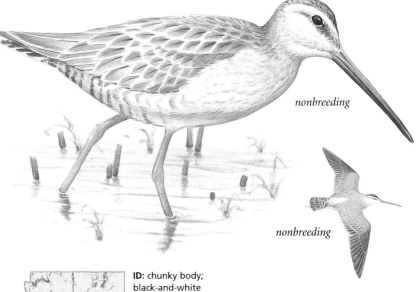

nonbreeding

nonbreeding

ID: chunky body; black-and-white barred tail; white rump extends onto back as wedge; long straight blackish bill; long, pale yellow legs and feet. *Breeding:* black and buffy speckled upperparts; orangish underparts, with black barring on flanks and undertail coverts. *Nonbreeding:* mostly plain gray upperparts, including head; darker crown; white eyebrow; darkish eye line. *Juveniles:* back and scapular feathers have buffy edges and black interiors.
Size: *L* 11–12½ in; *W* 19 in.
Status: common migrant to shores and mudflats throughout the region; locally common in winter in the south.

Habitat: mud flats, lakeshores and shallow marshes.
Nesting: does not nest in Arizona or New Mexico.
Feeding: wades in shallow water and rapidly probes bill into mud "sewing machine" fashion; feeds on freshwater worms, crustaceans, mollusks and aquatic insects.
Voice: call is a loud *keek*, given singly or in a series.
Similar Species: *Wilson's Snipe:* crown has median stripe; no white wedge on back; very different call.
Best Sites: *AZ:* Lower Colorado R.; Tres Rios Wetlands; Willcox L. *NM:* Bosque del Apache NWR; Bitterlake NWR; Percha Dam SP.

67

RING-BILLED GULL

Larus delawarensis

Few people can claim that they have never seen these common and widespread gulls. Ring-billed Gulls are omnivorous and will eat almost anything. They swarm parks, beaches, golf courses and fast-food parking lots looking for food handouts, making pests of themselves. However, Ring-bills also help out farmers by feasting on many crop pests. • During the winter, Ring-bills are the most common gull in Kansas. They are strikingly similar to California Gulls *(L. californicus)* in both range and appearance, but Ring-bills have a black ring around the tip of their bill, whereas the California Gull's bill is marked with red and black.

nonbreeding

nonbreeding

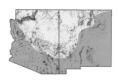

ID: gray upperparts; black wingtips with white spots; white underparts; yellow eyes; yellow bill with black ring near tip; yellow legs and feet. *Breeding:* white head. *Nonbreeding:* dusky streaking on nape, crown and cheek. *Immature:* variable plumage; juvenile mostly brown with blackish tail tip, wingtips, eyes and bill; pale pink legs and feet; resembles adult by second winter, except that head and breast are heavily streaked.
Size: *L* 18–20 in; *W* 4 ft.
Status: *AZ:* common migrant and locally common winter visitor to larger lakes and rivers statewide, especially along the lower Colorado River. *NM:* common migrant and locally common winter visitor to large lakes statewide.

Habitat: virtually any type of open water habitat; also landfills; often roosts in parking lots.
Nesting: does not nest in Arizona or New Mexico.
Feeding: plucks prey off the surface of the water or ground, or plunge-dives for prey; often begs for handouts from beachgoers, catching food tossed into the air; feeds on crabs, small fish, shrimp, carrion, insects, garbage and human foods.
Voice: call is a high-pitched *splee.*
Similar Species: only nonbreeding adult plumages are considered here. *California Gull:* much larger; no ring on bill; black and red spot near tip of lower mandible; dark eyes. *Herring Gull:* larger and less numerous; red spot near tip of lower mandible; no black ring on bill; pinkish legs and feet.
Best Sites: *AZ:* Lower Colorado R.; Roosevelt L.; Willcox L. *NM:* Bosque del Apache NWR; Bitterlake NWR; Percha Dam SP.

BAND-TAILED PIGEON

Patagioenas fasciata

Though similar in size, form and behavior to the familiar Rock Pigeon *(Columba livia)*, the Band-tailed Pigeon has a distinctive white crescent on its nape as well as a unique yellow bill and yellow legs. Through much of its extensive range in the Americas—from nearly the southeastern tip of Alaska to northern Argentina—the Band-tailed Pigeon inhabits foothills and lower mountains. • Suburban backyards edging stands of tall trees support their share of Band-tailed Pigeons, but these birds also inhabit more secluded forests. They are fond of acorns and generally are most numerous in forests with a strong oak component. Band-tailed Pigeons feed by clinging clumsily to twigs that may scarcely support their weight while plucking at nuts and fruits. • A heavy slapping of broad wings may reveal this bird's presence high within the canopy.

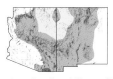

ID: varying shades of gray overall; dark eyes; white half-collar on iridescent green nape; black-tipped, yellow bill; purplish head and breast; dark gray tail is broadly tipped with pale gray band; yellow legs. *In flight:* pale underparts; long tail.
Size: *L* 13–15 in; *W* 26 in.
Status: *AZ:* uncommon summer resident of Pine Oak regions of the eastern mountains south to southeastern Arizona. *NM:* uncommon to common summer resident of mountain regions statewide.
Habitat: ponderosa pine or oak woodlands and adjacent farmland or riparian areas.
Nesting: on a forked branch; fragile platform of sticks has minimal lining; pair incubates one white egg for 18–20 days; young are fed "pigeon milk."
Feeding: gleans vegetation for nuts, especially acorns; also eats other seeds and insects during migration; most foraging is done in trees.
Voice: generally quite silent; very deep, hollow *Ooh, uh-WOO.*
Similar Species: *Rock Pigeon:* typically has white rump and dark bill; no gray band on dark tail. *White-winged Dove* (p. 70): smaller; white leading edges of wings show as upperwing patches in flight; blue orbital ring; red eyes. *Mourning Dove* (p. 71): smaller and more slender; pale brown overall; longer, white-fringed tail; lacks purple head and glossy green nape; whistling wingbeats.
Best Sites: *AZ:* White Mts.; Mt Lemmon. *NM:* Sangre de Cristo Mts.; Sondin Mts.; San Juan Mts.

WHITE-WINGED DOVE

Zenaida asiatica

The glowing light of early morning is sometimes punctuated by the soothing coos of the White-winged Dove. The piercing glance of hot red eyes contained in cooling pools of azure skin make this a captivating bird to observe at close range. • In the late 1800s, the lower Rio Grande Valley was home to several million White-winged Doves, but their numbers rapidly declined at the turn of the century owing to excessive hunting and clearing of their native brushland nesting habitat. They are one of few birds that have been able to recover from the destruction of much of their traditional habitat. In recent decades, they have adapted well to human-altered environments and are rapidly expanding their range northward. Though most retreat to Central America for the winter, increasing numbers are overwintering in our urban centers.

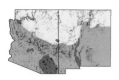

ID: stocky body with short, rounded tail; pale grayish brown plumage; blue orbital ring; red eyes. *In flight:* white leading edge of wing shows as upperwing patch.
Size: *L* 11–12 in; *W* 19 in.
Status: *AZ:* fairly common summer resident of Sonoran and riparian zones south of the Mogollon Rim. *NM:* fairly common summer resident in Sonoran habitats in the southwest.
Habitat: a variety of semi-open habitats including farmland, townsites and suburbs, brushlands, tree groves, riparian woodlands and chaparral.

Nesting: flimsy, stick platform is built on a horizontal limb or in the fork of a tree or shrub; pair alternates incubation of 1–4 (usually 2) white or pale buff eggs for 13–14 days; rarely colonial.
Feeding: mostly terrestrial; feeds on seeds, grain, insects and some fruit; visits bird feeders.
Voice: *who cooks for you?* and other cooing calls.
Similar Species: *Mourning Dove* (p. 71) and *Common Ground-Dove:* no white patches in wings; dark spots on upperwings; ground-dove is smaller. *Rock Pigeon:* stockier; white rump; black tail band.
Best Sites: *AZ:* Sonoran deserts around Phoenix and Tucson; Desert Botanical Garden; Arizona Sonora Desert Museum. *NM:* Bosque del Apache NWR; Percha Dam SP.

MOURNING DOVE

Zenaida macroura

The Mourning Dove's soft cooing, which filters through broken woodlands and suburban parks, is often confused with the sound of a hooting owl. Novice birders who track down the source of the calls are often surprised to find the streamlined silhouette of a perched dove. • This popular game animal is common throughout our region and is one of the most abundant native birds in North America. Its numbers and range have increased since human development created more open habitats and food sources, such as waste grain and bird feeders. • Two other smaller, stockier doves are found in our region. The Inca Dove *(Columbina inca)* is a common, local resident along the lower Colorado River and in urban areas of central and southern Arizona and southern New Mexico. The Common Ground-Dove *(Columbina passerina)* is a common permanent resident of the lower Colorado River and central and southeastern Arizona.

Nesting: on the ground or in a tree, flower pot or gutter of a house; female builds a fragile, shallow platform of grass (on the ground) or twigs (in a tree) supplied by the male; pair incubates 2 white eggs for 14 days; young are fed "pigeon milk"; multiple broods per year.

Feeding: gleans the ground and vegetation for seeds; visits feeders.

Voice: well-known, mournful, slow 6-note song.

Similar Species: *White-winged Dove* (p. 70): larger and stockier; short, rounded tail; red iris with blue orbital ring; white wing stripe. *Inca Dove:* gray-brown plumage with scaled appearance; long, white-edged tail and rufous primaries in flight. *Common Ground-Dove:* shorter, slightly white-cornered tail; plain gray back, belly and flanks; large, dark spots on upperwings; rufous primaries in flight.

Best Sites: widespread.

ID: slender dove; long, pointed, white-trimmed tail; gray-brown plumage; small head; dull red legs; dark bill; pale underparts; black upper-wing spots.

Size: *L* 11–13 in; *W* 18 in.

Status: common migrant and abundant resident in open and semi-open habitats regionwide; less common in winter in the far north.

Habitat: virtually any open or semi-open upland habitat, especially residential areas, open fields and agricultural regions.

GREATER ROADRUNNER

Geococcyx californianus

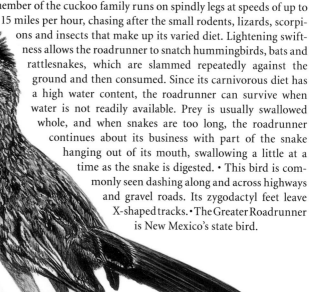

Celebrated for its appearance, speed and ability to catch rattlesnakes, the Greater Roadrunner is one of our region's most fascinating birds. This terrestrial member of the cuckoo family runs on spindly legs at speeds of up to 15 miles per hour, chasing after the small rodents, lizards, scorpions and insects that make up its varied diet. Lightening swiftness allows the roadrunner to snatch hummingbirds, bats and rattlesnakes, which are slammed repeatedly against the ground and then consumed. Since its carnivorous diet has a high water content, the roadrunner can survive when water is not readily available. Prey is usually swallowed whole, and when snakes are too long, the roadrunner continues about its business with part of the snake hanging out of its mouth, swallowing a little at a time as the snake is digested. • This bird is commonly seen dashing along and across highways and gravel roads. Its zygodactyl feet leave X-shaped tracks. • The Greater Roadrunner is New Mexico's state bird.

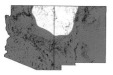

ID: streaky brown and whitish plumage; long, thick bill with hooked tip; raised crest; bare, blue and red skin patch behind eye; thick, scaly legs; short, rounded wings; very long tail.

Size: *L* 23 in; *W* 22 in.

Status: rare to uncommon but widespread resident regionwide; mostly in lower elevation arid desert regions of the south.

Habitat: thorn forest, desert and arid woodlands of pinyon-pine and juniper; agricultural lands and urban areas.

Nesting: usually in a cactus, dense shrub or low tree; cup-shaped stick nest is lined with vegetation and feathers (may include snakeskin and dried cow manure); pair incubates 3–6 white eggs for 20 days; may mate for life and defend breeding territory year-round.

Feeding: varied diet; catches insects, small mammals, lizards, snakes and small birds by running them down; also eats scorpions, snails, fruit and seeds.

Voice: descending, dovelike cooing; loud bill clattering.

Similar Species: none.

Best Sites: *AZ:* widespread in open desert around Phoenix and Tucson; Sycamore Creek near Sunflower; Boyce Thompson Arboretum; Phoenix Desert Botanical Garden; Sonoran Desert Museum. *NM:* Bosque del Apache NWR; Redrock Gila R.; Mangas Springs.

BARN OWL

Tyto alba

The haunting look of this night hunter has inspired superstitions among many people. Naked faces and black, piercing eyes give downy nestling Barn Owls an eerie look. In truth, however, the dedicated hunting efforts of these residents helps to keep farmlands and even city yards free from undesirable rodents.
• The Barn Owl is often associated with urban and agricultural areas and is widely known in the Old World for nesting in church steeples or barn lofts. Its nocturnal habit, taste for small rodents and general tolerance of humans have allowed this adaptable bird to prosper on six continents. • Normally these nocturnal birds hunt alone or in pairs, but during the winter months they may gather at local feeding sites. Owls have night vision 100 times stronger than that of humans, and they are able to locate prey using sound alone.

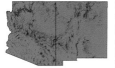

ID: appears all white; golden brown upperparts spotted with black and gray; heart-shaped facial disc; dark eyes; black-spotted, white underparts; long legs; white underwings.
Size: *L* 12½–18 in; *W* 45 in.
Status: uncommon resident throughout the region's southern deserts; uncommon migrant and summer resident elsewhere.
Habitat: roosts and nests in hollow trees, barns and other buildings, and groves of trees; forages over open habitats, especially agricultural fields.
Nesting: in a natural or artificial cavity, often in a sheltered, secluded hollow of a building; may dig a hole in a dirt bank or use an artificial nest box; no actual nest is built; female incubates 3–8 whitish eggs for 29–34 days; male feeds incubating female.
Feeding: strictly nocturnal; forages more by sound than sight; eats mostly mammals,

especially rodents, but also takes birds and occasionally other vertebrates.
Voice: harsh, raspy screeches and hisses; also makes metallic clicking sounds; often heard flying high over cities and residential areas late at night.
Similar Species: *Short-eared Owl:* less common; boldly streaked upperparts; yellow eyes; black wrist patches.
Best Sites: *AZ:* Boyce Thompson Arboretum; Lower Gila R. *NM:* Bosque del Apache NWR.

GREAT HORNED OWL

Bubo virginianus

The highly adaptable and superbly camouflaged Great Horned Owl has sharp hearing and powerful vision that allow it to hunt at night as well as by day. It will swoop down from a perch onto almost any small creature that moves. This bird apparently has a poorly developed sense of smell, which might explain why it is the only consistent predator of skunks. • An owl has specially designed feathers on its wings to reduce noise. The leading edge of the flight feathers are fringed rather than smooth, which interrupts airflow over the wing and allows the owl to fly silently. • Great Horned Owls begin their courtship as early as January, and by February and March, the females are already incubating their eggs. When other birds are beginning to fledge, Great Horned owlets are learning to hunt. • The large eyes of an owl are fixed in place, so to look up, down or to the side, the bird must move its entire head. As an adaptation to this situation, an owl can swivel its neck 180 degrees to either side and 90 degrees up and down!

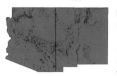

ID: stocky; prominent "horns"; heavily mottled brown body; rufous facial disc; yellow eyes; densely barred underparts; feathered feet; powerful talons.

Size: *L* 18–25 in; *W* 3–5 ft.

Status: fairly common and widespread permanent resident throughout the region.

Habitat: pine flatwoods, mixed oak-pine forests, agricultural land with scattered tall trees, riparian woodlands and wooded suburban areas.

Nesting: primarily during winter; usually uses an existing large nest (sometimes after evicting its rightful owners—often Bald Eagles); adds little or no material to the nest; mainly the female incubates 2 whitish eggs for 28–35 days.

Feeding: mostly nocturnal; usually swoops from a perch; eats a wide variety of usually vertebrate prey (even fish!), chiefly birds and mammals.

Voice: song consists of usually 4–6 low, deep hoots; juvenile's begging call an often-repeated, high, wheezy, scratchy note.

Similar Species: *Long-eared Owl:* smaller; thinner; vertical breast streaks; "ear" tufts are close together. *Western Screech-Owl:* much smaller; vertical breast streaks.

Best Sites: *AZ:* residential Tucson and Phoenix. *NM:* residential Albuquerque.

BURROWING OWL

Athene cunicularia

Easily identified by their long legs and oversized eyes, Burrowing Owls are loyal inhabitants of the plains and desert. Their favorite haunts are heavily grazed pastures in intensively cultivated regions and disturbed areas in extensive grasslands. They nest in underground burrows abandoned by other animals and are often seen perched atop fence posts or rocks near their burrow entrances. • Since Burrowing Owls use abandon animal burrows for nesting, the extermination of ground squirrels in the Great Plains has greatly reduced the number of suitable owl nest s ites. Collisions with vehicles, the effect of agricultural chemicals and the conversion of native grasslands to cropland are thought to be some of the other challenges facing this endangered bird. • When winter brings an influx of raptors to our state, Burrowing Owls spend much of the day underground to avoid predation. These owls become increasingly nocturnal at this time, risking short, low flights to capture rodents, birds and insects.

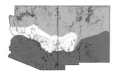

ID: brownish black body with white spotting; no ear tufts; large, yellow eyes; dark brown barring on white underparts; long legs.
Size: *L* 8–9 in; *W* 20–24 in.
Status: *AZ:* rare to locally common resident in the southern deserts; rare to locally common summer resident above the Mogollon Rim. *NM:* rare resident in the southern deserts and southeastern plains; rare to locally common summer resident nearly statewide.
Habitat: pastures, ballparks, road shoulders and airports; native dry prairies.
Nesting: often loosely colonial; digs a burrow that extends 4–8 ft underground; may add grass, sticks or other debris, such as dried cow dung to the nest site; female incubates 3–8 white eggs for 28–30 days.

Feeding: dusk to dawn; pounces on prey on the ground or swoops down in flight or from a fence post perch; eats mostly terrestrial insects; also takes crayfish, small vertebrates and even carrion.
Voice: call is a harsh *chuk* or *QUEE! kuk-kuk-kuk-kuk-kuk.* *Male:* courtship call a mournful, whistled *coo-coo.*
Similar Species: none.
Best Sites: *AZ:* agricultural areas surrounding Yuma and along the Lower Colorado River Valley. *NM:* the Eastern Plains surrounding Las Cruces.

COMMON NIGHTHAWK

Chordeiles minor

The Common Nighthawk is a member of the nightjar, or goatsucker, family, which have mottled brown plumage, long, narrow, pointed wings and a tiny bill. This aerial bird has adapted to catching insects in midair; its large, gaping mouth is surrounded by feather shafts that funnel insects into its bill. A nighthawk can eat over 2600 insects in one day. Look for nighthawks foraging for insects at nighttime baseball games. • Every May and June, the male Common Nighthawk makes an unforgettable booming sound as it flies high overhead. In an energetic courtship display, the male dives, then swerves skyward, making a hollow *vroom* sound with its wings. • The Lesser Nighthawk *(C. acutipennis)* is very similar to the Common Nighthawk and the two species are best distinguished by voice; the Common often gives a nasal "peent" during its aerial foraging, whereas the Lesser gives a low gutteral trill, most often while sitting on the ground.

ID: long, narrow, pointed wings; tiny bill; mottled dark brown body; white (male) or buffy (female) forecollar; heavily barred underparts.
In flight: white patches near tip of primaries; male has white patches on undertail; bounding, erratic flight.
Size: *L* 8½–10 in; *W* 24 in.
Status: *AZ:* uncommon to fairly common summer resident from May to September above the Mogollon Rim in open upper Sonoran zone. *NM:* uncommon to fairly common summer resident from May to September in high plains and most mountain ranges statewide.
Habitat: *Foraging:* most natural habitats; also in suburban areas. *Breeding:* open fields, prairies or the sandy margins of ponds.

Nesting: on bare ground or a gravel rooftop; no nest is built; female incubates 2 heavily marked, creamy white eggs for about 19 days; both adults feed the well-camouflaged young.
Feeding: feeds exclusively on insects captured in flight, mostly at dusk and dawn, but may be seen during the day, especially on cloudy days or after storms.
Voice: frequently repeated, nasal *peent* and a rarely-uttered *pit-pit. Male:* nonvocal "booming" sound during courtship dives.
Similar Species: *Lesser Nighthawk:* flies lower to ground; perched birds show buffy spotting in primaries. *Whip-poor-will:* found in forests; lack white "wrist" patches; shorter, rounder wings; rounded tail.
Best Sites: *AZ:* Sunrise Campground (White Mts.); San Francisco Mts. *NM:* Sangre de Cristo Mts.; San Juan Mts.

BROAD-TAILED HUMMINGBIRD
Selasphorus platycercus

Broad-tailed Hummingbirds breed in higher elevation, mountainous regions of the western United States and overwinter in Mexico and Central America. In our region, they are locally common summer residents of pine oak woodlands throughout. They migrate out of the region, but individuals occasionally overwinter at feeders. • Best known for the metallic trill produced by the male's wings, Broad-tailed Hummingbirds are often heard before they are seen. They breed during the short montane flowering season and are able to conserve energy during food shortages or cool nights by lowering their respiration rate and body temperature. • While most hummingbirds survive three to five years in the wild, one female Broad-tailed Hummingbird lived a record 12 years.

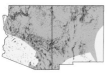

ID: bright, iridescent green crown and back; white underparts; long, straight bill. *Male:* rosy red throat; green and buffy wash to underparts; dark tail; wings whistle in flight. *Female:* dark streaking on cheeks and throat; buffy sides; broad, dark tail with rufous base and white tips.
Size: *L* 4 in; *W* 5¼ in.
Status: common summer resident to the mountains and foothills regionwide.
Habitat: subalpine meadows and montane forests, especially cypress-pine-oak or pinyon-juniper-oak woodlands; often near streams; gardens.

Nesting: on a branch, often overhanging a stream; female builds a cup nest of plant material and lines it with spider webs or plant down, then decorates it with lichen or bark; female incubates 2 white eggs for 14–17 days; may have 2 broods.
Feeding: flower nectar and small insects; favors red tubular flowers; visits hummingbird feeders.
Voice: high *chip* notes; male's wings produce a unique, metallic trill in flight.
Similar Species: *Black-chinned Hummingbird:* male has deep purple gorget and black mask; does not produce wing trill in flight. *Rufous Hummingbird* and *Allen's Hummingbird:* smaller size and smaller tail with more rufous than female Broad-tailed Hummingbird.
Best Sites: *AZ:* Prescott; Flagstaff; White Mts. *NM:* Santa Fe; Sangre de Cristo Mts.; Taos.

ELEGANT TROGON

Trogon elegans

The Elegant Trogon is an unusual perching bird with parrotlike colors and a long, narrow tail. This bird often perches quietly amongst the foliage, tilting its head slightly, then quickly darting out to catch insects or pluck fruit. • The Elegant Trogon reaches the northern limit of its range in mountain canyons of southeastern Arizona and southwestern New Mexico, where it is a summer resident only. Throughout its permanent range in Mexico and Central America, it inhabits a variety of habitats including tropical lowland forests, high-elevation riparian areas and arid scrublands. • The name *trogon* is derived from the Greek word for "gnawer" and refers to this bird's hooked bill.

ID: brightly colored plumage; red orbital ring; stout, yellow bill; long, narrow tail; metallic iridescence on back and tail. *Male:* black face; green upperparts; bright red underparts; white breast band; gray wings. *Female:* gray head and upperparts; white marking behind eye; whitish underparts; reddish undertail coverts.

Size: *L* 14 in; *W* 24 in.

Status: *AZ:* locally uncommon summer resident of foothills and canyons of extreme southeast. *NM:* rare and local summer resident of the mountains and canyons of the extreme southwest.

Habitat: cottonwood and sycamore riparian woodlands in mountain canyons; also uses pinyon, juniper and oak woodlands.

Nesting: secondary cavity nester, often in a sycamore in AZ; no nest material is added; both adults incubate 2–3 dull white or bluish white eggs for 17–22 days; both parents tend the young.

Feeding: gleans foliage or flycatches for a variety of insects; also eats fruit.

Voice: a repeated croak: *ko-ah, ko-ah.*

Similar Species: *Eared Trogon:* extremely rare; green upperparts and wings; broad tail has large white patch on underside.

Best Sites: *AZ:* Madera Canyon, Ramsey Canyon Preserve and Garden Canyon (Huachuca Mts.). *NM:* Peloncillo Mts.

BELTED KINGFISHER

Ceryle alcyon

Perched on a bare branch over a productive pool, the Belted Kingfisher utters a scratchy, rattling call. Then, with little regard for its scruffy hairdo, it plunges headfirst into the water, snatching a fish or a frog. Back on land, the kingfisher flips its prey into the air and swallows it headfirst. Similar to owls, kingfishers regurgitate the indigestible portion of their food as pellets, which can be found beneath favorite perches. • A pair of kingfishers typically takes turns excavating the nest burrow. The birds use their bills to chip away at an exposed sandbank and then kick loose material out of the tunnel with their feet. The female kingfisher has the traditional female reproductive role for birds but is more colorful than her mate—she has an extra red band across her belly. • Nestlings have closed eyes and are featherless for the first week, but after five days they are able to swallow small fish whole.

ID: bluish upperparts; shaggy crest; blue-gray breast band; white collar; long, straight bill; short legs; white underwings; small, white patch near eye. *Female:* rusty breast band. *Male:* no breast band.

Size: *L* 11–14 in; *W* 20 in.

Status: uncommon migrant and winter visitor regionwide.

Habitat: lakes, rivers, marshes and quarries, especially near exposed soil banks, gravel pits or bluffs.

Nesting: in a cavity at the end of an earth burrow, which is often up to 6 ft long; pair digs cavity with their bills and claws; pair incubates 6–7 white eggs for 22–24 days; both adults feed the young.

Feeding: dives headfirst into water, either from a perch or from hovering flight; eats mostly small fish, aquatic invertebrates and tadpoles.

Voice: fast, repetitive, cackling rattle, a little like a teacup shaking on a saucer.

Similar Species: *Green Kingfisher:* little range overlap; much smaller; green overall; long bill; white outer tail feathers in flight. *Blue Jay:* more intense blue color; smaller bill and head; behaves in completely different fashion.

Best Sites: *AZ:* Verde R.; Salt R.; Roosevelt L. *NM:* Bosque del Apache NWR; Percha Dam SP; Navajo Reservoir.

LEWIS'S WOODPECKER

Melanerpes lewis

The Lewis' Woodpecker is unique among woodpeckers, not only for its green and pink coloration, but because it does much of its foraging as flycatchers do, catching insects on the wing. It frequently perches solitarily in semi-open country on the tops of oaks or pines or atop poles and snags. • Lewis's Woodpeckers often fly in crowlike fashion, crossing the sky with slow, floppy wingbeats. • Competition with European Starlings and loss of extensive snag habitat through modern wildlife suppression has greatly diminished this woodpecker's numbers. Fall and winter concentrations still occur in areas with abundant oak mistletoe, a favored cold-weather berry source. • These large, dark woodpeckers were named for Meriwether Lewis, co-leader of the western "Expedition of Discovery" in the early 1800s. Although Lewis was not formally trained as a naturalist, his diary details a great many concise and original observations of natural history.

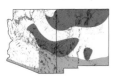

ID: dark green upperparts; dark red face; pale gray breast and collar; pinkish belly; dark undertail coverts; sharp, stout bill. *Immature:* brown head, face and breast; no red in face; no gray collar.
Size: *L* 11 in; *W* 21 in.
Status: *AZ:* uncommon and local summer resident of open pine-oak woodlands in the northeast; rare and erratic winter transient away from summering areas. *NM:* uncommon and local summer resident of open pine in the north and west; rare and erratic winter transient away from summering areas.
Habitat: broken or burned-over pine forests, pinyon pine-juniper and gray pine-oak woodlands, open riparian woodlands, ranch windbreaks and isolated groves.
Nesting: excavates a cavity in a dead or dying tree; pair incubates 6–7 white eggs for about 15 days.
Feeding: flycatches for flying invertebrates; probes into cracks and crevices for invertebrates; eats acorns and mistletoe berries locally in winter.
Voice: nearly silent away from nest; utters a harsh series of *chur* notes.
Similar Species: no other woodpecker is dark green in color; all other woodpeckers fly with pronounced undulations.
Best Sites: *AZ:* Lakeside; San Francisco Peaks. *NM:* Zuni Mts.; Chuska Mts.

ACORN WOODPECKER

Melanerpes formicivorus

Highly social Acorn Woodpeckers are well known for their unique, communal lifestyle. These woodpeckers live in family groups of a dozen or more birds, which cooperate to protect shared food-storage sites and nesting cavities. Groups include both breeding birds and nonbreeding helpers, usually young from the previous year. Though mating systems vary between populations, up to seven breeding males typically vie for one to three egg-laying females. Competition is especially intense among females who share a joint nest cavity, and females regularly remove and then eat eggs laid by their co-breeders. Nonbreeding group members help to raise the young and protect the group's feeding territory. • Acorn Woodpeckers eat a variety of food items, but almost half of their diet consists of acorns that are hoarded in hole-studded "granary trees" for later consumption. An oak or sycamore snag serving as a larder may be perforated with up to 50,000 holes.

ID: white patches on face and throat; pale eyes; glossy black upperparts; white underparts streaked with black; throat is often yellowish; white wing patches and rump. *Male:* red crown and nape. *Female:* red only on nape.
Size: *L* 9 in; *W* 17½ in.
Status: common local resident of mountains and canyons with oak, pine and sycamore.
Habitat: closely associated with many species of oak; oak and pine-oak woodlands; also found in riparian woodlands and parks.
Nesting: group excavates a cavity in a standing dead tree or branch; breeding adults and occasionally nonbreeding helpers incubate 4–6 white eggs for 11 days; young are raised communally.
Feeding: omnivorous diet; insects (especially ants) are caught in flight or gleaned from foliage; harvests and stores acorns in holes drilled into bark or standing deadwood; also eats fruit, seeds and bird eggs; drills small, shallow sap wells.
Voice: call is a raucous *ja-cup, jap-cup, jap-cup*, often becoming a chorus.
Similar Species: *Red-headed Woodpecker:* ranges do not overlap; all-red head; large white patch on back.
Best Sites: *AZ:* Madera Canyon, Ramsey Canyon Preserve and Miller Canyon (Huachuca Mts.). *NM:* Sitgreaves National Forest; Animas Mts.; Peloncillo Mts.

GILA WOODPECKER
Melanerpes uropygialis

Another specialty of the Southwest, the Gila Woodpecker is an essential link in the ecological chain of desert life. A variety of cavity-nesting birds, lizards, snakes and mice are some of the many creatures that use the old excavations of Gilas in giant saguaro cacti, ancient cottonwoods and large mesquite trees. • Freshly excavated nest cavities may not be used until the following year, especially in cactus, where a hardened skin must form on the surface of the pulpy innards before the cavity can be used for nesting. • Gila Woodpeckers are regularly observed taking sugar water from hummingbird feeders.

ID: tan head and underparts; black and white barring on wings, back and tail. *Male:* red crown patch. *Female:* no crown patch.
Size: *L* 8–9 in; *W* 16 in.
Status: *AZ:* common permanent resident in Phoenix and Tucson and of saguaro forests in the southern regions. *NM:* common permanent resident of saguaro forests in the southwestern regions.
Habitat: desert habitats including washes and lowlands with large mesquite trees and saguaro cacti, and streamside cottonwood-willow groves; also townsites.
Nesting: both adults excavate a nest cavity in a saguaro cactus, cottonwood tree or large mesquite, palm or willow tree; pair incubates 3–4 white eggs for about 14 days; 2–3 broods each year.
Feeding: insects, cultivated and cactus fruit, berries, seeds, nectar, worms, small eggs and small reptiles; gleans trees and shrubs, the ground and feeders.
Voice: calls include a distinctive *churr* and *kek-kek-kek*.
Similar Species: *Ladder-backed Woodpecker* (p. 83): black and white striping in face; streaky sides and flanks. *Northern Flicker* (p. 85) and *Gilded Flicker:* brown-and-black barred upperparts; black spots on underparts; black necklace patch.
Best Sites: Phoenix; Tucson; Verde R.; Gila R. *NM:* Poncho Villa SP; Guadalupe Canyon; Animas Valley.

LADDER-BACKED WOODPECKER

Picoides scalaris

The Ladder-backed Woodpecker is a common visitor to ranches and rural towns throughout the southwestern United States, taking over areas that the equally numerous Downy Woodpecker avoids. Formerly called the "Cactus Woodpecker," the Ladder-back frequently feeds and nests in cacti. This small, speckled woodpecker also flits between small scrub, dried riverbeds and pine-oak woodlands. • Male and female Ladder-backed Woodpeckers seem to use different foraging techniques and feed on different plant species, possibly because of limited food availability in their arid habitats. Females prefer to glean the tops and outer branches of trees or mesquite, while males are more likely to feed closer to the trunk or near the ground.

ID: black back with thick, white horizontal stripes turning to spots on wings; white or buffy underparts with black spotting; black tail with white-and-black striped outer coverts; white face and throat; black eye line joins black bill line; faint white moustache. *Male:* red crown with white dots on forehead. *Female:* black crown. *Juvenile male:* smaller red crown patch.
Size: *L* 7–7½ in; *W* 13 in.
Status: *AZ:* fairly common resident in desert riparian and mesquite bosques except in the northeast. *NM:* fairly common resident in the desert riparian and mesquite bosques of the south and east.
Habitat: mesquite, desert savanna, scrubland and thorn forests.
Nesting: in a cavity; uses trees, cacti, agave, yucca or utility poles; cavity is likely drilled by the male and lined with woodchips; pair incubates 2–7 creamy white eggs for up to 13 days.

Feeding: mainly eats insects such as ants and beetles; also eats cactus flowers; may feed on or near the ground or dig under bark.
Voice: drums quickly; quick descending laugh with a raspy ending; contact call is a quick *chip*.
Similar Species: *Downy Woodpecker* (p. 84): male has red patch on back of crown; black upper back and nape; white patch on upper back; white underparts, shorter bill.
Best Sites: *AZ:* Phoenix; Tucson; Boyce Thompson Arboretum; Phoenix Desert Botanical Garden. *NM:* Bosque del Apache NWR; Redrock Gila R.; Mangas Springs; Poncho Villa SP.

DOWNY WOODPECKER

Picoides pubescens

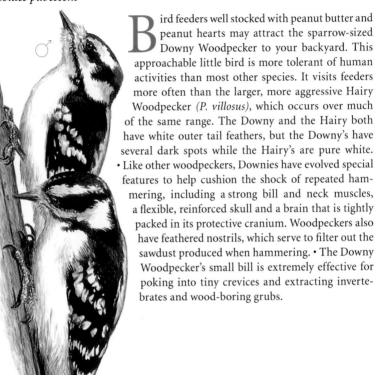

Bird feeders well stocked with peanut butter and peanut hearts may attract the sparrow-sized Downy Woodpecker to your backyard. This approachable little bird is more tolerant of human activities than most other species. It visits feeders more often than the larger, more aggressive Hairy Woodpecker *(P. villosus)*, which occurs over much of the same range. The Downy and the Hairy both have white outer tail feathers, but the Downy's have several dark spots while the Hairy's are pure white. • Like other woodpeckers, Downies have evolved special features to help cushion the shock of repeated hammering, including a strong bill and neck muscles, a flexible, reinforced skull and a brain that is tightly packed in its protective cranium. Woodpeckers also have feathered nostrils, which serve to filter out the sawdust produced when hammering. • The Downy Woodpecker's small bill is extremely effective for poking into tiny crevices and extracting invertebrates and wood-boring grubs.

most mountain ranges south to the Mogollon and Sacramentos.

Habitat: all wooded habitats, even suburban backyards.

Nesting: pair excavates a cavity in a dying or decaying trunk or limb and lines it with wood chips; pair incubates 4–5 white eggs for 11–13 days; both adults feed the young.

Feeding: forages mostly on smaller branches and twigs, or trunks of saplings and shrubs; chips and probes for insects or spiders; also eats nuts and seeds.

Voice: call a quiet *pik* or a whiny *queek, queek*; drumming is shorter but more frequent than that of the Hairy Woodpecker.

Similar Species: *Hairy Woodpecker:* larger; bill is as long as head is wide; no spots on white outer tail feathers. *Ladder-backed Woodpecker* (p. 83): black and white horizontal barring on back; buff underparts streaked with black; barring on white outer tail feathers.

Best Sites: *AZ:* White Mts. *NM:* Bosque del Apache NWR; Pecos Wilderness; Taos.

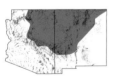

ID: short, stubby bill; white back; black wings with bold white spots or bars; white head with black crown, eye stripe, and mustache stripe; black-spotted, white outer tail feathers.
Male: red nape patch.

Size: *L* 6–7 in; *W* 12 in.

Status: *AZ:* local and uncommon resident above the Mogollon Rim and the White Mts. *NM:* rare to uncommon resident in

NORTHERN FLICKER

Colaptes auratus

Unlike other woodpeckers, the Northern Flicker is frequently seen on the ground, searching for insects, particularly ants. With robinlike hops, it investigates anthills, grassy meadows and forest clearings. • Flickers often bathe in dusty depressions. The dust particles absorb oils and bacteria that can harm the birds' feathers. To clean themselves even more thoroughly, flickers squash ants and preen themselves with the remains. Ants contain formic acid, which kills small parasites on the birds' skin and feathers. • There are two forms of the Northern Flicker: the western, "Red-shafted Flicker" is found throughout most of our region, where as the eastern "Yellow-shafted Flicker" is an uncommon winter resident in eastern New Mexico only. • Another species, the Gilded Flicker *(C. chrysoides)* occurs in the desert woodlands and saguaro stands of southern Arizona and northern Mexico. This flicker adapted to a different range during the ice age when it was glacially separated, but it now liberally interbreeds with the Red-shafted Flicker.

"*Red-shafted Flicker*"

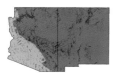

ID: *Red-shafted form:* brown back and wings barred with black; gray face with brown crown and nape; black "bib"; pale buffy underparts with bold, black spots; male has red mustache stripe. *Yellow-shafted form:* brown face with gray crown and nape; male has black mustache stripe.
Size: *L* 12½–13 in; *W* 20 in.
Status: common migrant and winter visitor regionwide; occurs in summer at higher elevations throughout both states.
Habitat: open woodlands, forest edges and wetlands; survives poorly in suburban areas.
Nesting: pair excavates a cavity in a dead or dying deciduous tree and lines it with wood chips; may use a nest box; pair incubates 5–8 white eggs for 11–16 days.
Feeding: forages on the ground for ants and other terrestrial insects; probes bark; also eats berries and nuts; occasionally flycatches.

Voice: loud, laughing, rapid *kick-kick-kick-kick-kick-kick; woika-woika-woika* issued during courtship.
Similar Species: *Gilded Flicker:* slightly smaller; cinnamon crown; yellow underwings and undertail; paler back with thinner barring. *Gila Woodpecker* (p. 82): smaller; black and white barring on back and central tail feathers; male has small red cap.
Best Sites: Boyce Thompson Arboretum; Desert Botanical Garden; Mogollon Rim; Huachuca Mts. *NM:* Albuquerque; Santa Fe; Pecos Wilderness.

WESTERN WOOD-PEWEE

Contopus sordidulus

The Western Wood-Pewee introduces the largest order of birds—the Passeriformes—usually known as "passerines," song birds or perching birds. The first passerine family found in our region is the flycatchers, itself a large family. There are thirty regularly occurring species of flycatchers in our region. The Western Wood-Pewee breeds from southern Alaska throughout western North America to Mexico and winters in South America. • Following this bird's characteristic, downslurred call often leads to a high, conspicuous perch, where the Western Wood-Pewee sings persistently throughout the day. When it's not singing, it launches itself in long, looping, foraging ventures. The Western Wood-Pewee is not as faithful to its perch as many other flycatchers; after launching out after an insect, it sometimes alights upon a different perch from the one it left. • The similar looking, but larger and heavier, Olive-sided Flycatcher *(C. cooperi)* is an uncommon summer resident in the mountains of northern Arizona and western New Mexico. It may be distinguished by its characteristic *quick-three-beers* song.

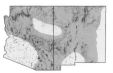

ID: dark olive brown upperparts; light underparts; 2 faint, white wing bars; no eye ring; light-colored lower mandible; light under-tail coverts; grayish throat.
Size: *L* 6¼ in; *W* 10½ in.
Status: common migrant and fairly common summer resident of wooded canyons throughout our region.
Habitat: open woodlands and deciduous, ponderosa pine and riparian forests.
Nesting: on a horizontal tree limb; small cup nest is made with plant fibers and is bound with spider silk; female incubates 3 creamy white or pale yellow eggs for 12–13 days.

Feeding: flycatches insects.
Voice: plaintive whistled *peeeyou* that drops off at the end; song is *fee-rrr-eet*.
Similar Species: *Olive-sided Flycatcher:* larger; white rump tufts; explosive song and calls. *Greater Pewee:* larger; pointed crest. *Townsend's Solitaire:* larger; gray overall; white eye ring; peach-colored wing patches; pale rump; long, thin, black tail with white outer feathers.
Best Sites: *AZ:* Oak Creek Canyon; Mt. Lemmon; White Mts. *NM:* widespread in the Sangre de Cristo Mts. and Sandia Mts.

GRAY FLYCATCHER

Empidonax wrightii

The Gray Flycatcher is one of eight species of *Empidonax* that are found in our region. The "empids" are among the most challenging birds to identify, and many individuals cannot be identified specifically. Empids are small flycatchers that often flip up their tails. Vocalisations are key to identifying these species. • The Gray's deliberate downward tail-bobbing, slender proportions and tendency to drop to the ground frequently in pursuit of insects help to distinguish this empid from its nearly identical relatives, the Dusky Flycatcher *(E. oberholseri)* and Hammond's Flycatcher *(E. hammondii).* The Hammond's Flycatcher breeds in the high coniferous forests of northwestern New Mexico, and the Dusky Flycatcher breeds in pine-oak woodlands and open pine stands of northern and eastern Arizona and western New Mexico.

ID: drab grayish upperparts; whitish underparts; faint eye ring; 2 thin, white wing bars; pale lower mandible with dark tip; long tail with thin, white border.
Size: *L* 5¼–6 in; *W* 8¾ in.
Status: *AZ:* fairly common migrant and winter visitor in central and southeast regions; fairly common summer resident in the mountain foothills above the Mogollon Rim in the northeast. *NM:* fairly common migrant statewide; fairly common summer resident in mountain foothills statewide.
Habitat: dry conifer woodlands with an understory of tall sagebrush or bitterbrush; mesquite woodlands.
Nesting: in a vertical fork of a sagebrush branch or on a horizontal branch of a pinyon pine or juniper; mostly the female builds deep, bulky cup nest of grasses, twigs and strips of bark, and lines it with feathers, fur and plant down; female incubates 3–4 creamy white eggs for 14 days.
Feeding: insects are taken by hawking, hovering or after a short flight to the ground.
Voice: call is a loud *whit; chawip seeahl* song (1st note often doubled, 2nd note often omitted) is often followed by an aspirated *whea* or liquid *whilp.*
Similar Species: *Dusky Flycatcher:* usually darker and plumper overall; restricted pale area on lower mandible; more contrast between upper- and underparts; does not bob its tail downward. *Hammond's Flycatcher:* darker, with more contrasting "vest"; plumper; tiny bill is entirely dark; often flicks its wings and short, thin tail. *Willow Flycatcher:* browner upperparts; lower mandible is entirely pale; bolder wing bars.
Best Sites: *AZ:* Patagonia Lake SP (winter); Oak Creek Canyon. *NM:* Rio Grande Nature Center; El Morro National Monument.

CORDILLERAN FLYCATCHER

Empidonax occidentalis

Cordilleran Flycatchers are western birds, similar to the Yellow-bellied Flycatcher *(E. flaviventris)* of the East. They breed in the mountain forests of the western U.S. and Mexico, but much remains to be learned about this species' distribution and migration. • The Cordilleran Flycatcher and the Pacific-slope Flycatcher *(E. difficilis)* were formerly lumped together into one species, the "Western Flycatcher." Although they have been regarded as a distinct species since 1989, their similar field characteristics remain a troubling issue that perpetuates their uncertain status. • *Empidonax* is a wonderful name for this confusing, but endearing, group of flycatchers—it means "king of the gnats"—a reflection of their amazing insect-catching abilities. • The scientific name *occidentalis* is Latin for "western."

ID: olive green upperparts; 2 white wing bars; yellowish throat and underparts; light-colored eye ring; orange lower mandible.

Size: *L* 5½ in; *W* 8 in.

Status: fairly common summer resident of higher elevation forests regionwide.

Habitat: coniferous and riparian woodlands or shady deciduous forests in the mountains, often near seepages and springs.

Nesting: in a cavity in a small tree, bank, bridge or cliff face; cavity is lined with moss, lichens, plant fibers, bark, fur and feathers; female incubates 3–4 creamy-white, cinnamon-spotted eggs for 15 days.

Feeding: flycatches for insects.

Voice: male's call is a chipper whistle: *swee-deet.*

Similar Species: *Willow Flycatcher* and *Western Wood-Pewee* (p. 86): no eye ring. *Least, Hammond's,* and *Dusky flycatchers:* lack the almond-shaped eye ring and the completely orange lower mandible; songs are very useful in field identification.

Best Sites: *AZ:* Mt. Lemmon; Sunrise Campground (White Mts.). *NM:* Sandia Crest; Water Canyon (Magdalena Mts.).

BLACK PHOEBE

Sayornis nigricans

The dark, handsome Black Phoebe is a routine resident of shady streamsides and other semi-open, moist habitats at lower and middle elevations throughout the Southwest. Like other phoebes, it has no wing bars and habitually pump its tail downward. • Black Phoebes are most often seen sitting alert on exposed low perches, such as fences, posts, stumps and the eaves of buildings. In the manner of other phoebes, they collect a large proportion of their invertebrate prey by delicate sallies from perch to ground. In eroded streambeds with no overhanging tree limbs, they resort to flycatching from stones ranging in size from larger boulders to streamside cobble. • During cold weather, Black Phoebes tend to concentrate in protected lowlands, often around houses, outbuildings and on southern exposures. They scatter throughout suburban and urban areas in winter, occurring in greatest numbers about small lakes, ponds, parks and gardens.

ID: mostly black plumage; white belly and undertail coverts; thin, white edgings to tail. *Immature:* dark brown precedes black adult plumage; cinnamon wing bars and rump are retained well into fall.
Size: *L* 6¾ in; *W* 11 in.
Status: *AZ:* fairly common migrant and resident below the Mogollon Rim; uncommon and local summer resident at elevations above the Mogollon Rim. *NM:* uncommon to fairly common resident in the south to the Mongolllon Mts., especially along the Rio Grande Valley; range extends farther north in migration and summer.
Habitat: semi-open habitats near water, including riparian woodlands, steep-walled canyons, cities and farmlands with wet areas.

Nesting: on cliffs, bridges, buildings and culverts; cup-shaped or semi-circular nest of vegetation, animal hair and mud is usually placed on a flat surface or vertical face with shelter from above; female incubates 4–5 white eggs for 16–18 days; pair raises the young; may return to same nest site over successive years.
Feeding: flycatches for aerial insects; gleans plant foliage by fluttering or snatching; commonly takes insects from the ground or from the water's surface; regurgitates indigestible parts of prey as pellets.
Voice: call note is a penetrating *tsip!* or *tsee*; song is an exclamatory *f'BEE, f'BEER!*.
Similar Species: none.
Best Sites: *AZ:* Boyce Thompson Arboretum; Sweetwater Wetlands; Patagonia Lake SP. *NM:* Bosque del Apache NWR; Percha Dam SP; Rio Grande Nature Center.

SAY'S PHOEBE

Sayornis saya

Unlike its close relative the Black Phoebe, this flycatcher is partial to dry environments. The Say's Phoebe thrives in sun-parched grassy valleys and hot, dry canyons—the agricultural lands and plains of the Southwest provide this sweet songster with all the amenities. Abandoned buildings provide a secure, sheltered nesting site that can be reused every year, and livestock conveniently stir up insects that the Say's Phoebe hawks from a fence post or other low perch. • The Say's Phoebe is the only bird whose common name and both Latin names are derived from one person, Thomas Say. A versatile naturalist, Say's primary contributions were in the field of entomology. • The name "phoebe" comes from the call of a close relative, the Eastern Phoebe *(S. phoebe)*.

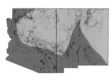

ID: dark tail; apricot buff belly and undertail coverts; brown-gray breast and upperparts; dark head; no eye ring; very faint wing bars; constantly bobs its tail.
Size: *L* 7½ in; *W* 13 in.
Status: fairly common migrant and summer resident throughout the region. *AZ:* common winter resident at lower elevations statewide. *NM:* common winter resident at lower elevation deserts in the south.
Habitat: hot, dry canyons, ravines, rimrocks, valleys and gullies dominated by grasses and shrubs; may also use scrublands and agricultural areas.

Nesting: in a niche on a cliff face or beneath an eave or bridge; nest of grass, moss and fur; white eggs, rarely with brown or reddish spots; female incubates 4–5 eggs for up to 17 days.
Feeding: flycatches for aerial insects; also gleans buildings, vegetation, streamsides and the ground for insects; sometimes runs short distances in pursuit of prey.
Voice: call is a softly whistled *pee-ur;* song is *pitseedar.*
Similar Species: *other flycatchers:* all lack apricot belly.
Best Sites: *AZ:* Phoenix Desert Botanical Garden; Hassayampa River Preserve; Patagonia Lake SP. *NM:* Bosque del Apache NWR; Percha Dam SP; Rio Grande Nature Center.

VERMILION FLYCATCHER

Pyrocephalus rubinus

The adult male Vermilion Flycatcher is one of the most brilliantly colored birds in the Southwest. *Pyrocephalus* or "fire head" and *rubinus* or "ruby-red" accurately describe the stunning appearance of his plumage. • In our region, Vermilion Flycatchers are found in open areas, such as marshes, pastures, fields and golf courses, invariably close to a pond or stream. They often perch on fences or trees, from which they watch for prey. • A foraging Vermilion Flycatcher acrobatically chases grasshoppers, beetles and butterflies through the woodlands, boomeranging back to its perch. After crunching down large insects, this flycatcher coughs up owl-like pellets containing the indigestible parts of its prey.

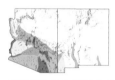

ID: *Male:* brownish black back and wings; bright red head and underparts; brownish black ear patch and nape; short, black bill. *Female:* grayish brown upperparts and head; white eyebrow; dark mask; white throat; white breast narrowly streaked with brown; dark pinkish lower belly and undertail coverts. *Immature:* male has variably patchy red plumage; female has yellowish lower belly and undertail coverts.
Size: *L* 6 in; *W* 10 in.
Status: *AZ:* fairly common migrant and local summer resident of cottonwood riparian areas below and along the Mogollon Rim; common resident in central and southern areas of the state. *NM:* uncommon to fairly common migrant and local summer resident of cottonwood riparian areas and oasis in the south; rare in winter.

Habitat open habitats with scattered trees and near open water.
Nesting: in the fork of a horizontal tree or shrub branch; female constructs a cup-shaped nest of twigs, vegetation, hair, spider webs and lichen; female incubates 2–4 cream-colored, speckled eggs for 12–14 days; both adults raise young; male may tend first brood while female begins a second nest.
Feeding: sallies for insects on or near the ground.
Voice: call is a sharp *pitsk;* courtship flight song is a soft *pit-a-see pit-a-see.*
Similar Species: none if seen well. *Say's Phoebe* (p. 90): superficially similar to adult female, but larger with a gray throat and unstreaked gray breast.
Best Sites: *AZ:* Patagonia Lake SP; Hassayampa River Preserve. *NM:* Bosque del Apache NWR; Percha Dam SP; Rattlesnake Springs.

ASH-THROATED FLYCATCHER

Myiarchus cinerascens

The Ash-throated Flycatcher is a characteristic species of the Southwest. Its infrequent, whistled calls echo from the shadows of heat-hazed oak and mesquite stands, representing the voice of the dry woodland. • As opportunistic as any other secondary cavity nester, Ash-throated Flycatchers will use a bluebird box, old machinery or an unused mailbox if a tree cavity cannot be found. These flycatchers are most numerous, however, in communities that offer an abundance of natural nest cavities. Encouraging landowners and urban planners to leave large, dead trees standing (where they do not pose a safety hazard) can benefit many animals that depend on tree cavities for shelter and nesting. • Another of the large *Myiarchus* flycatchers, the Brown-crested Flycatcher *(M. tyrannulus)*, extends its range from Mexico into our region. It is found in riparian woodlands south of the Mogollon Rim.

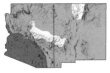

ID: gray-brown upperparts; gray throat and breast; yellow belly and undertail coverts; stout, dark bill; fluffy crown; 2 whitish wing bars; no eye ring; ample dark brown tail shows some rufous in webbing.
Size: *L* 7–8 in; *W* 12 in.
Status: common summer resident throughout the region. *AZ:* uncommon in winter in the south.
Habitat: *Breeding:* oak groves and woodland, riparian corridors with large, old trees. *In migration:* occurs in a wide variety of tree and shrub associations.
Nesting: in a natural or artificial cavity; pair amasses a nest of soft vegetation, hair and feathers; female incubates 4–5 creamy white eggs, blotched with lavender and brown, for about 15 days; pair feeds the young.

Feeding: forages by flycatching from an inconspicuous perch; rarely catches prey in mid-air; tends to forage low among trees and shrubs; eats mostly insects but will take fruit, rarely small lizards and even mice.
Voice: distinctive, year-round *prrrt* call; song is a series of similar calls; also issues a burry *ka-BREER!* or a harsh, abrupt *ka-brick*; general quality of voice vaguely suggests a referee's whistle; often silent and easily overlooked in migration.
Similar Species: *Brown-crested Flycatcher:* slightly larger; heavier bill; brighter yellow underparts. *Western Kingbird* (p. 95): slightly larger; pale gray head; black tail with white outer edges; no wing bars. *Cassin's Kingbird:* gray head; dark tail lacks reddish highlights; bright yellow belly; very pale wing bars are usually inconspicuous.
Best Sites: *AZ:* Hassayampa River Preserve; Patagonia Lake SP; Kino Springs.
NM: Bosque del Apache NWR; Rio Grande Nature Center; Rattlesnake Springs.

SULPHUR-BELLIED FLYCATCHER

Myiodynastes luteiventris

The unique, boldly patterned Sulphur-bellied Flycatcher reaches the northern limit of its breeding range in the mountains of southeastern Arizona. This tropical bird inhabits lush riparian canyons and often nests in sycamore, walnut or oak trees. In Arizona, Sulphur-bellied Flycatchers usually time their nest building with the summer rainy season in early July, making them one of the last birds to nest in our region.

ID: large, boldly patterned flycatcher; heavy bill; striped head and upperparts; fine, dark streaks on pale underparts; rufous tail.

Size: *L* 8½ in; *W* 14½ in.

Status: *AZ:* fairly common but local summer resident of shady pine-oak canyons in the southeast. *NM:* rare; found only in a few pine-oak canyons in the extreme southeast.

Habitat: riparian canyons in the mountains and tropical deciduous forest.

Nesting: secondary cavity nester; female constructs a loose cup nest of small twigs inside cavity; female incubates 3–4 white or buff eggs, richly marked with red or purple, for 16 days.

Feeding: gleans foliage or flycatches for insects; also eats fruit.

Voice: song is a constantly repeated, soft, liquid *tre-le-re-re* or *chu-eer.*

Similar Species: none.

Best Sites: *AZ:* Madera Canyon (Santa Rita Mts.); Miller Canyon (Huachuca Mts.); Cave Creek (Chiricahua Mts.). *NM:* Guadalupe Canyon (rare).

93

THICK-BILLED KINGBIRD

Tyrannus crassirostris

Kingbirds are a group of flycatchers that perch on wires or fence posts in open habitats and fearlessly chase larger birds out of their breeding territories. Once you have witnessed a kingbird's brave attacks against much larger birds, such as crows and hawks, you'll understand why this rabble-rouser was awarded its regal common name. • Sometimes described as "Arizona's loudest bird," the Thick-billed Kingbird is a year-round resident of western Mexico and was not discovered breeding in the U.S. until 1958. Since the first breeding pair was found in the Guadalupe Canyon of southeastern Arizona, this species has become an uncommon summer resident in the area. • The combination of dark upperparts, pale underparts and a massive bill make this large kingbird instantly recognizable within its range. Other kingbirds usually have olive upperparts and bright yellow underparts.

ID: stocky overall; large, thick bill; dusky upperparts; pale whitish underparts. *Juvenile:* pale yellow underparts; rufous wash on wing tips.
Size: *L* 9½ in; *W* 16 in.
Status: *AZ:* uncommon and local summer resident in the southeast. *NM:* uncommon summer resident only in Guadalupe Canyon.
Habitat: cottonwood and sycamore riparian canyons.
Nesting: in a crotch of a tree; frail nest is built of grass and twigs; pair incubates 3–5 brown or lilac spotted, creamy white eggs for about 16 days.

Feeding: flycatches for insects.
Voice: loud, shrill *cut-a-reep* calls and other, variable vocalizations.
Similar Species: other kingbirds in region have bright yellow underparts. *Brown-crested Flycatcher:* slimmer overall; smaller bill; paler gray head and throat; rufous on wings and tail. *Eastern Kingbird:* range rarely overlaps; less stocky overall; smaller bill; black head and upperparts strongly contrast with white underparts.
Best Sites: *AZ:* Patagonia Roadside Rest Area. *NM:* Guadalupe Canyon.

WESTERN KINGBIRD

Tyrannus verticalis

The tumbling aerial courtship display of the Western Kingbird is a common sight throughout our region. At other times, the Western Kingbird is a more conventional performer and is often seen surveying for prey from fence posts, barbed wire and power lines. Once it spots a flying insect, especially a dragonfly, bee or butterfly, a kingbird will quickly give chase for 40 ft. or more until the prey is caught. • The scientific name *verticalis* refers to this bird's small, hidden, red crown patch that is flared in courtship and territorial displays. • Much of the Western Kingbird's range overlaps with the similar-looking, and equally common, Cassin's Kingbird *(T. vociferans)*, which is absent only from southwestern Arizona and the eastern plains of New Mexico.

and plant down; female incubates 3–4 heavily mottled, white to pinkish eggs for 18–19 days.

Feeding: sallies for insects captured in flight or on the ground; also eats fruit.

Voice: alarm and threat calls are a rapid, rising series of shrill, sputtering *widik* and *pik* notes or twittering *kit* repetitions; male's song is a high-pitched, squeaky *pidik pik pidik peekado.*

Similar Species: *Eastern Kingbird:* local and uncommon in NM; black upperparts; white underparts; white-tipped tail. *Tropical Kingbird:* large bill; no white outer tail feathers. *Cassin's Kingbird:* dark gray throat emphasizes narrow white chin. *Say's Phoebe* (p. 90): smaller; pale rufous belly and undertail; dull gray upperparts; all-dark tail; wags tail.

Best Sites: widespread. *AZ:* Willcox Playa; San Rafael Grasslands; Organ Pipe Cactus National Monument. *NM:* Bosque del Apache NWR; Carlsbad Caverns NP; Rattlesnake Springs.

ID: greenish gray back and wings; gray head with small, black mask and white throat; short, black bill; gray breast; yellow belly and undertail coverts; black tail with white outer tail feathers.

Size: *L* 8–9 in; *W* 15–16 in.

Status: common migrant and summer resident throughout the region.

Habitat: fields, pastures and other open areas.

Nesting: usually on a horizontal branch against or near a tree trunk, or on a human-built structure; cup is built of available materials and is lined with hair, cotton

LOGGERHEAD SHRIKE

Lanius ludovicianus

Shrikes are small, predatory songbirds with very acute vision. They often perch atop trees and on wires to scan for small prey, which is caught in a fast, direct flight or a swooping dive. • Because the shrike lacks the talons and strong feet of hawks and owls, it impales its prey on barbed wire fences or thorny vegetation, earning itself the colloquial name "Butcher Bird." Impaling prey also indicates the hunting prowess of a male shrike, which helps him attract a mate. • Loggerhead Shrikes are found in a variety of open habitats but seem unable to survive in developed areas, probably because many are struck by vehicles as they swoop down to capture prey. Populations are declining across the continent at about 7% per year, and as a result, some populations are now endangered.

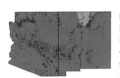

ID: large head; hooked bill; gray back and crown; wide, black mask; white throat and underparts; long, black tail with white corners; black wings with white primary patch; *Juvenile:* barred, brownish gray underparts. *In flight:* fast wingbeats; white patches in wings and tail.
Size: *L* 9 in; *W* 12 in.
Status: common resident in open habitats throughout the region and less common in the far north.
Habitat: open habitats such as pastures, fields and prairies; also ball fields and cemeteries.
Nesting: in the crotch of a shrub or tree; bulky cup nest of twigs and grass is lined with animal hair, feathers and rootlets;

female incubates 5–6 darkly spotted, pale buff to grayish white eggs for 15–17 days; raises 2 broods.
Feeding: swoops down on prey from a perch or attacks in pursuit; takes mostly large insects; regularly eats small birds and other vertebrates.
Voice: call a harsh *shack-shack*; song a series of warbles, trills and other notes.
Similar Species: *Northern Mockingbird* (p.): much thinner bill; no black mask; lighter wings; wingbeats slower and buoyant. *Northern Shrike:* rare winter resident in northern AZ and NM; adult is larger; fine barring on sides and breast; more sinuous black mask does not extend above hooked bill.
Best Sites: widespread. *AZ:* Sulphur Springs Valley; Roosevelt L.; Patagonia Lake SP. *NM:* Bosque del Apache NWR; Carlsbad Caverns NP.

GRAY JAY

Perisoreus canadensis

There are few birds in our region that rival Gray Jays for boldness. Small family groups glide slowly and unexpectedly out of mountain conifer forests, attracted by the slightest commotion or movement in the woods. These endearing birds are surprisingly confiding, and they will quickly welcome themselves to any passersby. Gray Jays are easiest to find in campgrounds and picnic areas, where they will win your admiration as they steal your lunch! • The friendly, mischievous Gray Jay has dark gray plumage and a long, elegant tail. This bold bird forms a strong pair bond, and after an absence, partners will seek each other out and touch or nibble bills. • Gray Jays lay their eggs and begin incubation as early as late February, allowing the young to get a head start on learning to forage and store food. These birds cache food for the winter, and their specialized salivary glands coat the food with a sticky mucus that helps to preserve it.

ID: dark bill; white forehead, cheek and throat; dark gray nape and upperparts; fluffy, pale gray breast and belly; white undertail coverts; fairly long tail.

Size: *L* 11–13 in; *W* 18–19 in.

Status: *AZ:* uncommon and local resident of high elevation coniferous forests above 9000 ft. in the White Mts. *NM:* fairly common resident of high elevation coniferous forests of the Jemez, San Juan and Sangre de Cristo mts.

Habitat: dense and open coniferous and mixed forests, bogs and fens; picnic sites and campgrounds generally above 9000 ft.

Nesting: in a conifer; insulated nest is made of plant fibers, roots, moss, twigs, feathers and fur; female incubates 3–4 speckled, pale gray to greenish eggs for 17–22 days.

Feeding: searches the ground and vegetation for insects, fruit, songbird eggs and nestlings, carrion and berries; stores food; steals unguarded human food.

Voice: complex vocal repertoire; soft, whistled *quee-oo;* chuckled *cla-cla-cla;* also imitates other birds, especially the Northern Pygmy-Owl.

Similar Species: *Clark's Nutcracker* (p. 102): larger, heavy black bill; black and white wings and tail. *Loggerhead Shrike* (p. 96) and *Northern Shrike:* black mask; black and white wings and tail; open country resident.

Best Sites: *AZ:* Sunrise Campground (White Mts.). *NM:* Wheeler Peak.

STELLER'S JAY

Cyanocitta stelleri

With a dark crest and velvet blue feathers, the stunning Steller's Jay is a resident jewel in our coniferous woodlands. Generally noisy and pugnacious, this bird suddenly becomes silent and cleverly elusive when nesting. • Bold Steller's Jays will not hesitate to steal food scraps from inattentive picnickers and scatter smaller birds at feeders. Their ability to adapt, learn and even take advantage of situations suggests that corvids are very intelligent birds. • Steller's Jays occur west of and in the Rocky Mountains, while the similar looking Blue Jay (*C. cristata*) lives east of the Rockies. • When George Wilhelm Steller, the first European naturalist to visit Alaska, saw his first Steller's Jay, its similarity to paintings of the Blue Jay convinced him that he had arrived in North America.

ID: glossy, deep velvet blue plumage; black head, nape and back; large, black crest; bluish forehead streaks; barred wings and tail. *In flight:* grayish underwings with blue linings; round-tipped, blue tail.

Size: *L* 11–12 in; *W* 19 in.

Status: common resident in high elevation coniferous and mixed forests regionwide.

Habitat: coniferous forests and pine-oak woodlands; townsites and exotic tree plantations.

Nesting: in the fork of a conifer; bulky stick and twig nest is lined with mud, grass and conifer needles; female incubates 4 brown-marked, pale greenish blue eggs for 16 days.

Feeding: searches the ground and vegetation for insects, small vertebrates and other food items; forages in treetops for nuts, berries and other birds' eggs; visits feeders during winter.

Voice: harsh, far-carrying *shack-shack-shack;* a grating *kresh, kresh.*

Similar Species: *Western Scrub-Jay* (p. 99) and *Pinyon Jay* (p. 101): no crest or barring on tail or wings; lack black head, nape and back. *Gray Jay* (p. 97): in-flight silhouette looks longer-tailed and rounder-winged; slow glides.

Best Sites: *AZ:* Mt. Lemmon; San Francisco Mts.; White Mts. *NM:* Sangre de Cristo Mts.; Jemez Mts.; Sandia Mts.

WESTERN SCRUB-JAY

Aphelocoma californica

This slender jay is often seen foraging among leaf litter or surveying its tree-dotted habitat from a perch atop a tall shrub. • Oak mast is a staple of the Western Scrub-Jay's winter diet. Each fall, this jay harvests fallen acorns and stores them individually in holes that it has dug in the ground with its strong bill. This intelligent bird often uses a rock or concrete slab as an "anvil" to assist in cracking open the shielding coat. At the end of the winter, uneaten acorns are not wasted—many germinate, regenerating the stand. • The Western Scrub-Jay has recently been granted full species status and is now separated from the Florida Scrub-Jay *(A. coerulescens)* and the Island Scrub-Jay *(A. insularis),* an endemic species of southern California's Santa Cruz Island.

ID: slim body; gray back on otherwise sky blue upperparts; long, unmarked tail; streaked white throat bordered by a bluish "necklace"; light gray underparts; dark, heavy bill; dark cheek patch; faint white eyebrow.
Size: *L* 11½ in; *W* 15½ in.
Status: common resident of mountain foothills and pinyon-juniper woodland throughout the region.
Habitat: chaparral and dry, brushy open areas of oak and pinyon-juniper woodlands, mixed oak-coniferous forests, broken mixed deciduous-coniferous woodlands and riparian woodlands; also found in suburban parks and gardens and urban shrubbery.
Nesting: in a small conifer or shrub; pair builds a bulky stick nest, usually with an inner cup lined with moss, grass and fur; female incubates 3–6 eggs for 15–17 days.
Feeding: forages on the ground for insects and small vertebrates; also eats other birds' eggs and nestlings, as well as acorns, pinyon nuts and many fruits.
Voice: perch call is a harsh, repetitive *ike-ike-ike;* in flight, a rough, frequently repeated *quesh, quesh, quesh.*
Similar Species: *Pinyon Jay* (p. 101): blue back and underparts; shorter tail. *Steller's Jay* (p. 98): local; large, black crest; dark head, nape and back; blue underparts; barred wings and tail. *Mexican Jay* (p. 100): local; blue head; bluish back; whitish throat; gray underparts.
Best Sites: *AZ:* Boyce Thompson Arboretum; Sycamore Creek; Mt. Ord; Red Rock SP. *NM:* Three Gun Spring Canyon (Sandia Mts.); Water Canyon (Magdalena Mts.).

MEXICAN JAY

Aphelocoma ultramarina

Within the U.S., the Mexican Jay is a specialty of southeastern Arizona and extreme southwestern New Mexico, with a disjunct population along the Mexican border in Texas. These separate populations seem to have originated in Mexico but developed in isolation from one another and have since learned to survive in distinct habitats, resulting in different nesting behavior, egg color, bill color of young and voice. • In both populations, nesting and feeding territories are protected year-round and over generations by a flock of related family members. In Arizona, two to four females within the flock may nest in a given season. A number of males may engage in breeding activity, but a single male attends the breeding female group. Young birds are typically fed and tended by both parents and other members of the flock. • This bird was previously known as the "Gray-breasted Jay" and the "Arizona Jay."

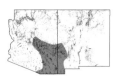

ID: long bill; blue upperparts; light gray underparts; no crest.
Size: *L* 11½–13 in; *W* 19½ in.

Status: *AZ:* common resident of evergreen oaks in the mountains of southeastern Arizona, and local north to the Mogollon Rim. *NM:* common resident of evergreen oaks in the Animas Mts. and Peloncillo Mts.; uncommon and local further north to the Pinos Altos Mts. and Mogollon Mts.
Habitat: open oak woodlands, canyons and lower mountain slopes.
Nesting: in a tree; pair builds bulky cup nest of twigs and sticks and lines it with soft plant fibers and rootlets; female incubates 4–5 pale green eggs, occasionally with brownish spots, for about 18 days; pair and other flock members feed young.
Feeding: omnivorous diet consists primarily of acorns, insects and seeds; may eat small reptiles, and rarely bird eggs, nestlings and small rodents.
Voice: various calls using different inflections and pitch variations include *weenk, weenk, weenk* and *drenk, drenk.*
Similar Species: *Western Scrub Jay* (p. 99): grayish back; thin white eyebrow; grayish-and-white-streaked throat bordered by blue necklace. *Pinyon Jay* (p. 101): is blue overall.
Best Sites: *AZ:* Madera Canyon, Ramsey Canyon Preserve and Garden Canyon (Huachuca Mts.). *NM:* canyons of the Peloncillo Mts. and Animas Mts.

PINYON JAY

Gymnorhinus cyanocephalus

Loud, social Pinyon Jays are seed caching birds found primarily in the pine forests of the foothills. When not breeding, these jays wander in sometimes enormous flocks that consist of many smaller family groups. Their sharp bill allows them to open pine cones and remove the seeds, while their specialized jaw absorbs the force of heavy pounding. • One bird can carry up to 40 whole, unhulled pine seeds in its expandable esophagus (a Western Scrub-Jay can carry only 5), and will transport the harvest to traditional caching grounds to be buried. A sharp memory allows individuals to accurately locate the hidden stores months later, even under snow. • The scientific name *Gymnorhinus* means "naked nose" and refers to the more exposed nostrils, an adaptation that keeps facial feathers free of pine pitch.

ID: dull gray blue plumage, brightest blue on head; long, dark, pointed bill; light streaks on throat; short tail; often flies in flocks.

Size: *L* 9–11½ in; *W* 19 in.

Status: *AZ:* fairly common resident of pinyon-juniper woodland in northern and central areas of the state generally north of the Mogollon Rim. *NM:* fairly common resident of pinyon-juniper woodland west of the eastern plains.

Habitat: *Breeding:* dry, open ponderosa pine, limber pine and juniper forest. *Foraging:* sagebrush flats and forests of pine and tall sagebrush.

Nesting: in loose colonies in pines, junipers and shrubs; pair builds large, bulky nest of twigs and fibers; female incubates 4–5 brown-marked, blue-green eggs for up to 17 days.

Feeding: searches the ground and vegetation for pinyon nuts, seeds and insects; also eats berries and other birds' eggs and nestlings.

Voice: flight call is a high, piercing mew or laughing, repeated *hah-hah;* warning call is low *krawk-krawk-krawk.*

Similar Species: *Western Scrub-Jay* (p. 99): light gray underparts; gray back; long tail. *Steller's Jay* (p. 98): large black crest; dark head, nape and back; barred wings and tail.

Best Sites: *AZ:* Flagstaff area; Sipe Wildlife Management Area (White Mts.); South Fork Little Colorado R. (White Mts.). *NM:* Pinos Altos Mts.; Pinyon Juniper woodlands of the Black Range and Sacramento Mts.

CLARK'S NUTCRACKER

Nucifraga columbiana

The Clark's Nutcracker has a long, sturdy bill for prying apart the cones of whitebark pine and other conifers and a special throat pouch for transporting the seeds to carefully selected storage spots. These caches might be eight miles or more apart and together may contain more than 30,000 seeds. Over winter and throughout the nesting cycle, nutcrackers use their phenomenal memory to relocate cache sites. • The whitebark pine is entirely dependent on the Clark's Nutcracker for seed dispersal, while the nutcracker relies on the pine's energy-rich seeds for successfully raising its young. • Captain William Clark of the Lewis and Clark expedition mistook this large-billed bird for a woodpecker and placed it in the genus *Picicorvus*, or "woodpecker-crow."

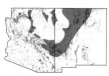

Other ID: light gray head, back and underparts; large, black bill; whitish face; black wings with flashy white secondaries; white undertail coverts; black and white tail feathers. *In flight:* stoops and tumbles unerringly along upper slopes of tall peaks.
Size: *L* 12–13 in; *W* 24 in.
Status: *AZ:* uncommon resident at or near timberline in the White Mts. and San Francisco Mts. *NM:* uncommon to fairly common resident at or near timberline in most major mountain ranges.
Habitat: *Breeding:* upper-elevation conifer forest; may use lower-elevation limber pine forest. *Nonbreeding:* may move to lower elevations.

Nesting: on a horizontal conifer limb; pair builds a stick platform nest lined with grass and strips of bark; pair incubates 2–4 darkly marked, greenish eggs for 16–22 days.
Feeding: forages on the ground and among trees for pinecones; hammers the cones with its bill; also eats insects; stores food for winter.
Voice: loud, unpleasant, grating *kra-a-a-a-a,* delivered mostly from perch.
Similar Species: *Gray Jay* (p. 98): smaller gray wings and tail; shorter bill. *Northern Mockingbird* (p. 126): much smaller; smaller bill; lighter underparts; white wing patch on the primary flight feathers; common in valleys and foothills.
Best Sites: *AZ:* San Francisco Peaks; Kaibab Plateau; Sunrise Campground (White Mts.). *NM:* Sandia Crest (Sandia Mts.); Wheeler Peak (Sangre de Cristo Mts.).

BLACK-BILLED MAGPIE

Pica hudsonia

Truly among North America's most beautiful birds, Black-billed Magpies are too often discredited because of their aggressive demeanor. Many westerners consider magpies a nuisance, whereas eastern visitors to our region are often captivated by their beauty and approachability. • The magpie is one of the most exceptional architects among birds. The domed compartment of its nest conceals and protects eggs and young from harsh weather and predators. Abandoned nests remain in trees for years and are often reused by other birds. • Magpies raised in captivity may learn how to imitate the human voice and "count" or tell apart different sized groups of objects. • Albino magpies occasionally occur. They have white bellies and light gray, instead of black, body feathers.

ID: black head, breast and back; large, black bill; white wing patch; iridescent wings may appear black; white belly; black under-tail coverts. *In flight:* rounded, black and white wings.
Size: *L* 18 in; *W* 25 in.
Status: *AZ:* uncommon and local resident in the extreme northeast corner of the state. *NM:* common resident in the northernmost regions of the state
Habitat: open forests, agricultural areas, riparian thickets, townsites and camp-grounds.

Nesting: in a tree or tall shrub; domed stick and twig nest is often held together with mud; female incubates 5–8 brown-spotted, greenish gray eggs for up to 24 days.
Feeding: omnivorous; forages on the ground for insects, carrion, human food waste, nuts, seeds and berries; picks insects and ticks from large ungulates; occasionally eats bird eggs; routinely scavenges vehicle-killed animals, including magpies.
Voice: loud, nasal, frequently repeated *ueh-ueh-ueh;* also many other vocalizations.
Similar Species: none
Best Sites: *AZ:* Teec-nos-pos. *NM:* Cochita L.; Taos; Las Vegas NWR.

AMERICAN CROW

Corvus brachyrhynchos

American Crows are wary, intelligent birds that have flourished despite considerable human effort, over many generations, to reduce their numbers. As ecological generalists, crows can survive in a wide variety of habitats and conditions. In January, when crows in our region are busy capturing lizards in the brushlands, crows in southern Canada are searching the snow-covered fields for mice or carrion. • Highly social Corvids have superb memories and are able to learn, make simple tools and problem solve. Crows will often drop walnuts or clams from great heights onto a hard surface to crack the shells, one of the few examples of birds using objects to manipulate food. They are also impressive mimics, able to whine like a dog, cry like a child, squawk like a hen and laugh like a human. Some crows in captivity are able to repeat simple spoken words. • In some places, thousands of crows may roost together on any given autumn night. These aggregations of crows are known as "murders." • The American Crow's cumbersome-sounding scientific name is Latin for "raven with the small nose."

ID: black plumage; large bill; broad wings.
Size: *L* 17–21 in; *W* 3 ft.
Status: *AZ:* locally common resident along the entire Mogollon Plateau; rare in winter to the lowland deserts. *NM:* locally common resident and winter visitor in the north and west.
Habitat: pastures, agricultural fields, oak and mixed oak-pine woodlands; wooded urban areas.
Nesting: in a tree or on a utility pole; large stick-and-branch nest is lined with fur and soft plant materials; female incubates 4–6 gray-green to blue-green eggs, blotched with brown and gray, for about 18 days.
Feeding: very opportunistic; feeds on carrion and animal prey as diverse as insects, bird eggs and nestlings, and other small vertebrates; also eats acorns and berries.
Voice: distinctive, far-carrying, repetitive *caw-caw-caw.*
Similar Species: *Common Raven* (p. 105) and *Chihuahuan Raven:* larger; heavier bill; shaggy throat; Chihuahuan Raven has white-based neck feathers.
Best Sites: *AZ:* widespread above the Mogollon Rim. *NM:* Bosque del Apache NWR; Las Vegas NWR.

COMMON RAVEN

Corvus corax

The Common Raven soars with a wingspan comparable to that of hawk's, traveling along coastlines, over deserts, along mountain ridges and even on the Arctic tundra. Few birds occupy such a large natural range. • Whether stealing food from a flock of gulls, harassing an eagle or scavenging from a carcass, the Common Raven is worthy of its reputation as a clever bird. Glorified in many cultures as a magical being, the raven does not act by instinct alone. From producing complex vocalizations to playfully sliding down snow banks, this raucous bird exhibits behaviors that many people once thought of as exclusively human. • Southeastern Arizona and southern New Mexico is also home to the Chihuahuan Raven *(C. cryptoleucus)*. Distinguishing the two species is difficult because the Chihuahuan Raven's white neck feathers usually remain hidden. The Chihuahuan Raven's calls are typically less varied, higher and more crowlike.

Size: *L* 24 in; *W* 50 in.
Status: *AZ:* fairly common to common resident of open areas statewide. *NM:* uncommon to common resident of open areas statewide.
Habitat: most habitats; tends to avoid habitats occupied by crows, such as urban parks, farmyards and orchards; forages locally in towns and cities, especially along highways and roads, seeking carrion.
Nesting: on steep cliffs, ledges, bluffs, power poles and tall conifers; large stick and branch nest is lined with fur and soft

ID: all-black plumage; heavy, black bill; wedge-shaped tail; shaggy throat; pointed wings.

plant materials; female incubates 4–6 eggs for 18–21 days.
Feeding: opportunistic omnivore; feeds on carrion, small vertebrates, other birds' eggs and nestlings, berries, invertebrates and human food waste.
Voice: many vocalizations, from deep gargling croaks to high twanging notes; deep, far-carrying, croaking *craww-craww* or *quork quork*; juveniles contact adults with a higher pitched croak.
Similar Species: *Chihuahuan Raven:* call is a higher pitched *craaaaag*; smaller body; thinner throat area; shorter bill; wedged tail is less distinct. *American Crow* (p. 104): smaller; smaller head and bill; shorter, rounder wings; fan-shaped tail; higher-pitched calls.
Best Sites: widespread. *AZ:* Boyce Thompson Arboretum; Arizona Sonora Desert Museum; Phoenix; Tucson. *NM:* Bosque del Apache NWR.

PURPLE MARTIN

Progne subis

The Purple Martin is the largest swallow in North America and a popular yard bird. Purple Martins historically bred in tree cavities and cliff crevices, but native Indians encouraged martins to nest in hollowed-out gourds hung on poles, and later North Americans introduced wooded or metal multi-room "apartment houses." As a result, most Purple Martins now nest in birdhouses or gourds. Residents who wish to attract martins should set out (or open up) their martin houses in early February and should routinely remove any House Sparrow nests that are built (the sparrows are a non-native species, so it is legal to remove their nests without a permit). • Despite a wide reputation as superb mosquito hawks, Purple Martins virtually never feed on mosquitoes. • The scientific name *Progne* refers to Procne, the daughter of the king of Athens who, according to Greek mythology, was transformed into a swallow.

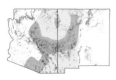

Habitat: large natural areas and undisturbed saguaro forests; may forage over any habitat.

ID: dark blue upperparts; shallowly forked tail. *Male:* dark blue overall. *Female and juvenile:* gray forehead; "scaly" dark and whitish underparts.

Size: *L* 7–8 in; *W* 18 in.

Status: *AZ:* uncommon migrant and uncommon and local breeder in undisturbed saguaro forests, and forested regions along the Mogollon Plateau. *NM:* rare to common summer resident of pine forests in the western mountains.

Nesting: communal; usually in an old woodpecker hole or cliff crevice; mostly the female builds a nest of feathers, grass, mud and vegetation; female incubates 4–5 white eggs for 15–18 days.

Feeding: aerial forager; feeds on flying insects such as ants, wasps and flies.

Voice: rich, pleasant chirping notes, often in flight.

Similar Species: none; large size, chirping calls and male's plumage distinct.

Best Sites: *AZ:* Roosevelt L.; Luna L. (White Mts.); Organ Pipe Cactus National Monument. *NM:* Lake Roberts (Pinos Altos Mts.); Bonito L. (Sacramento Mts.).

TREE SWALLOW

Tachycineta bicolor

Tree Swallows are most common during migration, appearing like huge clouds of smoke over marshes or fields. Swallows are swift and graceful fliers, routinely traveling at speeds of 30 miles per hour. • Tree Swallows are more cold hardy than other swallows, which explains their presence along the Colorado River Valley, AZ, during winter. They readily switch to a diet of berries when insects become scarce. • In bright spring sunshine, the iridescent back of the Tree Swallow appears dark blue, but in fall it appears green. Unlike other North American swallows, female Tree Swallows do not acquire their full adult plumage until their second or third year. • The range and habitat of the Tree Swallow overlaps with the nearly identical Violet-green Swallow *(T. thalassina)* in extreme northern Arizona and New Mexico and in migration. To differentiate the two, pay attention to the face and rump. The Tree Swallow has a dark cap that encompasses the eye and a dark rump in flight. The Violet-green's white cheek surrounds the eye, and it has noticeable white rump patches in flight.

ID: dark rump; iridescent dark blue or green upperparts; white underparts; shallowly forked tail.

Size: *L* 5½ in; *W* 14½ in.

Status: common migrant regionwide from February to early May and August to October. *AZ:* local in summer in the higher mountain ranges above Mogollon Rim; common winter resident along the Lower Colorado R. *NM:* local in summer, chiefly in the San Juan Mts.

Habitat: forages over any habitat.

Nesting: in a tree cavity or nest box lined with weeds, grass and feathers; female incubates 4–6 white eggs for up to 19 days.

Feeding: plucks flying insects from the air, or gleans foliage (especially that of Wax Myrtle) for berries.

Voice: alarm call is a metallic, buzzy *klweet*. *Male:* song is a liquid, chattering twitter.

Similar Species: *Violet-green Swallow:* white on face extends above eye; emerald green back; white rump patches. *Barn Swallow:* some birds appear wholly white below, but note deeply forked tail.

Best Sites: widespread in migration. *AZ:* Kaibab Plateau (summer). *NM:* San Juan Mts. (summer).

NORTHERN ROUGH-WINGED SWALLOW

Stelgidopteryx serripennis

Northern Rough-winged Swallows are more widespread in our region than most people realize. They typically nest in sandy banks along rivers and streams, excavating their own nesting burrow or reusing a burrow dug by another bird or rodent. Vertical cuts created by interstate highways have provided additional nesting crevices for these dusky little birds. Watch for Rough-wings zipping through busy intersections near banks, culverts and bridges. • Unlike other swallows, male Northern Rough-wings have curved barbs along the outer edge of their primary wing feathers. The purpose of this saw-toothed edge remains a mystery, but may be used to produce sound during courtship displays. Its English and scientific names relate to this structure; *Stelgidopteryx* means "scraper wing" and *serripennis* means "saw feather."

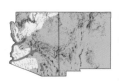

ID: dull brown upperparts; indistinct brown wash on breast; whitish underparts. *Juvenile*: wide, rufous wing bars. *In flight*: short, notched tail.

Size: *L* 5½ in; *W* 14 in.

Status: fairly common migrant from January to May and August to October and uncommon summer resident along streams and waterways throughout the region.

AZ: uncommon to fairly common in winter along the Lower Colorado R. and around Phoenix and Tucson.

Habitat: *Foraging:* over most habitats, especially near water. *Nesting:* in riverbanks, drain pipes, exhaust pipes (!) or other artificial cavities.

Nesting: sometimes in small colonies but usually solitary; pair excavates a burrow in an earthen bank and lines the nesting chamber with leaves and dry grass; mostly the female incubates 4–8 white eggs for 12–16 days.

Feeding: catches flying insects on the wing.

Voice: call a short, squeaky note.

Similar Species: *Bank Swallow:* brown breast band; white underparts. *Tree Swallow* (p. 107): some birds drab, appearing brown above, but note pure white underparts.

Best Sites: widespread in migration. *AZ:* Lower Colorado R. *NM:* Bosque del Apache NWR; Percha Dam SP.

CLIFF SWALLOW

Petrochelidon pyrrhonota

If the Cliff Swallow were to be renamed in the 20th century, it would probably be called "Bridge Swallow," because so many bridges have a colony living under them. In recent decades, Cliff Swallows have expanded their range across eastern North America, nesting on various human-made structures including bridges, culverts and under eaves. • Cliff Swallows roll mud into balls with their bills and press the pellets together to form their characteristic gourd-shaped nests.

As brooding parents peer out of the circular neck of the nest, their white forehead patch warns intruders that somebody is home. • Agricultural fields and marshes are favorite foraging sites for Cliff Swallows, which catch insects on the wing. Watch for their square (not forked) tail, cinnamon-colored rump patch and distinctive flight pattern of ascending with rapid wing-strokes then gliding gracefully down. • In our region, the Cliff Swallow's range overlaps with the Barn Swallow *(Hirundo rustica),* and the two may be found nesting in similar habitats. The Barn Swallow is easily distinguished by its long, deeply forked tail, visible on both perched and flying birds.

ID: orange rump; blackish back and wings; pale collar; blackish crown; white forehead; orange cheek and ear patches; black throat; pale underparts; black tail.

Size: *L* 5½ in; *W* 13½ in.

Status: common migrant and summer resident in lowlands throughout the region.

Habitat: *Foraging:* over most habitats. *Nesting:* over water.

Nesting: colonial; under bridges over water or on buildings built in water; pair builds a gourd-shaped mud nest with a small opening near the bottom; pair incubates 4–5 brown-spotted, white to pinkish eggs for 14–16 days.

Feeding: catches flying insects on the wing.

Voice: call is a twittering *churrr-churrr.*

Similar Species: *Barn Swallow:* deeply forked tail; dark rump; usually has rust-colored underparts and forehead. *Cave Swallow:* darker forehead; pale throat. *Other swallows* (pp. 107–08): lack buff forehead and rump patch.

Best Sites: *AZ:* Lower Colorado R.; Roosevelt L.; Patagonia Lake SP. *NM:* Bosque del Apache NWR; Percha Dam SP.

MOUNTAIN CHICKADEE

Poecile gambeli

This year-round resident of high-elevation forests spends much of its time feeding on seeds and insects high in a canopy of conifers. During harsh winter weather, many Mountain Chickadees move to lower elevations in search of warmer temperatures and more abundant food. • The Mountain Chickadee breeds at higher elevations than most other chickadees. It routinely nests in subalpine conifers and is often seen foraging up to the treeline. During winter, feeders in mountain townsites offer excellent viewing opportunities. • The scientific descriptor *gambeli* honors William Gambel, a 19th-century ornithologist who died of typhoid fever in the Sierra Nevada at the age of 28. • Two other chickadees are found in our region, but both lack the Mountain Chickadee's white eyebrow. The Black-capped Chickadee *(P. atricapillus)* is a common to uncommon summer resident in northern New Mexico. The Mexican Chickadee *(P. sclateri)* reaches the northern extension of its range in the Chiricahua Mountains, AZ, and the Animas Mountains, NM. Good viewing sites for this chickadee are Rustler Park in the Chiricahuas, AZ, and the Animas Mountains of NM.

ID: white eyebrow through black cap; white cheek; black "bib"; light gray upperparts and tail; drab, gray wings; light gray or tan underparts.

Size: *L* 5¼ in; *W* 8½ in.

Status: AZ: common resident of pine and spruce-fir forests in the higher mountain ranges from southeastern Arizona north across the Mogollon Plateau and Kaibab Plateau. **NM:** common resident of pine and spruce-fir forests in the higher mountains nearly statewide.

Habitat: montane coniferous forests and lower portions of subalpine forests; irregular downslope flights to lowlands and foothills.

Nesting: in natural cavity or abandoned woodpecker nest; can excavate cavity in soft, rotting wood; lines nest with fur, feathers, moss and grass; female incubates 5–9 unspotted white eggs for up to 14 days.

Feeding: gleans vegetation, branches and the ground for small insects and spiders; visits backyard feeders for seeds; also eats conifer seeds and invertebrate eggs.

Voice: call is a drawling *chick a-day, day, day;* song is a sweet, clear, whistled *fee-bee-bay.*

Similar Species: *Black-capped Chickadee:* lacks white eyebrow; buffy sides. *Mexican Chickadee:* lacks white eyebrow; gray sides.

Best Sites: AZ: Kaibab Plateau; Sunrise Campground (White Mts.); widespread across the Mogollon Plateau. **NM:** widespread in most mountain ranges statewide.

BRIDLED TITMOUSE

Baeolophus wollweberi

Titmice are small, crested birds that are often found in small flocks. Their crest is usually held in a relaxed, upright position, with a flattened crest indicating apprehension and an erect crest signaling a territorial dispute. The crest, combined with the unique facial pattern, easily distinguishes the Bridled Titmouse from all other similar birds in our region. • Of the 11 titmouse and chickadee species found in North America, the Bridled Titmouse and Mexican Chickadee have the southernmost range. The Bridled Titmouse inhabits montane woodlands from southeastern Arizona and southwestern New Mexico to the Oaxaca region of Mexico. • Outside of the breeding season, titmice are often found in mixed-species flocks with chickadees, kinglets, vireos and other songbirds. The Bridled Titmouse plays a leadership role in the flock and is often the first to sound alarm calls.

ID: dark gray upperparts; pale gray underparts; black throat; distinctive black stripe pattern on white face; black and gray crest.
Size: *L* 4½–5 in; *W* 8 in.
Status: *AZ:* common resident of mid elevation riparian and pine-oak woodlands of southeastern and central Arizona north to the Mogollon Rim. *NM:* fairly common resident of mid-elevation riparian and pine-oak woodlands in the southwest.
Habitat: higher elevation oak or pine-oak woodlands; riparian canyons.
Nesting: in a natural tree cavity or old woodpecker hole in a live or standing dead tree; occasionally uses artificial nest boxes;

nest is lined with grass, lichen, leaves, plant down, hair and other soft materials; female incubates 5–7 white eggs for 13–14 days.
Feeding: takes insects from stems, branches and leaves of trees and shrubs; often swings upside down on branch ends; also takes seeds from ground or from feeders.
Voice: contact call is a descending series of harsh, scolding, short notes; *chick-a-dee-dee-dee* call and *fee-bee* whistle often given; song is a variable, repeated series of 1–2 syllables.
Similar Species: *Juniper Titmouse* (p. 112): lacks black and white facial pattern. *Black-capped, Mexican* and *Mountain* (p. 110) chickadees: no crest; black cap; Mountain Chickadee has white eyebrow.
Best Sites: *AZ:* Madera Canyon, Garden Canyon and Ramsey Canyon Preserve (Huachuca Mts.). *NM:* Clanton Canyon (Peloncillo Mts.)

JUNIPER TITMOUSE

Baeolophus ridgwayi

Despite the Juniper Titmouse's plain, somber plumage, its disposition is bright and cheerful. The Juniper Titmouse is a denizen of pinyon-juniper woodlands, and it often acknowledges visitors with an inquisitive raise of its head crest. • These birds spend much of their time dangling upside down among green foliage, pecking at bark or prying into every little crack or crevice in search of aphids, leafhoppers, caterpillars, beetle larvae, spiders, seeds and berries. In winter, these birds are common at sunflower seed feeders. • "Titmouse" is a term that reflects these birds' high-pitched calls and their mouse-like, scurrying habits.

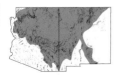

ID: uniform gray plumage; small, pointed crest; dark eye; no wing bars or eye ring.

Size: *L* 5¾ in; *W* 9 in.

Status: *AZ:* fairly common resident of pinyon-juniper woodlands from the Chiricahuas Mts. north and across the Mogollon Plateau and Kaibab Plateau; absent from the southwestern deserts. *NM:* fairly common resident of pinyon-juniper woodlands nearly statewide; absent from the southeastern plains.

Habitat: mature pinyon-juniper woodlands of the hills, foothills and mountains.

Nesting: excavates a cavity in soft, rotting wood or uses a natural cavity or an abandoned woodpecker nest (chosen by the female); cavity is lined with fur, feathers, moss and grass; female incubates 6–8 eggs for 14–16 days.

Feeding: gleans vegetation, branches and the ground for small insects and spiders; also eats seeds.

Voice: call is a chickadee-like *tsick-a-dee-dee;* song is a clearly whistled *witt-y witt-y witt-y.*

Similar Species: Bushtit (p. 114): no crest; brown cheek patch; darker legs. *Mountain Chickadee* (p. 110): black cap; white eyebrow; black "bib." *Blue-gray Gnatcatcher* (p. 122): white eye ring; longer tail with white outer feathers; no crest. *Phainopepla* (p. 129): female is much larger, with longer tail and red eyes.

Best Sites: *AZ:* Sycamore Creek; Superstition Mtns. *NM:* Three Gun Spring Canyon (Sandia Mts.); Lake Roberts (Pino Altos Mts.).

VERDIN

Auriparus flaviceps

Scientific classification of the Verdin continues to challenge ornithologists. Once considered to be a member of the chickadee family, it is now given the status of North America's only member of the Remizidae family—the Old World tits. • During breeding season, males build several nests, only one of which will be used for brooding. The other nests provide shaded daytime roosts or nighttime protection. Nests built early in spring face away from the wind for added warmth, but nests constructed later face toward the wind and allow breezes to cool eggs hatched under the intense summer sun. Young Verdins leave the nest when they are about 21 days old. Both adults and immatures may return to the main nest or use alternate nest sites at any time of the year for roosting. • Planting or growing healthy native trees, shrubs, cacti and wildflowers in your yard can provide attractive habitat for Verdins and a wide range of other beautiful bird species. Thorny shrubs such as palo verde, mesquite, hawthorn and cholla cactus are particular favorites of the Verdin.

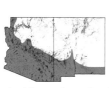

ID: gray overall, paler underparts; yellow head and throat; dark lores; short, black bill; dark eyes; red shoulder patch may be obscure.

Size: *L* 4–4½ in; *W* 6½ in.

Status: *AZ:* common resident of the lower Sonoran desert and lowland deserts statewide. *NM:* fairly common resident of deserts in the southwest.

Habitat: desert, thorny scrub thickets, riparian woods and low elevation mesquite woodlands; common inhabitant of townsites and suburban parks and gardens.

Nesting: female chooses among many nests built by male; in a thorny shrub, low tree or cholla cactus; hollow, spherical to oval nest of thorny twigs is lined with grass, leaves, feathers and spider silk; female incubates 4–5 green to blue-green eggs, with reddish brown spots, for about 10 days.

Feeding: catches insects during active foraging among foliage, stems and branches, or on the wing; forages in flocks outside of breeding season; may eat berries, seeds and spiders; often takes nectar from flowers or hummingbird feeders.

Voice: call is a rapid series of *chip* notes; song is 3–4 loud, whistled notes (2nd note is higher) *tsee-tsee-tsee*.

Similar Species: *Bushtit* (p. 114): brown cheek patch; black bill; adults lack yellow on head and red shoulder patch; female has light-colored eyes.

Best Sites: *AZ:* widespread in Phoenix and Tucson. *NM:* Bosque del Apache NWR; Percha Dam SP.

BUSHTIT

Psaltriparus minimus

I t is often said that the quality of the home reflects the character of its occupant. If this is true, then the tiny Bushtit is a noble resident. The intricate weave and elaborate shape of its hanging nest is an example of splendid architecture that is worthy of admiration and respect. • Intruders that violate the sanctity of a nest site can force the adults to switch mates, desert the nest or build a new one in a different location. • The Bushtit is best described as a hyperactive, gray cotton ball with a long, narrow tail. It seems to be constantly on the move, bouncing from one shrubby perch to another, looking for something to keep its hungry little engine running. • When they are not fully engrossed in the business of raising young, Bushtits travel in bands of up to 40 birds, filling the brushlands and woodlands with their charming bell-like tinkles. • *Psaltriparus* is derived from the Greek word *psaltris*, meaning "player of the lute" (or zither) and *parus*, the former Latin generic name for a titmouse.

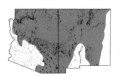

ID: uniform, gray plumage; light brown cheek patch; long tail; no crest.
Male: dark eyes.
Female: light-colored eyes.
Size: *L* 4½ in; *W* 6 in.
Status: fairly common resident of mid-elevation mixed oak and pinyon-juniper woodlands nearly regionwide. *AZ:* absent from deserts in the southwest. *NM:* absent from the southeastern plains.
Habitat: a variety of brushlands and woodlands including pinyon-juniper-mahogany woodlands, riparian thickets, oak savanna, open oak woodlands and chaparral.
Nesting: in a tree or bush, suspended from a forked twig; pair builds a socklike, hanging nest, woven with moss, lichens, cocoons, spider silk, fur and feathers, which can take up to 50 days to complete; pair incubates 5–7 eggs for 12 days.
Feeding: gleans vegetation for insects; also eats small seeds.
Voice: trilled alarm call; excited lisping notes.
Similar Species: *Juniper Titmouse* (p. 112): small crest; relatively shorter tail; lighter-colored legs; no brown cheek patch. *Ruby-crowned Kinglet* (p. 121): greenish overall; distinct wing bars and eye ring; persistently flicks its wings.
Best Sites: *AZ:* Sycamore Creek; Oak Creek Canyon. *NM:* Three Gun Spring Canyon (Sandia Mts.); Lake Roberts (Pino Altos Mts.).

WHITE-BREASTED NUTHATCH

Sitta carolinensis

Nuthatches are curious little birds that have unique foraging styles. Like woodpeckers and a few other species, they forage mostly on the trunk and larger branches of pines or other trees. But unlike other species, they often are seen moving down a trunk headfirst! Whereas woodpeckers and creepers use their tails to brace themselves against tree trunks, nuthatches grasp trees through foot power alone. • The White-breasted Nuthatch will occasionally visit backyard feeders that offer peanut butter. • Two other, smaller nuthatches are found in our region. The Red-breasted Nuthatch *(S. canadensis)* is an uncommon and irruptive permanent resident in our higher elevation, coniferous and mixed woodlands. Its distinctive *yank-yank-yank* call resembles a tin horn. The Pygmy Nuthatch *(S. pygmaea)* is most often found in montane, ponderosa pine woodlands. Its piping, high-pitched voice is quite unlike the nasal, rhythmic calls of the other nuthatch species.

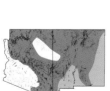

ID: small, short-tailed, tree-climbing bird; gray back and wings; white head with bold black (male) or grayish (female) crown and nape; white underparts with rusty undertail coverts.
Size: *L* 5½–6 in; *W* 11 in.
Status: common resident of montane forests regionwide.
Habitat: pinewoods, mixed oak/pine woods and wooded backyards.
Nesting: in a natural cavity or an abandoned woodpecker nest in a large, deciduous tree; female lines the cavity with bark, grass, fur and feathers; female incubates 5–8 brown-spotted, white eggs for 12–14 days.

Feeding: forages on tree trunks and branches for insects, spiders and pine seeds; also visits bird feeders.
Voice: song is a nasal *yank-hank, yank-hank,* lower than the Red-breasted Nuthatch.
Similar Species: *Chickadees* (p. 110): black "bib"; smaller bill. *Red-breasted Nuthatch:* smaller; irruptive; white eyebrow and black eye line; rusty underparts. *Pygmy Nuthatch:* smaller; gray cap extends over eye; buffy underparts.
Best Sites: widespread in pine-oak woodland habitats. *AZ:* Madera Canyon (Santa Rita Mts.); Mt. Lemmon; Red Rock SP. *NM:* widespread in the Sandia Mts. and Sangre de Cristo Mts.

BROWN CREEPER

Certhia americana

There are many species of creepers in Europe and Asia, but the Brown Creeper is the only member of its family that is found in North America. Creepers are small songbirds that forage by ascending tree trunks in a spiral fashion. • The cryptic Brown Creeper is never easy to find. Inhabiting old-growth forests for much of the year, it often goes unnoticed until a flake of bark suddenly takes the shape of a bird. If a creeper is frightened, it will freeze and flatten itself against a tree trunk, becoming even more difficult to see. • The Brown Creeper feeds by slowly spiraling up a tree trunk, searching for hidden invertebrates. When it reaches the upper branches, the creeper floats down to the base of a neighboring tree to begin another foraging ascent. Its long, stiff tail feathers prop it up against vertical tree trunks as it hitches its way skyward. • The thin whistle of the Brown Creeper is so high pitched that many birders often fail to hear it. To increase the confusion, the creeper's song often takes on the boisterous, warbling quality of a wood-warbler song.

Nesting: under loose bark; nest of grass and conifer needles is woven together with spider silk; female incubates 5–6 whitish eggs, dotted with reddish brown, for 14–17 days.
Feeding: hops up tree trunks and large limbs, probing loose bark for adult and larval invertebrates.
Voice: call is a high *tseee*; song is a faint, high-pitched *trees-trees-trees see the trees.*
Similar Species: plumage of creeper is unique. *Nuthatches* (p. 115); forage on trunks but do not ascend trunks in a spiral fashion.
Best Sites: *AZ:* widespread above Mogollon Rim; Madera Canyon (Santa Rita Mts.); Mt. Lemmon; Red Rock SP. *NM:* widespread in the Sandia Mts. and Sangre de Cristo Mts.

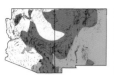

ID: mottled brown and white upperparts; brown head with pale eyebrow; white throat; short, downcurved bull; white underparts with buffy undertail coverts.
Size: *L* 5–5½ in; *W* 7½ in.
Status: fairly common resident of coniferous forests regionwide.
Habitat: mature deciduous, coniferous and mixed forests and woodlands, especially in wet areas with large, dead trees; also found near bogs.

CACTUS WREN

Campylorhynchus brunneicapillus

Wrens are small songbirds with very short tails, often held up at an angle, and loud "bubbly" songs. There are 74 species in the New World, with seven of these occurring in Arizona and New Mexico. • The Cactus Wren is active throughout the hot southern days, while most desert creatures are seeking shade. Perched upon a thorny bush, it utters loud, harsh calls throughout the day. This bold, curious wren is often approachable and has even been known to forage for dead or dying insects stuck to the front grills of parked cars. • These large wrens weave their football-shaped nests tightly within an impregnable fortress of cactus spines or thorny shrubs. The needle-sharp spines protect the nestlings from a host of predators, including snakes, lizards, mammals and larger birds. As the female incubates the eggs, the male may build several other nests to use as roosting sites. These wrens may mate for life.
• The Cactus Wren is Arizona's state bird.

ID: larger than typical wrens; prominent white eyebrow below dark crown; long, curved bill; streaked back; black and white barring on wings and tail; densely spotted underparts.
Size: *L* 8½ in; *W* 11 in.

Status: *AZ:* common resident of the lower Sonoran Desert and lowland deserts below the Mogollon Rim. *NM:* common resident of the lower Sonoran Desert and lowland deserts in the south.

Habitat: arid desert habitats, chaparral and townsites with an abundance of cacti (especially cholla cactus), yucca, mesquite and other thorny shrubs.

Nesting: nests among the spines of a cholla cactus or thorny shrub; pair builds a bulky, domed, elongated nest of vegetation, animal hair and feathers; female incubates 4–5 pale, purple-spotted eggs for 15–18 days; both adults raise the young.

Feeding: forages on the ground or along the base of tree trunks; probes for insects and spiders; may also eat small lizards and plant material including nectar, berries, seeds and small fruit.

Voice: song is a low, harsh series of notes: *chur chur chur chur chur*, heard year-round and at any time of the day.

Similar Species: *Thrashers* (p. 127): larger; no white eyebrow; unstreaked, gray-brown back; no black and white barring on wings or tail. *Canyon Wren:* smaller; no white eyebrow; very long bill; rufous overall with white throat and upper breast.

Best Sites: *AZ:* widespread around Phoenix and Tucson. *NM:* widespread south of the Mogollon Mts; Bosque del Apache NWR; Percha Dam SP.

ROCK WREN

Salpinctes obsoletus

R ock Wrens are typically identified at long range by their habit of bobbing atop prominent boulders, but these secretive birds can be difficult to spot initially. Singing males are experts at remaining concealed while bouncing their buzzy, trilling songs off canyon walls, maximizing the range and aural effect of the sound. • Rock Wren nests may be built in a sheltered, rocky crevice, in an animal burrow or even in an abandoned building. Nest entrances are typically "paved" with a few small pebbles, bones or other debris. Occasionally the entrances contain up to 1600 small items! Whether paving protects the nest from moisture, makes the nest easier to find in confusing rocky terrain or serves some other purpose is unclear. • The Canyon Wren *(Catherpes mexicanus)* is another long-billed wren that is found on talus slopes and rocky canyons throughout our region.

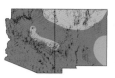

ID: blue-gray to gray-brown upperparts with intricate light and dark fleck-ing; cinnamon rump and tail; light underparts; finely streaked white throat and breast; slender bill; short white eyebrow; tail trimmed with buff-colored tips.

Size: *L* 6 in; *W* 9 in.

Status: fairly common resident in rocky canyons and rocky habitats regionwide.

Habitat: talus slopes, scree, outcrops, stony barrens and similar substrate with abundant crevices.

Nesting: in a crevice, hole or burrow; often places small stones at the opening; nest of grass and rootlets is lined with a variety of items; female incubates 5–6 white, speckled eggs for up to 14 days.

Feeding: forages among rocks, boulders, logs and on the ground for insects and spiders.

Voice: alarm call is *tick-EAR;* repeated, accented 1–2-note phrases: *tra-lee tra-lee tra-lee.*

Similar Species: *Canyon Wren:* rufous over-all; clean, white throat; no eyebrow; very long bill. *House Wren:* much smaller; no flecking on brown upperparts; shorter bill. *Bewick's Wren* (p. 119): gray-brown upper-parts and rump; bold, white eyebrow bor-ders dark eye line; clean, white throat and breast.

Best Sites: *AZ:* Boyce Thompson Arboretum; Patagonia Lake SP; Oak Creek Canyon. *NM:* Bosque del Apache NWR; Percha Dam SP.

BEWICK'S WREN

Thryomanes bewickii

This charming, brown mite seems to investigate all the nooks and crevices of its territory with endless curiosity and exuberant animation. As the Bewick's Wren briefly perches to scan its surroundings for sources of food, its long, narrow tail flits and waves from side to side, occasionally flashing with added verve as the bird scolds an approaching intruder. • Bewick's Wren populations west of the Mississippi River are better off than those to the east, where numbers are declining because of habitat loss. • John James Audubon chose to honor Thomas Bewick in the name of this spirited bird. A respected friend of Audubon, Bewick was an exceptionally talented wood engraver and the author and illustrator of *A History of British Birds.*

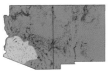

ID: long, bold, white eyebrow; long tail trimmed with white spots; rich brown or gray-brown upperparts; clean, whitish underparts; slender, downcurved bill.

Size: *L* 5¼ in; *W* 7 in.

Status: common resident of mid-elevation chaparral and pinyon-juniper woodlands regionwide.

Habitat: chaparral, riparian thickets, dense vines and shrubby tangles bordering woodlands, parks and gardens, brush piles, shrublands within pinyon-juniper woodlands and oak woodlands.

Nesting: often in a natural cavity or an abandoned woodpecker nest; also in bird boxes; nest of sticks and grass is lined with feathers; female incubates 5–7 eggs for up to 14 days.

Feeding: gleans vegetation for insects, especially caterpillars, grasshoppers, beetles and spiders.

Voice: alarm call is a peevish *dzeeeb* or *knee-deep;* bold and clear *chick-click, for me-eh, for you.*

Similar Species: *House Wren* and *Winter Wren:* shorter tail; faint buff eyebrow.

Best Sites: widespread in riparian, mesquite and chapparal habitats.

119

AMERICAN DIPPER

Cinclus mexicanus

When you come across a small, dark bird standing on an exposed boulder next to a fast-flowing mountain stream, you have no doubt found an American Dipper. This unique, aquatic songbird bends its legs incessantly, bobbing to the roar of the torrent, then suddenly dives into the water in search of aquatic insects. The dipper uses its wings to "fly" underwater, making its way along the streambed in search of hidden aquatic insect larvae. Fitted with scaly nose plugs, strong claws, dense plumage, inner eyelids to protect against water spray, and an oil gland to waterproof its feathers, the American Dipper survives a lifetime of these ice-cold forays. It also walks easily in shallow water, using its long toes to grasp the gravelly bottom. • The dipper's well-constructed nest may be used year after year, by several generations. One nest in Europe was used continuously for over 100 years.

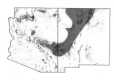

ID: stout body; slate gray plumage; head and neck darker than body; whitish eyelid visible when bird blinks; straight, black bill; pinkish legs; short tail. *Immature:* paler underparts and bill.
Size: *L* 7½ in; *W* 11 in. Male slightly larger than female.
Status: uncommon local resident of high mountains with fast, rushing, rocky streams.
Habitat: *Breeding:* swift, clear, cold permanent mountain streams with boulders and often waterfalls; subalpine tarns. *Winter:* also in larger, slower-flowing rivers and lowland lakes.

Nesting: built into rock ledge, overhang, uprooted tree or under a bridge; female builds bulky globe nest of moss and grass; nest entrance faces water; female incubates 4–5 white eggs for up to 17 days.
Feeding: wades through or dives into fast-flowing water for aquatic larval insects, fish fry and eggs.
Voice: vocal throughout year; alarm call is harsh *tzeet;* warbled song is clear and melodious.
Similar Species: none.
Best Sites: *AZ:* Sheeps Crossing; White Mts. *NM:* Rio Grande near Pilar; Sangre de Cristo Mts.

RUBY-CROWNED KINGLET

Regulus calendula

Kinglets are small, active songbirds that flick their wings frequently as they forage. Both of North America's two species are found in the Southwest. During winter, these energetic little birds visit bird feeders or flit among branches along with a colorful assortment of warblers and vireos. • The male Ruby-crowned Kinglet erects his red crown only during courtship and when defending his territory. For the rest of the year, his crown remains hidden among his dull gray head feathers. His bold, broken eye ring and two white wing bars are more useful field marks.
• In the northern parts of their wintering range, kinglets survive frigid winter temperatures by roosting together in groups or in vacant squirrel nests. Like chickadees, kinglets can lower their body temperatures at night to conserve energy.
• The Golden-crowned Kinglet *(Regulus satrapa)* is our smallest songbird, and except for humming-birds, is the smallest bird in the Southwest. It is a common summer resident in eastern Arizona and western New Mexico and an irruptive winter visitor throughout the region.

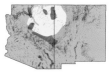

ID: tiny, active songbird with broken eye ring and tiny bill; grayish green upperparts, including head; black wings with 2 white wing bars; pale greenish gray underparts. *Male:* red crown patch (usually concealed). **Size:** *L* 4 in; *W* 7½ in.
Status: common migrant and winter visitor regionwide; uncommon summer resident of coniferous forests of the higher mountains.
Habitat: any wooded habitat, including suburban yards and city parks; often found near wet forest openings and edges.
Nesting: usually in a conifer; female builds hanging nest of lichen, twigs and leaves; female incubates 7–8 brown-spotted, white to pale buff eggs for 13–14 days.

Feeding: gleans and hovers for insects and spiders; also eats seeds and berries.
Voice: *Male:* song is an accelerating and rising *tea-tea-tea-tew-tew-tew look-at-Me, look-at-Me, look-at-Me.*
Similar Species: *Golden-crowned Kinglet:* boldly striped crown and face; no broken eye ring; has orange and yellow or yellow crown. *Orange-crowned Warbler:* no eye ring or wing bars. Empidonax *flycatchers* (pp. 88–89): eye ring complete in some species, absent in others; larger bill; foraging behavior very different.
Best Sites: widespread in a variety of habitats.

BLUE-GRAY GNATCATCHER

Polioptila caerulea

Gnatcatchers are essentially a subtropical genus, yet the tiny Blue-gray Gnatcatcher is a true migrant that has expanded into cool, temperate North America. A restless inhabitant of woodlands and brushy areas, the gnatcatcher flits from shrub to shrub with its long tail upraised and waving from side to side. • The two gnatcatchers that occur in our region may be distinguished by the amount of white on their tails and by their calls. The Blue-gray Gnatcatcher has mainly white undertail feathers and gives thin, high-pitched *see* chips or slurs. As its name implies, the Black-tailed Gnatcatcher *(P. melanura)* has a mainly black tail, with thin, white outer edges and two white spots on the end of the undertail. This species is usually seen in pairs, and its harsh calls resemble a crow calling at high speed.

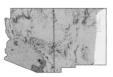

ID: blue-gray upperparts; long, thin, flexible tail is dark above with white outer feathers and appears nearly all white from below; white eye ring; pale gray underparts; dark legs; thin, dark bill (pale in winter). *Male:* black forehead.

Size: *L* 4½ in. (including tail); *W* 6½ in.

Status: common migrant and fairly common summer resident of mid-elevation oak and pinyon-pine woodlands throughout the region. *AZ:* fairly common winter visitor in central and southeastern regions. *NM:* rare in winter in the south.

Habitat: *Breeding:* abandoned pastures, urban parks, riverine floodplains and oak, upland and ravine woodlands; usually near swamps, ponds or rivers. *In migration:* scrubby growth and moist, riparian woods; occasionally in overgrown gardens and parks.

Nesting: in a shrub or small tree; neat cup nest of fibers, lichen and bark is bound with spider silk and lined with softer material; female incubates 4–5 pale, spotted eggs for 11–15 days.

Feeding: moves quickly through foliage, flicking its long tail, perhaps to flush concealed prey; gleans twigs or flycatches for small insects and spiders.

Voice: thin, high-pitched, single *see* notes or a short series of mewing or chattering notes; a very accomplished mimic of several species.

Similar Species: *Black-tailed Gnatcatcher:* black tail; breeding male has black cap. *Bushtit* (p. 114): grayer overall; tiny bill; lacks eye ring and white sides to tail; travels in flocks; female has white eyes.

Best Sites: *AZ:* Boyce Thompson Arboretum; Oak Creek Canyon. *NM:* Bosque del Apache NWR; Rio Grande Nature Center.

WESTERN BLUEBIRD

Sialia mexicana

The Western Bluebird's feathers, like the feathers of all blue birds, are not actually pigmented blue. The color is a result of the feathers' microscopic structure: shiny blues that change hue and intensity with the angle of view are produced by iridescence; dull blues come from "Tyndall scatter," the same process that produces the blue of the sky. • All three of the bluebird species that occur in North America are found in our region. The Western Bluebird is found throughout most of Arizona and western New Mexico but is replaced in our eastern region by the similar-looking Eastern Bluebird *(S. sialis)*. Our northern mountain meadows are home to the Mountain Bluebird *(S. currucoides)*, which lacks the chestnut throat and breast of the other species.

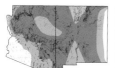

ID: chestnut red breast; light gray belly and undertail coverts; dark bill and legs; some chestnut on back. *Male:* deep blue head, back, wings and chin; chestnut red sides and flanks. *Female:* light eye ring; gray-brown head and back; bluish wings and tail.
Size: *L* 7 in; *W* 13 in.
Status: uncommon visitor to lower elevation canyons in winter. *AZ:* fairly common resident of foothills and montane habitats across the Kaibab and Mogollon plateaus. *NM:* fairly common resident of foothills and western mountains statewide.
Habitat: *Breeding:* broken oak and oak–conifer woodlands, oak savannas, riparian woodlands and open pine forests.

In migration and *winter:* lowland valleys, agricultural lands interspersed by woodlands and tree groves.
Nesting: in an abandoned woodpecker cavity, natural cavity or nest box; nest is built of stems, conifer needles and twigs; female incubates 4–6 eggs for up to 17 days.
Feeding: swoops from a perch to pursue flying insects; also forages on the ground for invertebrates. *In winter:* highly reliant on ground foraging or on mistletoe berries.
Voice: call is a soft *few* or a harsh *chuck;* song is a harsh *cheer cheerful charmer.*
Similar Species: *Eastern Bluebird:* little range overlap; chestnut throat; paler blue upperparts; no chestnut shoulder patch. *Mountain Bluebird:* lacks chestnut underparts; female is grayer overall. *Townsend's Solitaire:* grayish overall; white eye ring; peach-colored patches on wings and tail.
Best Sites: *AZ:* White Mts.; Mogollan Rim. *NM:* Sangre de Cristo, Mogollan and Sacrements Mts.

123

HERMIT THRUSH

Catharus guttatus

True to their English name, Hermit Thrushes are never encountered in groups, but are always found singly. They migrate later in fall and earlier in spring than do the other spotted thrushes. • This bird is considered to be one of the finest singers of all of North America's birds. Its song is almost always preceded with a single questioning note. • Though a rufous-colored tail is the trademark of the Hermit Thrushes, these birds are otherwise extremely variable in size, color and structure. The plumage of eastern populations is often tinged with reddish brown, while western birds are grayer. • The scientific name *guttatus* is Latin for "spotted" or "speckled," in reference to this bird's breast.

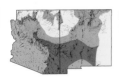

ID: brown upperparts including head; white eye ring; white underparts with black spotting on throat and breast; buffy flanks; rusty wings and tail.

Size: *L* 7 in; *W* 11½ in.

Status: fairly common migrant and uncommon summer resident of higher elevation coniferous and mixed coniferous forests regionwide. **AZ:** common winter resident of Sonoran zones of southern and central regions. **NM:** common winter resident to lowlands statewide.

Habitat: most brushy or wooded habitats with leaf litter, especially near water.

Nesting: in a small tree or shrub, or occasionally on the ground; female builds a bulky cup nest of vegetation; female incubates 4 light blue eggs for 11–13 days.

Feeding: gleans the ground or leaf litter for insects, spiders, worms and snails; also plucks fruit from trees or shrubs.

Voice: call is a dry *chuck;* song is a series of beautiful flutelike notes, both rising and falling in pitch; a small questioning note may precede the song.

Similar Species: *Swainson's Thrush:* upperparts including tail olive-brown without rusty tone; buffy face. *Fox Sparrow:* stockier build; conical bill; brown breast spots.

Best Sites: widespread in woodlands and thickets.

AMERICAN ROBIN

Turdus migratorius

Come spring, the familiar song of the American Robin may wake you early if you are a light sleeper. This abundant bird adapts easily to urban areas and often works from dawn until after dusk when there is a nest to be built or young mouths to feed. An adult with its bill stuffed full of earthworms and grubs is a sign that hungry young robins are somewhere close at hand. Young robins are easily distinguished from their parents by their disheveled appearance and heavily spotted underparts. • A hunting robin may appear to be listening for prey, but it is actually looking for movements in the soil—it tilts its head because its eyes are placed on the sides of its head. • English colonists named the American Robin after the Robin (*Erithacus rubecula*) of their native land. Both birds look and behave similarly, even though they are only distantly related. The American Robin's closest European relative is, in fact, the Blackbird (*T. merula*), which is identical in all aspects except plumage.

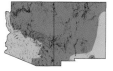

ID: gray-brown back; white throat streaked with black; white undertail coverts; incomplete white eye ring; black-tipped, yellow bill. *Male:* deep orangy red underparts; black head. *Female:* light orangy red underparts; dark gray head. *Juvenile:* paler upperparts with pale tips to feathers on back and wing coverts; dark-spotted, pale orange breast.
Size: *L* 10 in; *W* 17 in.
Status: uncommon to common migrant and winter visitor, irregular in winter in the south with numbers varying widely from year to year and common summer resident in forested canyons and mountainous regions regionwide.

Habitat: *Breeding:* open woodlands, including suburban yards and city parks. *In winter:* wooded habitat; often roosts on or near the ground.
Nesting: in a coniferous or deciduous tree or shrub; sturdy cup nest of grass, moss and loose bark is cemented with mud; female incubates 4 light blue eggs for 11–16 days; may raise up to 3 broods each year.
Feeding: forages on the ground and among vegetation for larval and adult insects, earthworms, other invertebrates and berries.
Voice: call is a rapid *tut-tut-tut;* song is an evenly spaced warble: *cheerily cheer-up cheerio.*
Similar Species: none; dark upperparts and orange underparts distinctive.
Best Sites: widespread in areas with extensive lawns and pastures.

125

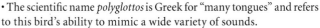

NORTHERN MOCKINGBIRD

Mimus polyglottos

The Northern Mockingbird has an amazing vocal repertoire that includes over 400 different song types, which it belts out incessantly throughout the breeding season, serenading into the night during a full moon. A mockingbird can imitate almost anything, from other birds and animals to musical instruments. In fact, it replicates notes so accurately that even computerized sound analysis may be unable to detect the difference between the original source and the mockingbird's imitation. • Whether perched comfortably on a power pole or singing from a street lamp, the Northern Mockingbird has adapted remarkably well to urban environments. It thrives in a variety of habitats ranging from lush gardens to arid deserts and is currently expanding its range northward. • The scientific name *polyglottos* is Greek for "many tongues" and refers to this bird's ability to mimic a wide variety of sounds.

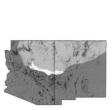

ID: medium-sized conspicuous songbird; gray back, nape and crown; pale face; white throat; yellow eyes; black wings with 2 narrow, white wing bars; whitish underparts; long blackish tail with white outer tail feathers. *Juvenile:* paler overall; lightly spotted breast. *In flight:* large white patch at base of primaries.
Size: *L* 10 in; *W* 14 in.
Status: common summer resident regionwide. *AZ:* winters widely, but mostly in the southern half of the state. *NM:* uncommon in winter in the south.
Habitat: any area with at least a scattering of trees or shrubs.
Nesting: in a shrub or small tree; cup nest is made of twigs, grass, fur and leaves; female incubates 3–4 brown-blotched, bluish gray to greenish eggs for 12–13 days.
Feeding: forages on or near the ground; feeds on a variety of berries and other fruit, and insects and other invertebrates.
Voice: calls include a harsh *check;* song is a medley of a wide variety of mimicked phrases, with the phrases often repeated three or more times.
Similar Species: *Loggerhead Shrike* (p. 97): smaller; black wings; black mask; thick, hooked bill.
Best Sites: *AZ:* widespread in residential Phoenix and Tucson. *NM:* widespread, including residential Albuquerque.

CURVE-BILLED THRASHER

Toxostoma curvirostre

Deserts filled with cholla, prickly-pear and saguaro cactus provide favored feeding, nesting and roosting habitat for this sassy, familiar bird. The Curve-billed Thrasher shares this harsh, sun-bleached habitat with the Cactus Wren and builds its nest among the yucca or cholla (pronounced choy-ah) cactus. Within this fortress of sharp spines, eggs and nestlings are protected from predators, but fledglings must quickly master flying or risk being fatally pricked as they enter or exit the nest. • A foraging Curve-billed Thrasher digs in the soil for insects, propping its tail against the ground for reinforcement then striking the soil with heavy, purposeful blows. • Six species of thrashers occur in Arizona and New Mexico. The Curved-billed Thrasher is most easily confused with the Crissal Thrasher *(T. crissale),* which shares much of the same range but is less common. Crissal Thrashers inhabit desert scrub, mesquite thickets and desert riparian areas.

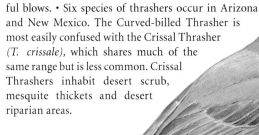

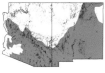

ID: long, dark, downcurved bill; bright yellow to orange eyes; pale brownish gray upperparts; brownish to buffy-gray underparts; large, blurry breast spots; long tail may have whitish corners; birds in eastern part of range may show white wing bars. *Juvenile:* dark bill is shorter.

Size: *L* 9½–11½ in; *W* 13–14 in.

Status: *AZ:* uncommon to common resident in lower Sonoran zone across the lower half of the state south of the Mogollon Rim. *NM:* uncommon to common resident of deserts and foothills across the southern portion of the state and of the eastern plains.

Habitat: arid, brushy lowlands, desert and grasslands with cholla cactus.

Nesting: loose, bulky cup of grasses, thorny twigs, feathers and animal hair is built in cholla cactus, yucca or thorny shrub; both adults incubate 3 blue-green, brown-spotted eggs for 12–15 days.

Feeding: forages on the ground for insects, berries and seeds; readily takes cactus fruit and seeds; often digs in soil with long bill.

Voice: call is a sharp, liquidy *whit-wheat;* song is a long series of variable whistled phrases.

Similar Species: *Crissal Thrasher:* unspotted buff-brown breast and belly; rufous under-tail coverts. *Sage Thrasher:* smaller, shorter bill; thin streaks on underparts.

Best Sites: *AZ:* widespread around Phoenix and Tucson. *NM:* Bosque del Apache NWR; Gila R. at Redrock.

127

CEDAR WAXWING

Bombycilla cedrorum

Waxwings are sleek-plumaged songbirds with distinct crests and yellow-tipped tails, and the tips of their secondary flight feathers look as though they are coated in red wax. • The Cedar Waxwing's splendid personality is reflected in its social feeding habits. If a bird's crop is full and it is unable to eat any more, it will continue to pluck fruit and pass it down the line like a bucket brigade, until the fruit is gulped down by a still-hungry bird. As flocks gorge on fermented berries in late winter and spring, birds will show definite signs of tipsiness. Mulberry, juniper or yaupon shrubs planted in your backyard can attract Cedar Waxwings and provide an opportunity to observe the striking plumage of these birds up close. • Practiced observers learn to recognize these birds by their high-pitched, trilling calls. Flocks are highly nomadic and numbers vary each year.

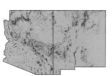

ID: slender body; gray rump; rich brown upperparts including head and crest; black mask and throat separated by white streak; gray wings with brown upperwing coverts; rich brown on breast shades to pale yellow belly; white undertail coverts; tail gray at base, then black with yellow tip. *Juvenile:* dull grayish brown above; pale throat; white underparts are streaked with grayish brown.
Size: *L* 7 in; *W* 12 in.
Status: erratic winter visitor regionwide with numbers fluctuating greatly from year to year.

Habitat: virtually any wooded habitat, especially those with abundant fruiting trees or shrubs.
Nesting: does not nest in Arizona or New Mexico.
Feeding: gleans foliage for berries and other fruit; also gleans for insects and sallies for flying insects.
Voice: faint, high-pitched, trilled whistle, often given in flight.
Similar Species: *Bohemian Waxwing:* rare in our region; larger; rufous undertail coverts.
Best Sites: widespread but erratic and unpredictable.

PHAINOPEPLA

Phainopepla nitens

The Phainopepla belongs to the Silky-flycatcher family, a small group of tropical, mainly fruit-eating birds. Despite its glossy plumage and saucy character, the Phainopepla leads a mysterious existence. • Much of this bird's life revolves around mistletoe, which provides nesting habitat and a food source. Once eaten, the pulpy, sticky-coated seeds slip through the bird's digestive system to be deposited on a new host tree or shrub branch, helping the parasitic plant colonize new territory. The mistletoe's tangled growth, sprouting in bushy tangles from elevated tree and shrub branches, also provides a concealing foundation for the Phainopepla's nest. This close, mutually beneficial relationship between plant and bird is known as "mutualism." • The name "Phainopepla" is derived from Greek words meaning "shining robe," referring to the male's elegant plumage.

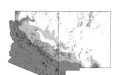

ID: raised crest; red eyes. *Male:* black plumage. *Female* and *immature:* dark wings and tail on an otherwise gray body. *In flight:* long, square tail; white (male) or pale gray (female) wing patch.

Size: *L* 7¾ in; 11 in.

Status: AZ: common resident of the lower Sonoran zone statewide. *NM:* uncommon resident in the southwest.

Habitat: broken mixed-oak and oak woodlands and riparian woodlands containing mistletoe and other berry-producing plants; occasionally attracted to exotic shrub plantings.

Nesting: in a mistletoe tangle or in the fork of a shrub or tree; male builds most of the shallow cup-shaped nest of twigs, vegetation, animal hair and spider webs; pair incubates 2–3 dark-spotted, pale gray or pinkish eggs; pair raises the young; may have 2 broods.

Feeding: eats mostly seasonally available berries and insects; takes insects by hawking or while flying or hovering.

Voice: call-note is a low, liquid *wurp?* with an upslurred effect; seldom-heard song is a short warble.

Similar Species: *Cedar Waxwing* (p. 128): immature has streaked underparts, flattened, swept-back crest and yellow-tipped tail.

Best Sites: widespread, especially in areas of dense mesquite with mistletoe.

OLIVE WARBLER

Peucedramus taeniatus

Although the colorful Olive Warbler looks and behaves like a typical wood-warbler, recent DNA evidence has classified it as the sole member of the family Peucedramidae. This warbler is found in high elevation pine forests and occupies a narrow band of mountain ranges that stretch from central Arizona and southwestern New Mexico south to Nicaragua. Those that breed in our region generally withdraw south for winter, but southern populations are nonmigratory. • Olive Warblers are birds of the upper canopy. They nest and feed high in pine trees, often creeping or hopping along the branches.

ID: medium sized warbler of upper canopy. *Male:* gray overall; orange head, neck and breast; 2 large, white wing bars. *Female:* similar to male but duller, with yellowish head, neck and breast.

Size: *L* 5 in; *W* 2–3 in.

Status: *AZ:* fairly common summer resident of higher elevation pine forests of central and southeastern regions; uncommon in winter within its summer range. *NM:* fairly common summer resident of higher elevation pine forests of the southwest; rare and local in winter within its summer range.

Habitat: high elevation coniferous and mixed woodlands.

Nesting: nests in conifers on outmost branches of upper canopy; female builds a cup nest with vegetation, lined with rootlets, moss, down and other soft materials; female incubates 3–4 heavily marked grayish or bluish eggs; both adults feed young.

Feeding: forages high in pine trees for insects and arthropods.

Voice: 2-syllable whistled or buzzy notes are repeated in a series.

Similar Species: *Hermit Warbler:* white belly; black on throat; no bold cheek patch.

Best Sites: *AZ:* Pinal Peak Recreation Area (Pinal Mts.); Mt. Lemmon (Catalina Mts.); Rustler Park (Chiricahua Mts.). *NM:* Signal Peak (Pinos Altos Mts.); Emory Pass (Black Mts.).

YELLOW WARBLER

Dendroica petechia

This species introduces the wood-warblers, a family of 54 species of small, active insectivorous birds, mostly with bright plumages. Yellow Warblers are typically inquisitive birds that flit from branch to branch in search of juicy caterpillars, aphids and beetles. Their lively courtship songs and golden plumage light up the landscape. • These birds are partial to lowland riparian woodlands while breeding, but occur in a variety of habitats including desert oases, mixed woodlands, urban gardens and farmyard orchards while in migration. • Yellow Warblers are among the most frequent victims of nest parasitism by Brown-headed Cowbirds. Unlike many birds, they can recognize the foreign eggs and many pairs will either abandon their nest or build another nest overtop the old eggs, creating bizarre, multilayered, high-rise nests. • The Yellow Warbler is often mistakenly called "Wild Canary" because of its bright yellow plumage.

ID: yellow overall; darker upper-parts, including nape and crown; darker wings have 2 yellow wing bars; black eyes. *Male:* bold orange streaking on breast and flanks. *Female:* faint orange breast streaks. *Juvenile:* plain buffy or gray overall.

Size: *L* 5 in; *W* 8 in.

Status: common summer resident of riparian areas regionwide.

Habitat: shrubby or wooded habitats, especially near water.

Nesting: in the fork of a deciduous tree or a small shrub branch; female builds a compact cup nest of grass, plant down, lichens and spider silk; female incubates 4–5 speckled, greenish white eggs for 11–12 days.

Feeding: gleans vegetation for insects and spiders; occasionally takes fruit.

Voice: call is a clear, loud *chip;* song is a series of 6–8 high, *sweet-sweet* notes with a rapid ending.

Similar Species: *Orange-crowned Warbler:* darker olive plumage overall; pale eyebrow; dark eye line; dusky streaking on breast and flanks. *Common Yellowthroat:* stays close to ground; female has olive upperparts, including nape and crown. *American Goldfinch* (p. 163): black wings and tail; male often has black forehead.

Best Sites: widespread in riparian cottonwood habitats. *AZ:* San Pedro River Conservation Area; San Pedro R.; Winkleman-Dudleyville; Boyce Thompson Arboretum. *NM:* Bosque Del Apache NWR; Rio Grande Nature Center; Percha Dam SP.

YELLOW-RUMPED WARBLER

Dendroica coronata

Yellow-rumped Warblers are the most abundant and widespread wood-warblers in North America. Apple, juniper and sumac trees laden with fruit attract these birds in winter. • This species has two forms: the yellow-throated "Aububon's Warbler," which is common in our region, and the less common, white-throated "Myrtle Warbler," which is found locally in winter. • For night migrants such as the Yellow-rumped Warbler, collisions with human-made structures including buildings and towers cause hundreds of fatalities each year. • The scientific name *coronata* is Latin for "crowned" and refers to this bird's yellow crown.

breeding

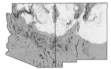

ID: both forms flash white corners in tail. *"Audubon's Warbler":* yellow crown, chin and throat, side patches and rump; white belly, undertail coverts and undertail patch; white wing highlights. *Breeding male:* blue-gray to blackish head and back; black streaks on back; blackish breast and sides. *Breeding female:* gray-brown upperparts; whitish underparts with faint brown breast streaks; fainter yellow patches. *"Myrtle Warbler":* white chin and throat; darker cheek; thin, white eye line; strongly streaked underparts.
Size: *L* 5–6 in; *W* 9 in.
Status: fairly common summer resident in high-elevation coniferous forests and common, widespread migrant and winter resident of lowland areas regionwide.
Habitat: *Breeding:* broken coniferous forests. *In migration and winter:* a variety of well-vegetated habitats in lowlands.

"Myrtle": most numerous in wax myrtle thickets. *"Audubon's":* more accepting of exotic vegetation and are found more widely.
Nesting: in a crotch or on a horizontal limb in a conifer; female constructs a compact cup nest with grass, bark strips, moss, lichens and spider silk; female incubates 4–5 brown- and gray-marked, creamy eggs for up to 13 days.
Feeding: hawks, hovers or gleans vegetation for beetles, flies, wasps, caterpillars, moths and other insects; sometimes eats berries.
Voice: call is a sharp *chip* or *check*. *Male:* variable song is a tinkling trill, often given in 2-note phrases that rise or fall at the end.
Similar Species: dull brown upperparts, yellow rump and yellow flank patch diagnostic. *Townsend's Warbler* (p. 134): yellow face and breast have black streaking; lacks yellow rump.
Best Sites: widespread in the south in winter.

BLACK-THROATED GRAY WARBLER

Dendroica nigrescens

The Black-throated Gray Warbler's shrill *weezy-weezy-weezy-wee-zee* song is very similar to the songs of its close relatives, the Townsend's Warbler and the Hermit Warbler *(D. occidentalis)*, both of which are easily distinguished from the Black-throated Gray by their conspicuous yellow features. • Male and female Black-throated Grays have very similar plumage, but the male is distinct because of his darker black markings. • This warbler is highly migratory, and its winter months are spent in Mexico and South America. • The Black-throated Gray Warbler is characteristic of juniper and pinyon pine stands.

ID: deep gray upperparts with black back streaks; black crown; white eyebrow and broad "mustache" stripe; yellow lores; sides streaked with black; white belly and undertail; black legs; 2 white wing bars. *Male:* black chin and "bib." *Female:* dark gray head; dark streaking on chin, throat and breast.
Size: *L* 5 in; *W* 7¾ in.
Status: fairly common summer resident of pinyon-juniper and oak woodlands regionwide. *AZ:* common, widespread migrant and uncommon winter resident of riparian areas in the south. *NM:* common, widespread migrant and rare winter resident of lowland areas in the southwest.
Habitat: *Breeding:* oak woodlands, juniper and pinyon stands and mountain mahogany. *In migration:* a variety of lowland woodlands, chaparral, farmyard and ranchland tree groves and windbreaks; suburban parks and gardens.

Nesting: usually on a horizontal branch in a conifer; small cup nest is made of grass, moss, lichens, feathers and fur; primarily the female incubates the 3–5 brown-marked, white eggs for 12 days.
Feeding: hawks, hover-gleans and gleans for insects.
Voice: lazy, oscillating *weezy-weezy-weezy-wee-zee*, often rising or falling at the end.
Similar Species: *Black-capped Chickadee* and *Mountain Chickadee* (p. 110): white breast; unstreaked sides; lighter, unstreaked upperparts. *Yellow-rumped Warbler* ("*Myrtle*") (p. 132): female has yellow on crown, sides and rump and has thin, white eye line rather than bold, white eyebrow.
Best Sites: *AZ:* Madera Canyon; Oak Creek Canyon (Sedona); Miller Canyon (Huachuca Mts.); Sycamore Creek and Mt. Ord (Sunflower). *NM:* Hondo Canyon (Sandia Mts.); Santa Fe Ski Basin (Sangre de Cristo Mts.).

TOWNSEND'S WARBLER

Dendroica townsendi

The Townsend's Warbler is a western species that seems to have found "greener pastures" in which to nest, but this colorful black and yellow bird still graces our region during migration. • Conifer crowns are preferred foraging sites for many wood-warblers, making warbler watching a neck-straining experience. Because they feed largely in tall trees during winter, Townsend's Warblers are often "underlooked." Sharp eyes, good birding instincts and a bit of luck will go a long way in helping you meet this striking warbler. • This bird bears the name of one of the West's pioneer ornithologists, John Kirk Townsend. • The Hermit Warbler is a closely related black-throated warbler that occasionally hybridizes with the Townsend's Warbler—hybrids usually have the yellow head of the Hermit and the darkly streaked yellow underparts of the Townsend's. The Hermit Warbler is also found in coniferous habitats and is an uncommon migrant throughout our region.

ID: yellow breast and sides are streaked with black; white lower belly and undertail coverts; black ear patch encompasses eye; olive greenish upperparts; 2 white wing bars. *Male:* black chin, throat and crown. *Female:* yellow chin and throat; white upper belly; dusky crown and ear patch. **Size:** *L* 5 in; *W* 8 in.
Status: rare to uncommon migrant from April to June and from September to October regionwide.
Habitat: lowland riparian and oak woodlands, mixed oak-coniferous forests, conifer and exotic tree groves and suburban parks and gardens. *In winter:* partial to semi-open, full-crowned lowland conifers.
Nesting: does not nest in our region.
Feeding: gleans vegetation and flycatches for beetles, flies, wasps and caterpillars.
Voice: call is an incisive, electronic *tzp;* male's song, rarely heard in our region, is wheezy, ascending and variable.
Similar Species: *Hermit Warbler:* gray back; white breast, belly and undertail; all-yellow face lacks dark ear patch.
Best Sites: *AZ:* Madera Canyon; Oak Creek Canyon (Sedona); Miller Canyon (Huachuca Mts.); Sycamore Creek and Mt. Ord (Sunflower). *NM:* Hondo Canyon (Sandia Mts.); Santa Fe Ski Basin (Sangre de Cristo Mts.).

RED-FACED WARBLER

Cardellina rubrifrons

Another of the unique birds that extends its breeding range into the highlands of Arizona and New Mexico, the striking Red-faced Warbler is a highlight for many birders in the Southwest. Its brilliant red face is framed by black, white and gray markings, a plumage pattern that is retained year round. • This active, tail-waving bird is one of the first migratory warblers to arrive, and nesting activity begins in April or May. The female Red-faced Warbler constructs a ground nest that is often covered by a roof of vegetation. Although pairs are monogamous and males aggressively defend their territory, it is common for other males to secretly slip into territories and father young. Seventy-five percent of all nests contain offspring fathered by a male from an adjacent territory. • Very little research has been conducted on this species, but U.S. populations may be in decline because of habitat degradation.

ID: gray upperparts; red face, throat, breast and half collar; black cap extends down side of head; grayish white belly; whitish nape, rump and 2 faint wing bars; often flicks tail sideways. *Immature:* duller with pinkish face.
Size: *L* 5½ in; *W* 8½ in.
Status: *AZ:* uncommon to fairly common summer resident of high elevation coniferous forests of the southeast and the Mogollon Rim. *NM:* uncommon to fairly common summer resident of high-elevation coniferous forests of the southwestern mountains.
Habitat: forests of spruce-fir and pine-oak above 6000 ft.
Nesting: mountain nest is well hidden under a log, rock or tree trunk; female builds a cup of grass, bark and other vegetation, lined with animal hair and soft plant fibers; female incubates 3–4 pinkish white eggs, flecked with brown, for 12–17 days; both parents feed the young.
Feeding: insects form bulk of diet; forages by gleaning outer foliage of conifers, by hovering or by hawking; readily forages in mixed species flocks outside of breeding season.
Voice: issues a low *tchip* call; song is a sweet, ringing series of rapid, variable *tsweet* or *tsi-wi* notes with an emphatic ending (often similar in pattern to Yellow Warbler song).
Similar Species: none.
Best Sites: *AZ:* Pinal Peak Recreation Area (Pinal Mts.); Mt. Lemmon (Catalina Mts.); Rustler Park (Chiricahua Mts.). *NM:* Signal Peak (Pinos Altos Mts.); Emory Pass (Black Mts.).

PAINTED REDSTART

Myioborus pictus

When the Painted Redstart's unwarblerlike call resonates from shaded riparian woodlands, you may think you are hearing a Pine Siskin (*Carduelis pinus*). But there is no mistaking this redstart for any other species once you spot the contrasting black, red and white plumage and its characteristic creeping behavior. This boldly colored bird often partially spreads its wings, revealing white wing patches, and fans its tail to show off its white outer tail feathers. Both the male and the female Painted Redstart share the same bold plumage, and both sexes are reported to sing. This redstart can sometimes be seen moving up or down the side of a tree trunk, foraging much like a nuthatch. • The Painted Redstart was named after Old World redstarts—in the flycatcher family—because of plumage similarities. "Start" originates from the Old English *steort*, which means tail.

ID: black plumage; white wing patch; white crescent under eye; bright red upper belly and lower breast; white undertail coverts and outer tail feathers. *Juvenile:* slaty gray-black lower breast and upper belly.

Size: *L* 5½ in; *W* 8¾ in.

Status: *AZ:* fairly common summer resident in pinyon-juniper and mixed pine-oak woodlands of the central and southeast regions. *NM:* fairly common summer resident in pinyon-juniper and mixed pine-oak woodlands in the southwest.

Habitat: pine-oak mountain woodlands and steep canyons with sycamores and streamside oaks.

Nesting: usually on a steep slope, canyon wall or embankment; ground nest is hidden under a tree, shrub or boulder; female builds cup nest of grass, leaves, pine needles and bark and lines it with hair and fine grasses; female incubates 3–4 creamy white eggs with fine brown spots for 13–14 days; raises 2 broods.

Feeding: insects are taken along the ground and among foliage by hopping, hawking or hovering; may take sugar water from hummingbird feeders; may move vertically along tree trunks like a nuthatch.

Voice: call is a clear, whistled *wheeoo;* song is a variable series of musical warbles: *weetle-weetle-weetle*, often ending in a higher *wheat-wheat-wheat*; may also sing *wheata-wheata-wheata-awheata-wee*.

Similar Species: none.

Best Sites: *AZ:* Madera Canyon; Oak Creek Canyon (Sedona); Miller and Garden Canyon (Huachuca Mts.). *NM:* Cherry Creek Campground (Pinos Altos Mts.).

YELLOW-BREASTED CHAT

Icteria virens

The Yellow-breasted Chat is our most unusual wood-warbler. At 7½ inches, it is by far our largest warbler. Its bill is thick and stocky, more like a tropical tanager, and its song and courtship displays are reminiscent of thrashers and mockingbirds. • Because of their skulking habits and preference for thick vegetation, Yellow-breasted Chats may be more numerous than observations suggest. Most birders in our region encounter a chat no more frequently than once or twice every few years. • The male Yellow-breasted Chat performs impressive courtship rituals. It sings a most unwarblerlike series of caws, squeaks, grunts, whistles and other sounds while flying up in the air and briefly hovering before dropping back down with dangling feet, pumping his tail and arching his wings above his body.

ID: olive-brown upperparts; white "spectacles"; short, stocky bill; yellow throat and breast; whitish belly. *Male:* black lores. *Female:* gray lores.
Size: *L* 7½ in; *W* 9½ in.
Status: *AZ:* uncommon to common summer resident in riparian and dense willow-mesquite thickets statewide. *NM:* uncommon and local summer resident in lowland riparian and dense willow-mesquite thickets statewide.
Habitat: dense thickets and woodland edges.
Nesting: in a dense tangle, often among thorny bushes; female builds a well-concealed cup nest of stems, vines and leaves, and lines it with fine grass; female incubates 3–6 (usually 5) spotted, white eggs for 11 days.
Feeding: gleans low vegetation for insects, spiders, small crustaceans and fruit.
Voice: calls include *whoit, chack,* and *kook*; song is a series of whistles, squawks, grunts, squeals, and various other sounds, uttered during an aerial display and sometimes at night.
Similar Species: none.
Best Sites: *AZ:* Boyce Thompson Arboretum; San Pedro R., Dudleyville-Winkelman. *NM:* Bosque del Apache NWR, Rio Grande Nature Center; Percha Dam SP.

HEPATIC TANAGER

Piranga flava

Tanagers are a large family of mostly tropical birds with highly variable, brightly colored plumage and fairly thick bills. In Central and South America, there are over 200 tanager species representing every color of the rainbow. Three of the five North American species visit our region to breed. • Our largest warbler, the Hepatic Tanager, is a restless, jumpy bird that may fly long distances in search of food. The unflattering title of "hepatic" means "relating to the liver" and refers to the male's liver-red plumage. The genus name of *Piranga* means "small bird" in an indigenous South American tongue, while the species name *flava*, Latin for "yellow," indicates that the female was probably the first of this species to be described. • Mixed wood riparian zones of the Colorado River, central Arizona and southern New Mexico are also home to the similar-looking, but brighter red, Summer Tanager *(P. rubra)*.

ID: longish, dark bill; distinctive gray cheek. *Male:* dull red overall with grayish wash. *Female and juvenile:* dull greenish gray overall; dull orange throat and forehead; male acquires red plumage gradually.

Size: *L* 8 in; *W* 12½ in.

Status: *AZ:* common summer resident of montane oak, pine and pinyon-juniper woodlands statewide. *NM:* fairly common summer resident of montane oak, pine and pinyon-juniper woodlands in the mountains of the southwest.

Habitat: mid-elevation oak and pine forests.

Nesting: in a forked branch high in a tree; saucer-shaped nest of grass is lined with flower petals; female incubates 3–5 bluish eggs for 12–14 days; both parents feed the young.

Feeding: gleans foliage for insects or sallies for flying insects.

Voice: call notes are *chuk* and *squeep*; bold, short phrases; varied whistles at even intervals.

Similar Species: *Summer Tanager:* brighter red plumage; pale bill; no dark cheek patch.

Best Sites: *AZ:* Rustler Park (Chiricahua Mts.); Madera Canyon; Oak Creek Canyon (Sedona); Miller and Garden Canyon (Huachuca Mts.). *NM:* McMillen Campground and Signal Peak (Pinos Altos Mts.); Emory Pass (Black Mts.).

WESTERN TANAGER

Piranga ludoviciana

With a golden body accentuated by black wings, a black tail and an orange-red face, the male Western Tanager brings a splash of color to the foothills and lower mountain slopes. The male and female of this species are unique among our region's tanagers in having one yellow and one white wing bar. • This western bird breeds locally in the mountains and foothills. The male's courtship song is difficult to identify because it closely parallels the phrases of an American Robin's song. The tanager's notes are somewhat hoarser, as if the bird had a sore throat, and end with a distinctive, hiccuplike *pit-a-tik*.

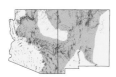

ID: 1 yellow and 1 white wing bar; stout, dull orangy bill. *Breeding male:* yellow underparts and rump; black back, wings and tail; orangy red face. *Female:* olive green overall; lighter underparts; darker upperparts; faint wing bars.
Size: *L* 7 in; *W* 11½ in.
Status: common summer resident of mid- to high-elevation coniferous forests and common and widespread migrant regionwide.
Habitat: *Breeding:* conifer or mixed-wood foothill and mountain forests from 3000 to 9000 ft. *In migration:* may appear in almost any stand of trees, no matter how small or isolated; also in thorn scrubland and riparian areas.
Nesting: in a fork or on a horizontal branch of a conifer, placed well out from the trunk; cup nest is loosely built of twigs, grass and other plant materials and lined with fine vegetation; female incubates 3–5 pale blue, brown-speckled eggs for 13–14 days.
Feeding: gleans vegetation and catches flying insects on the wing; eats wasps, beetles and other insects; also eats fruit; drinks from the ground.
Voice: call is a unique, crisp *pritik* or *pri-terik;* song is a hoarse, rapid series of dry 2- or 3-note phrases.
Similar Species: male is distinctive. *Bullock's Oriole* (p. 158): females have thinner, sharper bills and lack all-yellow underparts. *Summer Tanager:* female lacks white wing bars.
Best Sites: *AZ:* Madera Canyon; Oak Creek Canyon (Sedona); Miller Canyon, Ramsey Canyon Preserve and Garden Canyon (Huachuca Mts.); Sycamore Creek and Mt. Ord (Sunflower). *NM:* Hondo Canyon (Sandia Mts.); Santa Fe Ski Basin (Sangre de Cristo Mts.).

GREEN-TAILED TOWHEE

Pipilo chlorurus

Towhees are large, chunky sparrows with long tails. Arizona and New Mexico are home to four species of these colorful sparrows. • Green-tailed Towhees are birds of arid scrub habitats in the foothills and lower mountains. They can be common summer birds of hillsides and foothills, while remaining entirely unknown in the nearby valleys. The best time to see Green-tailed Towhees is in spring, when the males give clear, whistled notes, raspy trills or catlike *mew* calls from an exposed woody perch. Otherwise, they remain concealed in shrubby undergrowth, industriously scratching away debris with both feet in search of insects and hidden seeds. • Green-tailed Towhees often join up with White-crowned Sparrows during their fall migration to Mexican wintering grounds. • *Pipilo* is derived from a Latin word meaning "to twitter"; *chlorurus* means "green tail."

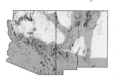

ID: yellowish green upperparts, most intense on wings and tail; orange rufous crown; dark stripe on white throat; sooty gray face and breast; conical, gray bill; gray legs. *Immature:* brownish overall; streaked upperparts and underparts; pale throat is bordered by dark stripe and white stripe.
Size: *L* 6½–7¼ in; *W* 9¾ in.
Status: common migrant in dense brush regionwide. *AZ:* fairly common summer resident of deciduous brush in the higher mountains to the north; common winter resident in dense brush in central and southeastern regions. *NM:* uncommon summer resident of deciduous brush in the higher mountains to the north; rare to uncommon winter resident in dense brush in the south.

Habitat: arid, shrubby hillsides featuring sagebrush, juniper or other well-spaced trees and shrubs; also found in dense, low thickets.
Nesting: on the ground or very low in a bush; deep, bulky, thick-walled cup nest of twigs, grass and bark shreds is lined with fine materials; female incubates 3–4 darkly spotted, white eggs for 11 days.
Feeding: scratches the ground for insects, seeds and berries; drinks morning dew from leaves; occasionally visits feeding stations.
Voice: call is a distinctive, nasal *mew*; song consists of clear, whistled notes followed by squealing, raspy trills: *swee-too weet chur cheee-churr.*
Similar Species: *Chipping Sparrow* (p. 143): smaller; white eyebrow; black eye line; no green back. *Rufous-crowned Sparrow:* reddish eye line; no green back.
Best Sites: *AZ: In winter:* Patagonia Lake SP; Boyce Thompson Arboretum. *NM: In winter:* Bosque del Apache NWR; Rio Grande Nature Center.

SPOTTED TOWHEE

Pipilo maculatus

Spotted Towhees are often heard before they are seen. These noisy foragers rustle about in dense undergrowth, craftily scraping back layers of dry leaves to expose the seeds, berries or insects hidden beneath. Towhees prefer tangled thickets and overgrown gardens, especially if there are blackberries or other small fruits for the taking. Many pairs breed in urban neighborhoods, where they take turns scolding the family cat. • Spotted Towhees rarely leave their sub-arboreal world, except to perform their simple courtship song or to furtively eye a threat to their territory.

♂

ID: *Male:* black hood, back, wings and tail; rufous flanks; dark, conical bill; bold, white spotting on wings; white tips on outer tail feathers; white belly and undertail. *Female:* somewhat drabber and paler overall.

Size: *L* 7–8½ in; *W* 10½ in.

Status: fairly common migrant and winter resident of brushy thickets regionwide.

AZ: fairly common summer resident of mid-elevation canyons and dense thickets statewide, except in the southwest.

NM: fairly common summer resident of mid-elevation canyons and dense thickets in the foothills west of the eastern plains.

Habitat: riparian thickets, chaparral, brushy ravines, shady canyons and thick undergrowth in suburban parks and gardens.

Nesting: low in a bush, on the ground under cover or in a brushy pile; cup nest of leaves, grass and bark shreds is lined with fine materials; primarily the female incubates 3–4 brown-speckled, white eggs for 12–13 days.

Feeding: scratches the ground vigorously for seeds and insects; periodically visits feeding stations; also eats berries and acorns, especially in winter; seldom feeds in trees.

Voice: call is a raspy or whining *chee* or *chwaay;* song is a simple, querulous trilling: *here here here PLEASE.*

Similar Species: *Black-headed Grosbeak* (p. 150): stockier; much heavier bill; dark eyes; rufous is restricted on sides. *Dark-eyed Junco* (p. 147): smaller; "Oregon" race has pale rufous on back and sides. *American Redstart:* much smaller, flittier; male has black breast, bright red sides and orange in wings and tail; no white wing spots.

Best Sites: *AZ:* Boyce Thompson Arboretum; Madera Canyon; Oak Creek Canyon (Sedona); Miller and Garden Canyon (Huachuca Mts.) *NM:* Bosque del Apache NWR (winter); Rio Grande Nature Center (winter); Sandia Mts.; Sangre de Cristo Mts.

CANYON TOWHEE

Pipilo fuscus

Few birds are as bold as the Canyon Towhee, well known for its scrappy, scolding disposition and habit of foraging among the gravel of parking lots, hopping underneath parked cars in search of shade and food. Like other towhees, it scratches the ground in a two-footed hopping motion to uncover a variety of seeds and insects. • A pair of adult Canyon Towhees may mate for life, foraging together year-round and staying within the boundaries of their loosely protected territory. A breeding pair may raise up to three broods each year, depending on the availability of food and water. • The closely related Abert's Towhee *(P. abertii)* is found in western and southern Arizona and southwestern New Mexico. It is loyal to the dense cover of the few riparian areas within the arid Southwest. Its song is a series of ascending whistles followed by a one- or two-part trill.

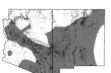

ID: rusty cap and undertail coverts; buffy throat, breast and sides; dark central breast spot and "necklace" of dark spots; white belly; gray upperparts.

Size: *L* 8½ in; *W* 11½ in.

Status: AZ: uncommon to fairly common resident of desert canyons and foothills generally below the Mogollon Rim. **NM:** uncommon to fairly common resident of desert canyons and foothills nearly statewide.

Habitat: canyons, chaparral, scrub desert and grassland, desert foothills and open pinyon-juniper woodlands.

Nesting: a bulky cup-shaped nest of twigs, bark, vegetation and animal hair is placed in a shrub, small tree or cactus; female incubates 3–4 sparsely marked, whitish or pale blue eggs for 11 days; both adults raise the young.

Feeding: seasonally available seeds and insects are found while foraging on ground, often under objects like parked cars, benches, shrubs and logs; occasionally scratches dirt.

Voice: *chiup* is a typical call; song is a chipping, musical trill.

Similar Species: *Abert's Towhee:* lacks rusty cap, white belly, dark central breast spot and "necklace" of dark spots. *Green-tailed Towhee* (p. 140): brighter, rufous cap; greenish wings and tail; white throat with two dark stripes.

Best Sites: AZ: Roosevelt L.; Patagonia Lake SP; Organ Pipe Cactus National Monument, South Mountain Park (Phoenix). **NM:** Bosque del Apache NWR; Rio Grande Nature Center; Percha Dam SP.

CHIPPING SPARROW

Spizella passerina

The Chipping Sparrow and Dark-eyed Junco do not share the same tailor, but they must have attended the same voice lessons, because their songs are very similar. Though the rapid trill of the Chipping Sparrow is slightly faster, drier and less musical than the junco's, even experienced birders can have difficulty identifying this singer. • The Chipping Sparrow has one of the most extensive breeding ranges of any sparrow in North America and is well known over most of the continent. It commonly nests at eye level, and it is well known for using animal hair to line its nest. • The closely related Brewer's Sparrow *(S. breweri)* is a desert species that breeds in the arid mountains of northeastern Arizona and northwestern New Mexico, and overwinters in the southern half of our region. It is gray-brown overall, with a white eye ring and faint streaking on the crown.

breeding

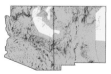

Habitat: open conifers or mixed woodland edges; often in yards and gardens with tree and shrub borders.

Nesting: usually nests at midlevel in a coniferous tree; female builds a compact cup nest of woven grass and rootlets, often lining it with hair; female incubates 4 pale blue eggs for 11–12 days.

Feeding: gleans the ground for insects, spiders and seeds; visits bird feeders during winter.

Voice: call is a high-pitched *chip;* song is a rapid, dry trill.

Similar Species: *Rufous-crowned Sparrow:* red eye line; gray eyebrow; black whisker mark. *Green-tailed Towhee* (p. 140): no black eye line; green back; black whisker mark. *American Tree Sparrow:* little seasonal overlap; dark central breast spot; rufous stripe extends behind eye; lacks bold, white eyebrow.

Best Sites: *AZ:* Mt. Lemmon; Catalina Mts.; Red Rock SP (Sedona). *NM:* Sangre de Cristo Mts.; Sandia Mts.

ID: short tail; often observed in flocks in trees; brown upperparts streaked with black; gray nape; brown crown streaked with black; pale eyebrow; black eye line; gray face; white throat; pinkish bill; brown wings with 2 white wing bars; grayish underparts. *Breeding*: bright rusty cap bordered with black; dark bill.

Size: *L* 5–6 in; *W* 8½ in.

Status: common summer resident of coniferous forests regionwide. *AZ:* common winter resident in the southern and central regions. *NM:* common winter resident in the south.

LARK SPARROW

Chondestes grammacus

The Lark Sparrow's unique, quail-like facial pattern and unique tail pattern distinguish it from all other sparrows. This large sparrow is typically seen in open, shrubby areas and edge habitats, but it occasionally ventures into meadows and wooded areas to join flocks of Vesper Sparrows *(Pooecetes gramineus)* and Savannah Sparrows. • Courting males are conspicuous and active, singing clear, buzzy trills and spreading their wing and tail feathers in a manner that reminded early naturalists of the famed Sky Lark of Europe. The males will challenge rivals near their nest but do not defend a large territory. • During migration, small flocks of Lark Sparrows are regularly seen foraging alongside juncos, sparrows and towhees in suburban parks and gardens.

ID: robust body; chestnut head with white throat, eyebrow and crown stripe edged with black; unstreaked pale breast with dark central spot; rounded tail with flashy white corners.
Size: *L* 6 in; *W* 11 in.
Status: fairly common summer resident in brushy desert areas with scattered trees and common migrant regionwide. *AZ:* fairly common winter resident throughout southern and central regions. *NM:* common migrant statewide; uncommon winter resident in the extreme south.
Habitat: semi-open shrublands, sandhills, sagebrush and occasionally pastures.
Nesting: on the ground or in a low bush; bulky cup nest is made of grass and twigs and lined with finer materials; occasionally reuses abandoned thrasher nests; female incubates 4–5 white eggs, with sparse dark markings, for 11–12 days.
Feeding: walks or hops on the ground, gleaning seeds; also eats grasshoppers and other invertebrates.
Voice: melodious and variable song that consists of short trills, buzzes, pauses and clear notes.
Similar Species: no other sparrow has the distinctive head pattern.
Best Sites: widespread in open habitats with scattered trees. *AZ:* Roosevelt L.; agricultural areas. *NM:* Bosque del Apache NWR.

BLACK-THROATED SPARROW

Amphispiza bilineata

The Black-throated Sparrow and the Sage Sparrow *(A. belli)* both prefer arid, sagebrush-dominated habitat. The close bond between these two species is further reflected in their similar preference for seeds and insects, and in the similar appearance of the juvenile Black-throated Sparrow and the adult Sage Sparrow. • Because of its hot, dry habitat, the Black-throated Sparrow is ordinarily without any source of standing or flowing water. To survive without drinking water, this sparrow has evolved a super-efficient physiology that allows it to extract and recycle moisture obtained from its food. • There is danger in building a nest near the ground—Black-throated Sparrow nestlings and eggs are a welcome food item for a number of lizards, snakes, ground squirrels and other animals.

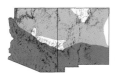

ID: gray cheek and cap; prominent white eyebrow; black chin, throat and "bib"; broad white jaw line; unstreaked, light underparts; dark bill. *In flight:* black tail with white edges to outer feathers. *Juvenile:* white chin and throat; dark streaking on upper breast; light lower mandible.
Size: *L* 4½–5½ in; *W* 9 in.
Status: *AZ:* common permanent resident of desert habitats statewide. *NM:* common permanent resident of desert habitats in the south.
Habitat: rocky hills and flatlands covered with sagebrush, greasewood, saltbrush and rabbit brush; also found on lower mountain slopes with pinyon-juniper woodlands and an understory of open sagebrush.
Nesting: on the ground under the shelter of tall weeds, in a rocky cliff crevice, in a shrub or low in a tree; open cup of twigs, grass and weeds is lined with hair, fine grasses and rootlets; female incubates 4–5 darkly spotted, creamy to grayish white eggs for 11–12 days; both adults feed the young.
Feeding: forages on the open ground by walking, often in small, loose flocks; may also forage in low shrubs and trees. *Summer:* eats mostly insects. *Winter:* takes seeds from the ground.
Voice: call is a series of faint, tinkling, chattery notes; simple but variable song often opens with a few clear notes followed by a light trill.
Similar Species: *Sage Sparrow:* shorter, thinner white eyebrow; distinct dark streaking on sides; fine streaking on head and back; runs on ground with its tail held high.
Best Sites: *AZ:* widespread in surrounding deserts of Tucson and Phoenix. *NM:* Tularosa Valley; Carlsbad Caverns National Monument.

WHITE-CROWNED SPARROW
Zonotrichia leucophrys

In winter, large, bold and smartly patterned White-crowned Sparrows brighten brushy hedgerows, overgrown fields and riparian areas. They typically appear singly, or in twos or threes, flitting through brushy fencerows and overgrown fields. • The White-crowned Sparrow is North America's most studied sparrow. Several races have been identified, although plumage differences are minor, and research has given science tremendous insight into bird physiology, homing behavior and the geographic variability of song dialects. • White-crowns breed in the far north and in alpine environments. This bird has a widespread distribution in North America, and populations in different parts of its range vary significantly in behavior and in migratory and nesting habits.

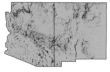

ID: distinctive orange bill; gray or brown back with dark streaking; gray nape; crown boldly marked with black and white; black eye line; gray throat and breast; pale underparts. *Juvenile:* head subtly marked with tan and gray; brown eye line.
Size: *L* 5½–7 in; *W* 9½ in.
Status: rare and local summer resident near treeline in a few restricted mountain ranges and common migrant and winter resident regionwide.
Habitat: woodlots, brushy tangles and riparian thickets.
Nesting: rare breeder; on the ground or in a shrub or small coniferous tree; female weaves a cup nest of twigs, grass, leaves and bark, and lines it with fine materials; female incubates 3–5 greenish eggs, with reddish blotches, for 11–14 days.
Feeding: scratches the ground to expose insects and seeds; also eats berries, buds and moss caps; may take seeds from bird feeders.
Voice: call is a high, thin *seet* or sharp *pink*; song, rarely heard in our region, is a frequently repeated variation of *I gotta go wee-wee now.*
Similar Species: *White-throated Sparrow:* bold, white throat; grayish bill; yellow lores; browner overall.
Best Sites: widespread in migration and in winter.

DARK-EYED JUNCO

Junco hyemalis

Juncos spend most of their time hopping on the ground, and they are readily flushed from wooded trails and backyard feeders. Their distinctive, white outer tail feathers flash in alarm as they seek cover in a nearby tree or shrub. • There are five closely related Dark-eyed Junco subspecies in North America that share similar habits but differ in coloration and range. All five subspecies are found in our region and interbreed where their ranges meet. The "Oregon" (*oreganus*) and Gray-headed (*caniceps*) subspecies are the most widespread. Yet another species, the Yellow-eyed Junco (*J. phaeonotus*) reaches the northern limit of its range in south-eastern Arizona. This southern specialty is known to walk, not hop, along the ground. Good viewing sites include Rustler Park in the Chiricahua Mts.

"Oregon Junco"

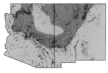

ID: white outer tail feathers; pale bill. *"Slate-colored" male:* dark gray upperparts; pink bill; white belly; white outer tail feathers. *"Slate-colored" female:* duller plumage, with some brown in wings. *"Oregon" male:* rusty upperparts and flanks strongly contrast with black head. *"Oregon" female:* muted colors; dark gray head. *"Gray-headed":* pale gray hood; gray upperparts; bright rufous patch on back.
Size: *L* 5½–7 in; *W* 9½ in.
Status: common migrant and winter visitor and common summer resident in coniferous forests throughout the region.

Habitat: shrubby woodland borders; also backyard feeders.
Nesting: on the ground, usually concealed; female builds a cup nest of twigs, grass, bark shreds and moss; female incubates 3–5 brown-marked, whitish to bluish eggs for 12–13 days.
Feeding: scratches the ground for inverte-brates; also eats berries and seeds.
Voice: call is a smacking *chip* note, often given in series; song is a long, dry trill, very similar to that of the Chipping Sparrow, but more musical.
Similar Species: none; plumage pattern, small size and ground-dwelling habits are distinctive.
Best Sites: Flagstaff; Mt. Lemmon; Red Rock SP (Sedona). *NM:* Sangre de Cristo Mts.; Sandia Mts.

NORTHERN CARDINAL

Cardinalis cardinalis

A bird as beautiful as the Northern Cardinal rarely fails to capture our attention and admiration: it is often the first choice for calendars and Christmas cards. • These birds prefer the tangled shrubby edges of woodlands and are easily attracted to backyards with feeders and sheltering trees and shrubs. • Northern Cardinals form one of the bird world's most faithful pair bonds and sing to one another year-round with soft, bubbly whistles. The female is known to sing while on the nest, and it is believed that she is informing her partner whether or not she and the young need food. The male is highly territorial and will often attack his own reflection in windows or shiny objects. • The Northern Cardinal owes its name to the vivid red plumage of the male, which resembles the red robes of Roman Catholic cardinals.

ID: pointed crest; thick, red-orange bill; rather long tail. *Male:* bright red overall; black face and eyes.
Female: warm brown back and head; less distinct black face; pale red wings; reddish brown breast; white belly; reddish tail.
Juvenile: resembles female with duller plumage; brown face; blackish bill.
Size: *L* 7½–9 in; *W* 12 in.
Status: *AZ:* uncommon to common permanent resident of riparian and dense thickets in central and southeast regions.
NM: uncommon to locally common permanent resident of riparian areas and dense thickets in the south.
Habitat: any shrubby or open wooded habitat; shuns dense woodlands.
Nesting: in a dense shrub, thicket, vine tangle or low in a coniferous tree; female builds an open cup nest of twigs, weeds, grass, leaves and rootlets and lines it with hair and fine grass; female incubates 3–4 profusely marked, whitish to greenish white eggs for 12–13 days.
Feeding: gleans low shrubs and the ground for seeds, insects and berries; visits feeders.
Voice: call is a loud metallic *tick*; song is a variable series of clear, whistled notes.
Similar Species: *Pyrrhuloxia* (p. 149): gray overall; longer, red-tipped crest; yellow-orange bill; male has red on face, underparts, wings and tail. *Juniper Titmouse* (p. 112): resembles juvenile but much smaller, with gray upperparts and pale underparts washed with buffy. *Summer Tanager:* mostly arboreal; male lacks crest and black face and has longer, paler bill.
Best Sites: *AZ:* widespread throughout Phoenix and Tucson. *NM:* Rattlesnake Springs; Carlsbad Caverns NP.

PYRRHULOXIA

Cardinalis sinuatus

The tropical-looking Pyrrhuloxia and its close relative the Northern Cardinal are crested birds with thick, stubby bills perfect for cracking seeds. These birds share similar habitats, behaviors and even songs, but the Pyrrhuloxia is found in drier, more open habitats. It is a year-round resident of the arid brush country and thorny desert scrub found throughout much of the Southwest. Lush suburban gardens bursting with juicy berries, seeds and fruits often serve as powerful attractants for this parrot-billed bird. • In winter, Pyrrhuloxia forage with other birds in large flocks, readily visiting feeders and wandering northward, outside of their breeding range. In early spring, males become increasingly aggressive and break away from flocks to establish breeding territories. They defend their territory until late summer by singing their clear, whistled *what-cheer* songs and chasing intruders.

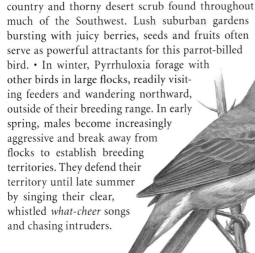

ID: *Male:* grayish overall; long, red-tipped crest; thick, stubby, orange-yellow bill; red on face, underparts, wings and tail. *Female:* similar to male but with much less red. *Immature:* duller version of female with dark bill and pale wing bars.
Size: L 8¾ in; *W* 12 in.
Status: *AZ:* fairly common to uncommon permanent resident in central and southeast regions. *NM:* uncommon permanent resident in the south.
Habitat: desert habitats including arid canyons, mesquite and acacia thickets, brushy washes and scrubby riparian areas; may wander into hedgerows, open woodlands and farmlands; may visit feeders during winter.

Nesting: in a thorny shrub, tree or tangle of mistletoe; female builds a cup-shaped nest of bark, thorny twigs and fine plant materials; female incubates 2–3 darkly spotted white or very pale green eggs for 14 days; both adults raise the young.
Feeding: forages on or near the ground, in shrubs or low trees; eats seeds, insects, berries and small fruits; may visit feeders; forms small flocks in winter.
Voice: common call is a sharp *chink*; song is a varied series of liquid whistles, shorter and thinner than the song of the Northern Cardinal: *what-cheer what-cheer.*
Similar Species: *Northern Cardinal* (p. 148): conical, red, unhooked bill; thicker, shorter crest; black face; male is red overall; female and immature are warm brown with reddish wings; immature birds have dark bill.
Best Sites: *AZ:* Arizona Sonora Desert Museum; Patagonia Lake SP. *NM:* Rattlesnake Springs; Carlsbad Caverns NP.

BLACK-HEADED GROSBEAK

Pheucticus melanocephalus

Anyone birding in our region during spring or summer quickly makes acquaintance with Black-headed Grosbeaks. These birds are marvelous singers, advertising breeding territories with extended bouts of complex, accented caroling. Brightly-colored males sing from slightly sheltered perches near the top of a tree, while duller females forage and conduct nesting chores within the cover of interior foliage, betraying their presence with frequent call-notes. • Black-headed Grosbeaks are most characteristic of riparian thickets, rich oak woodlands and broken conifer forests with a strong hardwood component but will also visit backyard feeders adjacent to dense woodlots. • The scientific name *Pheucticus* is thought to be derived from the Greek *phyticos*, meaning "painted with cosmetics," referring to the male's bright coloring.

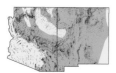

ID: large, dark, conical bill. *Male:* orange-brown underparts and rump; black head, back, wings and tail; white wing bars and undertail coverts. *Female:* dark brown upperparts; buff underparts; lightly streaked flanks; pale eyebrow and crown stripe.
Size: *L* 7–8 in; *W* 12 in.
Status: common migrant and fairly common summer resident throughout the region.
Habitat: *Breeding:* a variety of forests and forest-edge situations, preferring deciduous riparian, oak, mixed oak-coniferous woodlands, farmyards, parks and suburban tree groves. *In migration:* may appear in almost any stand of trees or tall brush.

Nesting: in a tall shrub or deciduous tree, often near water; female builds a loosely woven cup nest of twigs, stems and grasses; pair incubates 3–4 brown-spotted, pale blue eggs for 12–14 days.
Feeding: forages in the upper canopy for invertebrates and plant foods; occasionally visits feeding stations.
Voice: call is a high-pitched, penetrating *eek*; song is a loud, ecstatic caroling known for exceptionally rich quality and many accented notes.
Similar Species: male is distinctive. *Rose-breasted Grosbeak:* rare in our region; female has pale bill and streaked breast.
Best Sites: *AZ:* Madera Canyon, Miller Canyon and Ramsey Canyon Preserve (Huachuca Mts.); Boyce Thompson Arboretum. *NM:* Sangre de Cristo Mts.; Sandia Mts.; Percha Dam SP.

BLUE GROSBEAK

Passerina caerulea

Male Blue Grosbeaks owe their spectacular spring plumage not to a fresh molt but, oddly enough, to feather wear. While Blue Grosbeaks are wintering in Mexico, Central America or, infrequently, in our southern regions, their brown feather tips slowly wear away, leaving the crystal blue plumage that is seen as they arrive on their breeding grounds. The lovely blue color of the plumage is not produced by pigmentation, but by tiny particles in the feathers that reflect only short wavelengths in the light spectrum. • The Blue Grosbeak is more closely related to the Indigo Bunting *(P. cyanea)* than to other grosbeaks. A pair of rusty wing bars, visible even on first-winter birds, distinguishes the Blue Grosbeak from the similar-looking Indigo Bunting. • In spring, watch for the tail-spreading, tail-flicking and crown-raising behaviors that suggest the birds might be breeding. • *Caerulea* is from the Latin for "blue," a description that just doesn't grasp this bird's true beauty.

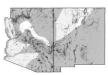

ID: large, conical bill; orange wing bars; characteristically flicks tail. *Male:* blue body; black face; dark wings with wide wing bars; plumage mottled with brown after breeding. *Female and juvenile:* rich brown overall; plain face; paler underparts; rump and shoulders washed with blue; male acquires adult plumage gradually.
Size: L 6–7½ in; *W* 11 in.
Status: common migrant and fairly common summer resident regionwide.
Habitat: thick brush, riparian thickets, shrubby areas and dense weedy fields near water.
Nesting: in a shrub or low tree; pair builds a cup nest of twigs, roots and grass and lines it with finer materials, including paper and occasionally a shed reptile skin; female incubates 2–5 pale blue eggs for 11–12 days.
Feeding: gleans the ground and foliage for insects; also eats seeds or fruit.
Voice: call is a loud *chink*; song is a series of sweet, melodious, warbling phrases that rise and fall.
Similar Species: *Indigo Bunting:* smaller body and bill; no orange wing bars; male lacks black face. *Brown-headed Cowbird* (p. 157): female is similar in plumage but mostly terrestrial, with longer tail often held upraised.
Best Sites: *AZ:* Patagonia Lake SP; San Pedro River Conservation Area. *NM:* Bosque del Apache NWR; Percha Dam SP; Gila R.; Red Rock.

LAZULI BUNTING

Passerina amoena

Small flocks of Lazuli Buntings migrate through much of our region, arriving on their breeding grounds in mid-May. Males set up territorial districts in which neighboring males copy and learn their songs from one another, producing "song territories." Each male within a song territory sings with slight differences in the syllables, producing his own acoustic fingerprint. • Two additional species of buntings occur in our region: the Indigo Bunting and the Varied Bunting *(P. versicolor)*. The Indigo Bunting is primarily an eastern bird that extends its breeding range into New Mexico, southeastern Arizona and locally along the Colorado River. Indigo-Lazuli hybrids commonly occur where their ranges overlap, producing offspring with extremely varied intermediate plumages. The Varied Bunting is an uncommon southern visitor that breeds in the mesquite and riparian thickets of southeastern Arizona.

Nesting: in an upright crotch low in a shrubby tangle; female weaves small cup nest of grass and lines it with finer grass and hair; female incubates 3–5 eggs for 12 days.

Feeding: gleans the ground and low shrubs for grasshoppers, beetles and other insects, and native seeds; visits bird feeders in some areas.

Voice: male's song is a brief complex of whispering notes: *swip-swip-swip zu zu ee, see see sip see see.*

Similar Species: *Indigo Bunting:* no wing bars; male lacks chestnut breast. *Blue Grosbeak* (p. 151): larger body and bill; male is blue; both male and female have rusty wing bars, blue on shoulder and white belly and undertail coverts. *Varied Bunting:* little range overlap; darker blue with red wash above; red patch on back of neck. *Western Bluebird* (p. 123): male is larger; slimmer bill; more extensive chestnut on breast; no wing bars.

Best Sites: *AZ:* Oak Creek Canyon; South Fork Little Colorado R. (White Mts.). *NM:* Sandia Mts.; Sange de Cristo Mts.

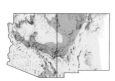

ID: stout, conical bill. *Male:* turquoise hood and rump; chestnut upper breast; white belly; dark wings and tail; 2 bold, white wing bars. *Female:* soft brown overall; hints of blue on rump.

Size: *L* 5–6 in; *W* 8 in.

Status: *AZ:* common migrant and fairly common local summer resident along the Mogollon Rim. *NM:* common migrant and fairly common local summer resident in the western mountain ranges.

Habitat: *Breeding:* expanses of low shrubs with elevated song perches, sagebrush, chaparral, forest edge and streamsides. *In migration:* lowland areas including foothill canyons.

RED-WINGED BLACKBIRD

Agelaius phoeniceus

Nearly every cattail marsh worthy of description in our region plays host to Red-winged Blackbirds for at least part of the year. Red-wings are year-round residents here, and few people have been denied a meeting with these abundant, widespread birds. • The male's bright red shoulders and short, raspy song are his most important tools in the often intricate strategy he employs to defend his territory from rivals. A flashy and richly voiced male who has managed to establish a large and productive territory can attract several mates to his cattail kingdom. In field experiments, males whose red shoulders were painted black soon lost their territories to rivals they had previously defeated. • After the male has wooed the female, she starts the busy work of weaving a nest amid the cattails. Cryptic coloration allows the female to sit inconspicuously upon her nest, blending in perfectly with the surroundings.

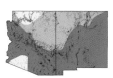

ID: dark bill, legs and feet. *Male:* black overall except for large red shoulder patch edged in yellow. *Female:* brown upperparts; pale underparts heavily streaked with dark brown; pale eyebrow and throat often tinged pinkish.
Size: *L* 7–9½ in; *W* 13 in.
Status: fairly common migrant and summer resident, and common winter resident throughout the region.
Habitat: any shrubby or brushy wetland; dry prairie.
Nesting: colonial; in cattails or a shoreline bush, usually by or over water; female weaves a deep cup nest of dried cattail leaves and grass and lines it with fine grass; female incubates 3–4 darkly marked, pale blue-green eggs for 10–12 days.

Feeding: gleans the ground for grain, other seeds and invertebrates; may visit bird feeders.
Voice: calls include a harsh *check* and a high *tseert*; song is a *konk-a-ree.*
Similar Species: plumage of male is distinctive; female resembles sparrow or finch but is much larger, is found in flocks in open habitats and has pointed bill. *Brown-headed Cowbird* (p. 157): female is dull gray-brown overall and has finely streaked underparts.
Best Sites: marshes and wetlands regionwide.

WESTERN MEADOWLARK

Sturnella neglecta

Meadowlarks are terrestrial songbirds with chunky bodies, short tails and rather long, pointed bills. North America's two species—the Eastern Meadowlark *(S. magna)* and the Western Meadowlark—are nearly identical in plumage. Both occur in Arizona and New Mexico, but the Western is more common and widespread. • The two meadowlark species are very similar in appearance, so birders must listen for their songs to distinguish them. The Eastern Meadowlark's clear song is a series of distinct whistles, while the song of the Western Meadowlark is more varied and ends with a gurgle. • The drab plumage of most female songbirds protects them during the breeding season, but the female meadowlark relies on her V-shaped "necklace" and bright yellow throat and belly to distract predators and lead them away from the nest. • The Western Meadowlark was overlooked by members of the Lewis and Clark expedition, who mistakenly thought it was the same species as the Eastern Meadowlark. This oversight is represented in the scientific name *neglecta*.

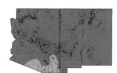

ID: short tail; strongly streaked upperparts; dark crown; white eyebrow; black eye line; yellow throat, breast and upper belly; bold, black "V" on breast; black flank streaking; mostly white tail.
Size: *L* 9–9½ in; *W* 14 in.
Status: common resident of grasslands and open habitats regionwide.
Habitat: open grassy habitats, with or without scattered trees, including suburban areas.
Nesting: on the ground, sometimes in a slight depression, concealed by dense grass; female builds a domed grass nest woven into surrounding vegetation; female

incubates 3–7 brown-speckled, white eggs for 13–15 days; raises 2 broods.
Feeding: forages on the ground; gleans for insects (especially grasshoppers and crickets) and spiders; also eats seeds.
Voice: calls include a rattle in flight and a high, buzzy *dzeart;* song is a rich series of 2–8 melodic, slurred whistles.
Similar Species: *Eastern Meadowlark:* best distinguished by song. *Dickcissel:* much smaller and less numerous; rarely seen on ground; yellow restricted to male's throat and upper breast; no streaking on flanks. *Bobolink:* smaller; seen only during migration; underparts buffy, not yellow; no black "V" on breast.
Best Sites: *AZ:* widespread around Phoenix and Tucson. *NM:* widespread.

YELLOW-HEADED BLACKBIRD

Xanthocephalus xanthocephalus

You might be taken aback by the pitiful grinding sound produced when the male Yellow-headed Blackbird perches on a cattail stalk and arches his dazzling golden head backward to "sing." A nonmuscial series of grating notes leave other sounds to be desired. • These birds often nest in small colonies and require a marsh with a 50:50 ratio of emergent vegetation and water in which to breed. Yellow-headed Blackbirds are strategic in sharing their soggy habitat with the smaller Red-winged Blackbirds; Yellow-heads tend to command the center of the wetland, pushing competitors to the periphery where predation is highest. • The bird's scientific name *xanthocephalus* means "yellow head."

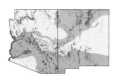

ID: *Male:* black body with yellow head and breast; black mask; white patch at base of primary coverts.
Female and juvenile: brown replaces black; dusky nape and crown; duller yellow face and breast; wing patch faint or absent.
Size: *L* 8–11 in; *W* 15 in.
Status: locally common migrant and summer resident. *AZ:* common winter resident in the south. *NM:* uncommon winter resident in the south.
Habitat: *In migration and winter:* agricultural fields, dairies and cattle feedlots. *Summer:* deep marshes, sloughs, lakeshores and river impoundments where cattails dominate.
Nesting: loosely colonial; female builds a deep basket of aquatic plants lined with

dry grass, woven into surrounding vegetation over water; female incubates 4 pale green or gray eggs, marked with gray or brown, for 11–13 days.
Feeding: forages on the ground for grain, other seeds and insects; may visit bird feeders.
Voice: call is a deep *croak;* song is a strained, metallic grating note followed by a descending buzz.
Similar Species: adult male is distinctive. *Great-tailed Grackle* (p. 156): female and juvenile resemble female or juvenile Yellow-headed Blackbird but are larger with longer tail, are buffy not yellow and lack white wing patch.
Best Sites: *AZ:* Gila R.; Arlington Valley; Lower Colorado River Valley. *NM:* Bosque del Apache NWR; Percha Dam SP.

GREAT-TAILED GRACKLE

Quiscalus mexicanus

The Great-tailed Grackle is the largest grackle in North America and is one of our larger all-black birds, second only to the ravens. The male Great-tailed Grackle has sacrificed function for beauty with a tail so long that it acts as a sail on windy days, continually pointing the bird into the wind. • Great-tailed Grackles are farmland feeders, devouring waste grain before heading into suburban areas at night, announcing their presence with squeaks and hoots in a noisy gang. These gangs, especially in winter, bully other birds from feeders. • In nesting colonies, females may steal nesting material from each other, and both sexes will stray from their mates, with females sometimes switching territories within a breeding season. • Since the 1960s, the Great-tailed Grackle population has expanded to northern Nebraska, southern Kansas and eastern Colorado.

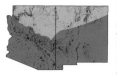

ID: yellow eyes. *Male:* black body with purple-blue iridescence; very long, wide tail. *Female:* gray-brown body, lighter below; shorter tail; light eyebrow.
Size: *Male: L* 18 in; *W* 23 in. *Female: L* 15 in; *W* 19 in.
Status: *AZ:* common to abundant resident of cities, towns and agricultural areas statewide. *NM:* uncommon to abundant resident of cities, towns and agricultural areas statewide; less common in winter in the far north.
Habitat: open to semi-open habitat; urban parks, farmland and wetlands.

Nesting: near water; in a tree or in cattails; tree nest is made of mud, moss and varied debris; wetland nest is made of cattails and thick vegetation; female incubates 3–4 darkly marked, pale blue eggs for 13–14 days.
Feeding: forages on or near the ground or in shallow water; gleans the water's surface or ground for prey; varied diet includes birds' eggs, grain, insects, crustaceans and other invertebrates.
Voice: very verbal; male screeches to proclaim his territory; ascending whistles, hoots and squeaks; noisy chattering in large groups, especially in winter.
Similar Species: *Common Grackle:* shorter tail and wings; much smaller body; limited iridescence.
Best Sites: *AZ:* widespread in Phoenix and Tucson, and in agricultural areas statewide. *NM:* urban and agricultural areas.

BROWN-HEADED COWBIRD

Molothrus ater

This nomad historically followed bison herds across the Great Plains (it now follows cattle), so it never stayed in one area long enough to build and tend a nest. Instead, the Brown-headed Cowbird lays its eggs in the nests of other birds, including 220 known species, making it the most successful brood parasite in North America. While not all nest parasitism is successful—some birds eject the cowbird eggs or build new nests elsewhere, and others, such as doves, cannot properly feed the young cowbird—nearly 150 of the species parasitized by the Brown-headed Cowbirds successfully raise the cowbird young. • This species has greatly expanded its range in the past century, as people have cleared forests and established cattle feedlots and dairy farms. It now breeds from southern Alaska to northern Mexico, and it winters in much of the continental U.S. and Mexico.

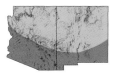

ID: short, squared tail; conical bill; raises tail when foraging on ground. *Male:* black body with green iridescence; brown head. *Female:* dull grayish brown overall; pale throat; faint streaking on breast. *Juvenile:* resembles female but back and wings appear "scaly"; streaked underparts. **Size:** *L* 6–8 in; *W* 12 in. **Status:** common migrant and summer resident regionwide. *AZ:* common winter resident in the south. **Habitat:** any habitat with scattered trees. *Winter:* large flocks at dairy farms and feedlots.

Nesting: brood parasite: female lays eggs in the nest of other birds; variably marked, whitish eggs hatch after 10–13 days. **Feeding:** forages on the ground for seeds; rarely takes insects. **Voice:** call is a high-pitched *seep*, often given in flight; song is a liquidy, tri-syllabic gurgle. **Similar Species:** *Bronzed Cowbird:* male has red eyes; female is uniformly dull black. *Brewer's Blackbird:* slimmer, longer bill; longer tail; lacks contrasting brown head and darker body. **Best Sites:** widespread.

BULLOCK'S ORIOLE

Icterus bullockii

Orioles are members of the blackbird family that have brilliant orange or yellow plumage. Of North America's nine species, five have occurred in our region, but two of these are rare. • Although Bullock's Orioles can be common and widespread in riparian woodlands throughout our region, most residents are unaware of their existence. The glowing orange, black and white of the male's plumage blends remarkably well with the sunlit and shadowed upper-canopy summer foliage, where the bird spends much of its time. Finding the drab olive, gray and white female oriole is even more difficult, especially for predators. • Orioles build very elaborate hanging pouch nests, and a nest dangling in a bare tree in fall is sometimes the only evidence that the bird was ever there. • The Hooded Oriole *(I. cucullatus)* is an uncommon summer resident in riparian areas and thorn forests of southern Arizona and southern New Mexico. The male's orange crown is distinctive, but the female is very similar to the Bullock's Oriole in appearance.

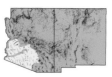

ID: *Male:* bright orange eyebrow, cheek, underparts, rump and outer tail feathers; black throat, eye line, cap, back and central tail feathers; large, white wing patch. *Female:* dusky yellow throat and upper breast; gray underparts; olive gray upperparts and tail; small, white wing patches.

Size: *L* 7–9 in; *W* 12 in.

Status: fairly common summer resident of lowland riparian areas throughout the region.

Habitat: deciduous riparian forests, willow shrublands and urban areas.

Nesting: high in a deciduous tree, suspended from a branch; hanging pouch nest is woven with fine plant fibers, hair and string and lined with horsehair, plant down, fur and moss; female incubates 4–5 grayish white eggs, scrawled with black markings, for 12–14 days.

Feeding: gleans shrubs and canopy vegetation for caterpillars, beetles, wasps and other invertebrates; also eats fruit and nectar; occasionally visits hummingbird feeders or feeders stocked with orange halves.

Voice: accented series of 6–8 whistled, rich and guttural notes.

Similar Species: *Hooded Oriole:* male lacks black cap and has smaller wing bars. *Western Tanager* (p. 139): yellow body plumage; no black cap or throat. *Summer Tanager* and *Hepatic Tanager* (p. 138): female has thicker, pale bill and no wing bars. *Baltimore Oriole:* rare; male lacks orange cheek and large, white wing patch.

Best Sites: *AZ:* Oak Creek Canyon; Patagonia Creek Preserve. *NM:* Bosque del Apache NWR; Percha Dam SP.

SCOTT'S ORIOLE
Icterus parisorum

Scott's Oriole was named after Winfield Scott, a major general of the U.S. Army, presidential nominee and mediator of many disputes and controversies in the 19th century. Scott had no interest in ornithology, but an admiring soldier who thought he had found a new species named it *Icterus scottii*, in honor of Scott. Because the ornithologist Bonaparte had previously assigned the species name *parisorum,* after the Paris brothers who collected the first specimens in Mexico, only the common name was kept. • This oriole spends its summers in the southwestern states, nesting near a water supply within stands of yucca, oak, sycamore or palm trees. Populations are slowly declining, but very little is known about this species, especially in relation to disturbances and habitat loss. • The name "oriole" comes from the Latin *aureolus,* meaning "golden"—most North American orioles are yellow or orange.

ID: yellow under-parts, undertail coverts and rump, with yellow leading into tail; 2 white wing bars; black tail; blue legs. *Male:* black head, back and breast. *Female and immature:* brown head and nape; female has dark throat.
Size: *L* 9 in; *W* 12½ in.
Status: fairly common summer resident of pinyon-juniper woodland statewide in both states.
Habitat: arid, open desert grasslands; semi-arid areas with yucca or Joshua trees; riparian woodland.

Nesting: within yucca, oak, Joshua tree or pinyon pine; female constructs hanging nest of yucca leaves; female incubates 24 darkly blotched, pale blue eggs for approximately 14 days.
Feeding: feeds on insects, fruit and berries; may be attracted to sugar-water feeders.
Voice: clear, fast whistle, with emphasis on the middle of the song.
Similar Species: *Hooded Oriole* and *Orchard Oriole* (rare): females have drabber upper-parts and yellow-green underparts; juvenile males have black throat and yellow head and nape.
Best Sites: *AZ:* Sycamore Creek (Sunflower); Cabeza Prieta NWR; Organ Pipe Cactus. *NM:* Carlsbad Caverns NP; Magdalena Mts.

GRAY-CROWNED ROSY-FINCH
Leucosticte tephrocotis

Three different forms of the rosy-finch are found in North America, but the Gray-crowned Rosy-Finch is the most abundant. It breeds on high elevation mountain slopes from Montana north to Alaska, likely breeding at higher elevations than any other North American bird. As winter approaches, this hardy pink and brown bird migrates southward to the lower mountains and foothills of the western United States, including the Sangre de Cristo Mountains of northern New Mexcio. It frequents feeders, especially during winter storms. During winter, rosy-finches roost at night in caves, tunnels, abandoned buildings, mine shafts and unused Cliff Swallow nests. • Two other rosy-finches also occur in the Sangre de Cristo Mountains. The Brown-capped Rosy-Finch *(L. australis)* may be a permanent resident, whereas the Black Rosy-Finch *(L. atrata)* is found only in winter. Both exhibit variable plumage.

breeding

ID: *Breeding:* dark, conical bill; black forehead and forecrown; conspicuous gray hindcrown; rosy shoulder, rump and belly; brown cheek, back, chin, throat and breast; short black legs; dark tail and flight feathers. *Nonbreeding:* yellow bill.
Size: *L* 5½–6½ in; *W* 13 in.
Habitat: shrubby lower elevation slopes, arid valleys, roadsides and townsites.
Status: *AZ:* extremely rare vagrant to the region. *NM:* rare to locally common winter visitor primarily to the Sangre de Cristo and San Juan Mts.

Nesting: does not nest in our region.
Feeding: Russian thistle, wild grass, mustard and sunflower. *Winter:* almost exclusively seeds.
Voice: song, rarely heard in our region, is long, goldfinchlike warble; calls are high, chirping notes and constant chattering.
Similar Species: *Brown-capped Rosy-Finch:* dark brown-black crown instead of gray. *Black Rosy-Finch* darker gray or black overall; less rosy on underparts. *Red Crossbill* and *Pine Grosbeak:* males are brighter red overall; black bill; no gray and black crown. *Cassin's Finch* and *House Finch* (p. 161): no gray and black crown; have reddish throat and breast; do not forage on or fly about summits or alpine snow.
Best Sites: *AZ:* none. *NM:* Sandia Crest House (Sandia Mts.).

HOUSE FINCH

Carpodacus mexicanus

Native to the western United States and Mexico, the House Finch was brought to eastern cities for the cage bird trade and sold as the "Hollywood Finch." When, in 1940, it became known that the House Finch was a protected species, some pet shop owners in New York City released their birds to avoid prosecution. From these few dozen birds, the population grew to exceed 10 million birds by the late 1990s, as the species colonized the entire eastern U.S. and extreme southern Canada! • The color of male House Finches varies from yellow to red, but females prefer the reddest-plumaged males. • The two species of *Carpodacus* finches found in our region look so similar that even experienced birders sometimes confuse them. In general, House Finches are bottomland birds seldom encountered in forested mountains, whereas Cassin's Finches (*C. cassinii*) live in the highest forests within the zone of heavy winter snowpack. Cassin's Finches are common summer residents in our northern, mountainous regions and irruptive winter residents elsewhere.

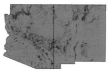

ID: streaked brown upperparts; 2 pale wing bars; whitish underparts with brown streaking. *Male:* brown crown; usually red (but may be orange or yellow) on forehead, throat and breast; reddish rump. *Female:* resembles male, but without red (or orange or yellow) areas.
Size: *L* 5–6 in; *W* 9½ in.
Status: *AZ:* common permanent resident in foothills and lowlands statewide. *NM:* common permanent resident in lowlands statewide.
Habitat: urban, suburban and agricultural areas.
Nesting: in a natural or artificial cavity or birdhouse; female builds a cup nest of twigs

and lines it with finer materials; female incubates 4–5 sparsely marked pale blue eggs for 12–14 days.
Feeding: gleans vegetation and the ground for seeds; also takes berries, buds and some flower parts; often visits feeders.
Voice: flight call is a sweet *cheer*, given singly or in a series; song is a bright, disjointed warble lasting about 3 seconds, often ending with a harsh *jeeer* or *wheer*.
Similar Species: *Cassin's Finch:* bright red cap; browner upperparts with distinct streaks; female has weak face pattern and narrow, crisp streaks on breast. *Red Crossbill* (p.): bill has crossed mandibles; male has more red overall and darker wings.
Best Sites: *AZ:* widespread in residential Phoenix and Tucson. *NM:* widespread in residential Albuquerque.

LESSER GOLDFINCH

Carduelis psaltria

Lesser Goldfinches are tiny, yellow and green birds found most often in pairs or small flocks. • Unlike the less common American Goldfinch, which is a winter resident, the Lesser Goldfinch occurs year-round in arid areas of our region. It occupies a variety of habitats near fresh water, including dry, brushy expanses, open oak woodlands and agricultural lands. • In early spring, Lesser Goldfinch pairs begin nesting in woodlands, savannas, forest edges and commonly in towns and cities. Family groups coalesce somewhat in fall and winter, concentrating in weedy thickets, untilled gardens, meadows and hillside seeps. They flock to a limited extent with other goldfinches and Pine Siskins.

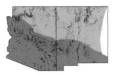

ID: lemon yellow underparts and undertail coverts; black wings and tail; small, stubby, black bill. *Male:* black cap and wings; white wing bars; white wing and tail patches. *Female:* greenish upperparts; pale, narrow wing bars.
Size: *L* 4–4½ in; *W* 8 in.
Status: common migrant and summer resident in both states. *AZ:* fairly common permanent resident below the Mogollon Rim. *NM:* uncommon winter resident in the south.
Habitat: inhabits a variety of semi-open habitats near water; most numerous in oak woodland, chaparral and suburban and rural edge habitats.
Nesting: saddled on the outer portion of a limb in a small tree or shrub; cup nest is woven with grass, plant fibers, bark strips,

moss and a few feathers; female incubates 4–5 pale bluish or bluish green eggs for 12–13 days.
Feeding: gleans ground and vegetation for seeds or insects; attracted to salt and mineral licks; readily visits birdbaths, garden hoses and feeders stocked with niger seed.
Voice: distinctive, breezy song of upslurred and downslurred *teeoo…tooee* notes; also chatters and mimics snatches of songs and calls from other species;
Similar Species: *American Goldfinch* (p. 163): white undertail coverts and rump; breeding male has black forehead and bright yellow body; nonbreeding male has olive brown back, yellow-tinged head and "shoulder" patches and gray underparts. *Pine Siskin* (p.): grayish olive overall with heavy streaking; yellow flashes in wings and tail.
Best Sites: *AZ:* Boyce Thompson Arboretum; Phoenix and Tucson. *NM:* Albuquerque; Rio Grande Nature Center; Bosque del Apache NWR.

AMERICAN GOLDFINCH

Carduelis tristis

The American Goldfinch is colloquially known as "Wild Canary" because of the male's bright plumage and musical song. It breeds in southern Canada and the northern two-thirds of the continental U.S., and it winters throughout the U.S. and northern Mexico. In Arizona, the American Goldfinch is an irruptive winter visitor, found throughout the state during most years. • American Goldfinches often remain in our region until late May or early June, by which time they have molted into their breeding plumage, and the males have begun singing. • The scientific name *tristis*, Latin for "sad," refers to the goldfinch's voice but seems a rather unfair choice for such a pleasing and playful bird • Although they also occur in natural habitats, American Goldfinches are common visitors to bird feeders that supply thistle or black niger seed.

ID: stocky body; bold wing bars. *Breeding male:* bright yellow body; black wings with white bars; black forehead and tail. *Breeding female:* resembles male but duller; no black cap. *Nonbreeding:* brownish or grayish upperparts; gray underparts; may show some pale yellow on head and breast.
Size: *L* 4½–5½ in; *W* 9 in.
Status: *AZ:* fairly common but sporadic migrant and winter visitor statewide.
NM: common migrant and winter visitor statewide.
Habitat: any weedy, shrubby or open woodland habitat, including suburbs.
Nesting: does not nest in Arizona or New Mexico.

Feeding: gleans ground and vegetation; feeds primarily on seeds but takes some fruit; commonly visits feeders that supply thistle seeds.
Voice: calls include *po-ta-to-chip* or *per-chic-or-ee* (often delivered in flight); song is a long, varied series of trills, twitters, warbles and hissing notes.
Similar Species: *Lesser Goldfinch* (p. 162): adult male has black cap, black back and larger white wing and tail patches; female has olive green upperparts and pale, narrow wing bars. *Evening Grosbeak:* much larger; massive bill; lacks black forehead.
Best Sites: *AZ:* Red Rock SP; Mt. Lemmon. *NM:* Albuquerque; Rio Grande Nature Center; Bosque del Apache NWR.

HOUSE SPARROW

Passer domesticus

A well-known resident of grocery store signs, fast-food parking lots and gas stations, the House Sparrow is a native of Europe and northern Africa. The House Sparrow was introduced to North America in the 1850s around Brooklyn, New York, as part of a plan to control the insects that were damaging grain and cereal crops. Contrary to popular opinion at the time, this sparrow's diet is largely vegetarian, so its effect on crop pests proved to be minimal. Since then, the House Sparrow has colonized most human-altered environments on the continent. It has benefited greatly from its close association with people. • This sparrow has been blamed for the decline of native cavity-nesting species such as Eastern Bluebirds, but its population has also been declining for decades. • House Sparrows belong to the large Old World family of sparrows (Passeridae), which are only distantly related to the family that contains the New World sparrows (Emberizidae).

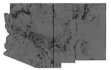

ID: stocky body. *Male:* gray crown; black bill, chin, throat and breast forms "bib"; chestnut nape; light gray cheek; white wing bar; dark, mottled upperparts; gray underparts. *Female:* plain gray-brown overall; buffy eyebrow; streaked upperparts.
Size: *L* 5½–6½ in; *W* 9½ in.
Status: widespread resident of cities, towns and urban areas in our region.
Habitat: usually restricted to areas around human habitation; does not flock with native sparrows.

Nesting: often communal; in a human-made structure, ornamental shrub or natural cavity; pair builds a large, dome-shaped nest of grass, twigs, plant fibers and litter and often lines it with feathers; pair incubates 4–6 whitish to greenish white eggs, dotted with gray and brown, for 10–13 days.
Feeding: gleans the ground and vegetation for seeds, insects and fruit; frequently visits feeders for seeds.
Voice: call is a short *chill-up;* song is a plain, familiar *cheep-cheep-cheep-cheep.*
Similar Species: unlikely to be confused with any other species; no native species shares nesting habitat.
Best Sites: widespread.

GLOSSARY

accipiter: a forest hawk (genus *Accipiter*), characterized by a long tail and short, rounded wings; feeds mostly on birds.

brood: *n.* a family of young from one hatching; *v.* to incubate the eggs.

brood parasite: a bird that lays its eggs in other birds' nests.

buteo: a high-soaring hawk (genus *Buteo*), characterized by broad wings and a short, wide tail; feeds mostly on small mammals and other land animals.

cere: a fleshy area at the base of the bill that contains the nostrils.

clutch: the number of eggs laid by the female at one time.

corvid: a member of the family Corvidae; includes crows, jays, magpies and ravens.

dabbling: a foraging technique used by some ducks, in which the head and neck are submerged but the body and tail remain on the water's surface; dabbling ducks can usually walk easily on land, can take off without running and have brightly colored speculums.

diurnal: most active during the day.

eclipse plumage: a cryptic plumage, similar to that of females, worn by some male ducks in fall when they molt their flight feathers and consequently are unable to fly.

endangered: a species that is facing extirpation or extinction in all or part of its range.

extirpated: a species that no longer exists in the wild in a particular region but occurs elsewhere.

flatwood: an ecoregion characterized by poorly drained, sandy soils, often with standing water during the rainy season; typical vegetation includes pines, saw palmetto, wax myrtle and wiregrasses.

flushing: when frightened birds explode into flight in response to a disturbance.

flycatching: a feeding behavior in which the bird leaves a perch, snatches an insect in mid-air and returns to the same perch; also known as "sallying" and "hawking."

gorget: a conspicuous area of the chin, throat and upper breast; is often iridescent.

irruption: a sporadic mass migration of birds into an unusual range.

lek: a place where males (especially grouse and similar species) gather to display for females in spring.

molt: the periodic shedding and regrowth of worn feathers (often twice a year).

polyandry: a mating strategy in which one female breeds with many males.

polygyny: a mating strategy in which one male breeds with many females.

precocial: a bird that is relatively well developed at hatching; precocial birds usually have open eyes, extensive down and are fairly mobile.

raptor: a carnivorous bird; includes eagles, hawks, falcons and owls.

riparian: habitat along rivers or streams.

speculum: a brightly colored patch on the wings of many dabbling ducks.

stoop: a steep dive through the air, usually performed by birds of prey while foraging or during courtship displays.

threatened: a species likely to become endangered in the near future in all or part of its range.

vagrant: a bird that has wandered outside of its normal migration range.

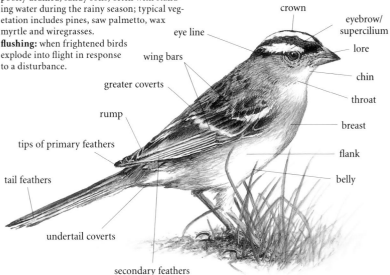

crown

eyebrow/supercilium

eye line

lore

wing bars

chin

throat

greater coverts

breast

rump

flank

tips of primary feathers

belly

tail feathers

undertail coverts

secondary feathers

CHECKLIST

The following checklist contains 564 species of birds that have been officially recorded in Arizona and/or New Mexico. Species are grouped by family and listed in taxonomic order in accordance with the A.O.U. *Check-list of North American Birds* (7th ed.) and its supplements.

The following categories are noted:

I = Introduced (6)
ex = extirpated (2)
en = endangered (2)
th = threatened (2)
AZ = only in Arizona (47)
NM = only in New Mexico (37)

Waterfowl (Anatidae)
- ❏ Black-bellied Whistling-Duck
- ❏ Fulvous Whistling-Duck
- ❏ Greater White-fronted Goose
- ❏ Snow Goose
- ❏ Ross's Goose
- ❏ Brant
- ❏ Cackling Goose (NM)
- ❏ Canada Goose
- ❏ Trumpeter Swan
- ❏ Tundra Swan
- ❏ Wood Duck
- ❏ Gadwall
- ❏ Eurasian Wigeon
- ❏ American Wigeon
- ❏ Mallard
- ❏ Blue-winged Teal
- ❏ Cinnamon Teal
- ❏ Northern Shoveler
- ❏ Northern Pintail
- ❏ Garganey
- ❏ Green-winged Teal
- ❏ Canvasback
- ❏ Redhead
- ❏ Ring-necked Duck
- ❏ Tufted Duck (AZ)
- ❏ Greater Scaup
- ❏ Lesser Scaup
- ❏ Harlequin Duck
- ❏ Surf Scoter
- ❏ White-winged Scoter
- ❏ Black Scoter
- ❏ Long-tailed Duck
- ❏ Bufflehead
- ❏ Common Goldeneye
- ❏ Barrow's Goldeneye
- ❏ Hooded Merganser
- ❏ Common Merganser
- ❏ Red-breasted Merganser
- ❏ Ruddy Duck

Grouse & Allies (Phasianidae)
- ❏ Chukar (AZ) (I)
- ❏ Ring-necked Pheasant (I)
- ❏ Gunnison Sage Grouse (NM) (ex)
- ❏ White-tailed Ptarmigan (NM)
- ❏ Dusky Grouse
- ❏ Sharp-tailed Grouse (NM) (ex)
- ❏ Lesser Prairie-Chicken (NM)
- ❏ Wild Turkey

Quails (Odontophoridae)
- ❏ Scaled Quail
- ❏ California Quail (AZ)
- ❏ Gambel's Quail
- ❏ Northern Bobwhite
- ❏ Montezuma Quail

Loons (Gaviidae)
- ❏ Red-throated Loon
- ❏ Pacific Loon
- ❏ Common Loon
- ❏ Yellow-billed Loon

Grebes (Podicipediae)
- ❏ Least Grebe (AZ)
- ❏ Pied-billed Grebe
- ❏ Horned Grebe
- ❏ Red-necked Grebe
- ❏ Eared Grebe
- ❏ Western Grebe
- ❏ Clark's Grebe

Albatrosses (Diomedeidae)
- ❏ Laysan Albatross (AZ)

Petrels & Shearwaters (Procellariidae)
- ❏ Sooty Shearwater (AZ)

Storm-Petrels (Hydrobatidae)
- ❏ Leach's Storm-Petrel (AZ)
- ❏ Black Storm-Petrel (AZ)
- ❏ Least Storm-Petrel

Tropicbirds (Phaethontidae)
- ❏ White-tailed Tropicbird (AZ)
- ❏ Red-billed Tropicbird (AZ)

Boobies & Gannets (Sulidae)
- ❏ Blue-footed Booby (AZ)
- ❏ Brown Booby (AZ)

Pelicans (Pelecanidae)
- ❏ American White Pelican
- ❏ Brown Pelican

Cormorants (Phalacrocoracidae)
- ❏ Neotropic Cormorant
- ❏ Double-crested Cormorant

Darters (Anhingidae)
- ❏ Anhinga

Frigatebirds (Fregatidae)
- ❏ Magnificent Frigatebird

Herons (Ardeidae)
- ❏ American Bittern
- ❏ Least Bittern
- ❏ Great Blue Heron
- ❏ Great Egret
- ❏ Snowy Egret
- ❏ Little Blue Heron
- ❏ Tricolored Heron
- ❏ Reddish Egret
- ❏ Cattle Egret
- ❏ Green Heron
- ❏ Black-crowned Night-Heron

❏ Yellow-crowned Night-Heron

Ibises (Threskiornithidae)
❏ White Ibis
❏ Glossy Ibis
❏ White-faced Ibis
❏ Roseate Spoonbill

Storks (Ciconiidae)
❏ Wood Stork

Vultures (Cathartidae)
❏ Black Vulture
❏ Turkey Vulture
❏ California Condor (AZ) (en)

Eagles, Kites & Hawks (Accipitridae)
❏ Osprey
❏ Swallow-tailed Kite
❏ White-tailed Kite
❏ Mississippi Kite
❏ Bald Eagle (th)
❏ Northern Harrier
❏ Sharp-shinned Hawk
❏ Cooper's Hawk
❏ Northern Goshawk
❏ Gray Hawk
❏ Common Black-Hawk
❏ Harris's Hawk
❏ Red-shouldered Hawk
❏ Broad-winged Hawk
❏ Short-tailed Hawk
❏ Swainson's Hawk
❏ White-tailed Hawk (AZ)
❏ Zone-tailed Hawk
❏ Red-tailed Hawk
❏ Ferruginous Hawk
❏ Rough-legged Hawk
❏ Golden Eagle

Falcons (Falconidae)
❏ Crested Caracara
❏ American Kestrel
❏ Merlin
❏ Aplomado Falcon
❏ Peregrine Falcon
❏ Prairie Falcon

Rails (Rallidae)
❏ Yellow Rail (NM)
❏ Black Rail (AZ)
❏ Clapper Rail (AZ)
❏ King Rail (NM)
❏ Virginia Rail
❏ Sora
❏ Purple Gallinule
❏ Common Moorhen
❏ American Coot

Cranes (Gruidae)
❏ Sandhill Crane
❏ Whooping Crane (NM) (en)

Plovers (Charadriidae)
❏ Black-bellied Plover
❏ American Golden-Plover
❏ Pacific Golden-Plover (AZ)
❏ Snowy Plover
❏ Semipalmated Plover
❏ Piping Plover (NM) (th)
❏ Killdeer
❏ Mountain Plover

Stilts & Avocets (Recurvirostridae)
❏ Black-necked Stilt
❏ American Avocet

Jacanas (Jacanidae)
❏ Northern Jacana (AZ)

Sandpipers (Scolopacidae)
❏ Greater Yellowlegs
❏ Lesser Yellowlegs
❏ Solitary Sandpiper
❏ Willet
❏ Wandering Tattler
❏ Spotted Sandpiper
❏ Upland Sandpiper
❏ Whimbrel
❏ Long-billed Curlew
❏ Hudsonian Godwit
❏ Marbled Godwit
❏ Ruddy Turnstone
❏ Red Knot
❏ Sanderling
❏ Semipalmated Sandpiper
❏ Western Sandpiper
❏ Little Stint (NM)
❏ Least Sandpiper
❏ White-rumped Sandpiper (NM)
❏ Baird's Sandpiper
❏ Pectoral Sandpiper
❏ Sharp-tailed Sandpiper
❏ Dunlin
❏ Curlew Sandpiper (NM)
❏ Stilt Sandpiper
❏ Buff-breasted Sandpiper
❏ Ruff
❏ Short-billed Dowitcher
❏ Long-billed Dowitcher
❏ Wilson's Snipe
❏ American Woodcock (NM)
❏ Wilson's Phalarope
❏ Red-necked Phalarope
❏ Red Phalarope

Jaegers, Gulls & Terns (Laridae)
❏ Pomarine Jaeger
❏ Parasitic Jaeger
❏ Long-tailed Jaeger
❏ Laughing Gull
❏ Franklin's Gull
❏ Little Gull (NM)
❏ Bonaparte's Gull
❏ Heermann's Gull
❏ Mew Gull
❏ Ring-billed Gull
❏ California Gull
❏ Herring Gull
❏ Thayer's Gull
❏ Lesser Black-backed Gull (NM)
❏ Yellow-footed Gull (AZ)
❏ Western Gull
❏ Glaucous-winged Gull
❏ Glaucous Gull
❏ Sabine's Gull
❏ Black-legged Kittiwake
❏ Gull-billed Tern (AZ)
❏ Caspian Tern
❏ Royal Tern (NM)
❏ Elegant Tern
❏ Common Tern
❏ Arctic Tern
❏ Forster's Tern
❏ Least Tern
❏ Black Tern
❏ Black Skimmer

Murrelets (Alcidae)
❏ Ancient Murrelet (NM)

Pigeons & Doves (Columbidae)
❏ Rock Pigeon (I)
❏ Band-tailed Pigeon
❏ Eurasian Collared-Dove (I)
❏ White-winged Dove
❏ Mourning Dove
❏ Inca Dove
❏ Common Ground-Dove
❏ Ruddy Ground-Dove

Parakeets (Psittacidae)
❏ Thick-billed Parrot (AZ)

Cuckoos & Anis (Cuculidae)
❏ Black-billed Cuckoo
❏ Yellow-billed Cuckoo
❏ Greater Roadrunner
❏ Groove-billed Ani

Barn Owls (Tytonidae)
❏ Barn Owl

Owls (Strigidae)
❏ Flammulated Owl

- ❏ Western Screech-Owl
- ❏ Eastern Screech-Owl (NM)
- ❏ Whiskered Screech-Owl
- ❏ Great Horned Owl
- ❏ Northern Pygmy-Owl
- ❏ Ferruginous Pygmy-Owl (AZ)
- ❏ Elf Owl
- ❏ Burrowing Owl
- ❏ Mottled Owl
- ❏ Spotted Owl
- ❏ Barred Owl (NM)
- ❏ Long-eared Owl
- ❏ Short-eared Owl
- ❏ Boreal Owl (NM)
- ❏ Northern Saw-whet Owl

Nightjars (Caprimulgidae)
- ❏ Lesser Nighthawk
- ❏ Common Nighthawk
- ❏ Common Poorwill
- ❏ Chuck-will's-widow (NM)
- ❏ Buff-collared Nightjar
- ❏ Whip-poor-will

Swifts (Apodidae)
- ❏ Black Swift
- ❏ Chimney Swift
- ❏ Vaux's Swift
- ❏ White-throated Swift

Hummingbirds (Trochilidae)
- ❏ Green Violet-ear (NM)
- ❏ Broad-billed Hummingbird
- ❏ White-eared Hummingbird
- ❏ Berylline Hummingbird
- ❏ Cinnamon Hummingbird
- ❏ Violet-crowned Hummingbird
- ❏ Blue-throated Hummingbird
- ❏ Magnificent Hummingbird
- ❏ Plain-capped Starthroat (AZ)
- ❏ Lucifer Hummingbird
- ❏ Ruby-throated Hummingbird (NM)
- ❏ Black-chinned Hummingbird
- ❏ Anna's Hummingbird
- ❏ Costa's Hummingbird
- ❏ Calliope Hummingbird
- ❏ Bumblebee Hummingbird (AZ)
- ❏ Broad-tailed Hummingbird

- ❏ Rufous Hummingbird
- ❏ Allen's Hummingbird

Trogons (Trogonidae)
- ❏ Elegant Trogon
- ❏ Eared Trogon (AZ)

Kingfishers (Alcedinidae)
- ❏ Belted Kingfisher
- ❏ Green Kingfisher (AZ)

Woodpeckers (Picidae)
- ❏ Lewis's Woodpecker
- ❏ Red-headed Woodpecker
- ❏ Acorn Woodpecker
- ❏ Gila Woodpecker
- ❏ Red-bellied Woodpecker (NM)
- ❏ Williamson's Sapsucker
- ❏ Yellow-bellied Sapsucker
- ❏ Red-naped Sapsucker
- ❏ Red-breasted Sapsucker (AZ)
- ❏ Ladder-backed Woodpecker
- ❏ Downy Woodpecker
- ❏ Hairy Woodpecker
- ❏ Arizona Woodpecker
- ❏ American Three-toed Woodpecker
- ❏ Northern Flicker
- ❏ Gilded Flicker (AZ)

Flycatchers (Tyrannidae)
- ❏ Northern Beardless-Tyrannulet
- ❏ Olive-sided Flycatcher
- ❏ Greater Pewee
- ❏ Western Wood-Pewee
- ❏ Eastern Wood-Pewee
- ❏ Yellow-bellied Flycatcher
- ❏ Acadian Flycatcher
- ❏ Willow Flycatcher
- ❏ Least Flycatcher
- ❏ Hammond's Flycatcher
- ❏ Gray Flycatcher
- ❏ Dusky Flycatcher
- ❏ Pacific-slope Flycatcher
- ❏ Cordilleran Flycatcher
- ❏ Buff-breasted Flycatcher
- ❏ Black Phoebe
- ❏ Eastern Phoebe
- ❏ Say's Phoebe
- ❏ Vermilion Flycatcher
- ❏ Dusky-capped Flycatcher
- ❏ Ash-throated Flycatcher
- ❏ Nutting's Flycatcher (AZ)
- ❏ Great Crested Flycatcher
- ❏ Brown-crested Flycatcher
- ❏ Great Kiskadee
- ❏ Sulphur-bellied Flycatcher

- ❏ Piratic Flycatcher (NM)
- ❏ Tropical Kingbird (AZ)
- ❏ Couch's Kingbird (NM)
- ❏ Cassin's Kingbird
- ❏ Thick-billed Kingbird
- ❏ Western Kingbird
- ❏ Eastern Kingbird
- ❏ Scissor-tailed Flycatcher

Becards (incertae sedis: family uncertain)
- ❏ Rose-throated Becard (AZ)

Shrikes (Laniidae)
- ❏ Loggerhead Shrike
- ❏ Northern Shrike

Vireos (Vireonidae)
- ❏ White-eyed Vireo
- ❏ Bell's Vireo
- ❏ Black-capped Vireo (NM)
- ❏ Gray Vireo
- ❏ Yellow-throated Vireo
- ❏ Plumbeous Vireo
- ❏ Cassin's Vireo
- ❏ Blue-headed Vireo
- ❏ Hutton's Vireo
- ❏ Warbling Vireo
- ❏ Philadelphia Vireo
- ❏ Red-eyed Vireo
- ❏ Yellow-green Vireo

Jays & Crows (Corvidae)
- ❏ Gray Jay
- ❏ Steller's Jay
- ❏ Blue Jay
- ❏ Western Scrub-Jay
- ❏ Mexican Jay
- ❏ Pinyon Jay
- ❏ Clark's Nutcracker
- ❏ Black-billed Magpie
- ❏ American Crow
- ❏ Chihuahuan Raven
- ❏ Common Raven

Larks (Alaudidae)
- ❏ Horned Lark

Swallows (Hirundinidae)
- ❏ Purple Martin
- ❏ Tree Swallow
- ❏ Violet-green Swallow
- ❏ Northern Rough-winged Swallow
- ❏ Bank Swallow
- ❏ Cliff Swallow
- ❏ Cave Swallow
- ❏ Barn Swallow

Chickadees & Titmice (Paridae)
- ❏ Black-capped Chickadee
- ❏ Mountain Chickadee

- ❏ Mexican Chickadee
- ❏ Bridled Titmouse
- ❏ Juniper Titmouse

Verdins (Remizidae)
- ❏ Verdin

Bushtits (Aegithalidae)
- ❏ Bushtit

Nuthatches (Sittidae)
- ❏ Red-breasted Nuthatch
- ❏ White-breasted Nuthatch
- ❏ Pygmy Nuthatch

Creepers (Certhiidae)
- ❏ Brown Creeper

Wrens (Troglodytidae)
- ❏ Cactus Wren
- ❏ Rock Wren
- ❏ Canyon Wren
- ❏ Carolina Wren
- ❏ Bewick's Wren
- ❏ House Wren
- ❏ Winter Wren
- ❏ Sedge Wren (NM)
- ❏ Marsh Wren

Dippers (Cinclidae)
- ❏ American Dipper

Kinglets (Regulidae)
- ❏ Golden-crowned Kinglet
- ❏ Ruby-crowned Kinglet

Gnatcatchers (Sylviidae)
- ❏ Blue-gray Gnatcatcher
- ❏ Black-tailed Gnatcatcher
- ❏ Black-capped Gnatcatcher (AZ)

Thrushes (Turdidae)
- ❏ Northern Wheatear (AZ)
- ❏ Eastern Bluebird
- ❏ Western Bluebird
- ❏ Mountain Bluebird
- ❏ Townsend's Solitaire
- ❏ Veery
- ❏ Gray-cheeked Thrush
- ❏ Swainson's Thrush
- ❏ Hermit Thrush
- ❏ Wood Thrush
- ❏ Clay-colored Robin (NM)
- ❏ White-throated Robin
- ❏ Rufous-backed Robin
- ❏ American Robin
- ❏ Varied Thrush
- ❏ Aztec Thrush (AZ)

Mockingbirds & Thrashers (Mimidae)
- ❏ Gray Catbird
- ❏ Northern Mockingbird
- ❏ Sage Thrasher
- ❏ Brown Thrasher

- ❏ Long-billed Thrasher (NM)
- ❏ Bendire's Thrasher
- ❏ Curve-billed Thrasher
- ❏ Crissal Thrasher
- ❏ Le Conte's Thrasher (AZ)
- ❏ Blue Mockingbird (AZ)

Starlings (Sturnidae)
- ❏ European Starling (I)

Pipits (Motacillidae)
- ❏ White Wagtail
- ❏ Red-throated Pipit (AZ)
- ❏ American Pipit
- ❏ Sprague's Pipit

Waxwings (Bombycillidae)
- ❏ Bohemian Waxwing
- ❏ Cedar Waxwing

Silky-Flycatchers (Ptilogonatidae)
- ❏ Phainopepla

Olive Warbler (Peucedramidae)
- ❏ Olive Warbler

Wood-Warblers (Parulidae)
- ❏ Blue-winged Warbler
- ❏ Golden-winged Warbler
- ❏ Tennessee Warbler
- ❏ Orange-crowned Warbler
- ❏ Nashville Warbler
- ❏ Virginia's Warbler
- ❏ Lucy's Warbler
- ❏ Northern Parula
- ❏ Tropical Parula (AZ)
- ❏ Yellow Warbler
- ❏ Chestnut-sided Warbler
- ❏ Magnolia Warbler
- ❏ Cape May Warbler
- ❏ Black-throated Blue Warbler (NM)
- ❏ Yellow-rumped Warbler
- ❏ Black-throated Gray Warbler
- ❏ Black-throated Green Warbler
- ❏ Townsend's Warbler
- ❏ Hermit Warbler
- ❏ Blackburnian Warbler
- ❏ Yellow-throated Warbler
- ❏ Grace's Warbler
- ❏ Pine Warbler
- ❏ Prairie Warbler
- ❏ Palm Warbler
- ❏ Bay-breasted Warbler
- ❏ Blackpoll Warbler
- ❏ Cerulean Warbler
- ❏ Black-and-white Warbler

- ❏ American Redstart
- ❏ Prothonotary Warbler
- ❏ Worm-eating Warbler
- ❏ Swainson's Warbler
- ❏ Ovenbird
- ❏ Northern Waterthrush
- ❏ Louisiana Waterthrush
- ❏ Kentucky Warbler
- ❏ Connecticut Warbler (AZ)
- ❏ Mourning Warbler
- ❏ MacGillivray's Warbler
- ❏ Common Yellowthroat
- ❏ Hooded Warbler
- ❏ Wilson's Warbler
- ❏ Canada Warbler
- ❏ Red-faced Warbler
- ❏ Painted Redstart
- ❏ Slate-throated Redstart
- ❏ Fan-tailed Warbler (AZ)
- ❏ Golden-crowned Warbler (NM)
- ❏ Rufous-capped Warbler (AZ)
- ❏ Yellow-breasted Chat

Tanagers (Traupidae)
- ❏ Hepatic Tanager
- ❏ Summer Tanager
- ❏ Scarlet Tanager
- ❏ Western Tanager
- ❏ Flame-colored Tanager (AZ)

Sparrows & Allies (Emberizidae)
- ❏ Green-tailed Towhee
- ❏ Spotted Towhee
- ❏ Eastern Towhee
- ❏ Canyon Towhee
- ❏ Abert's Towhee
- ❏ Rufous-winged Sparrow (AZ)
- ❏ Cassin's Sparrow
- ❏ Botteri's Sparrow
- ❏ Rufous-crowned Sparrow
- ❏ Five-striped Sparrow (AZ)
- ❏ American Tree Sparrow
- ❏ Chipping Sparrow
- ❏ Clay-colored Sparrow
- ❏ Brewer's Sparrow
- ❏ Field Sparrow
- ❏ Worthen's Sparrow (NM)
- ❏ Black-chinned Sparrow
- ❏ Vesper Sparrow
- ❏ Lark Sparrow
- ❏ Black-throated Sparrow
- ❏ Sage Sparrow
- ❏ Lark Bunting
- ❏ Savannah Sparrow
- ❏ Grasshopper Sparrow

Baird's Sparrow
Henslow's Sparrow (NM)
Le Conte's Sparrow
Nelson's Sharp-tailed
Sparrow (NM)
Fox Sparrow
Song Sparrow
Lincoln's Sparrow
Swamp Sparrow
White-throated Sparrow
Harris's Sparrow
White-crowned Sparrow
Golden-crowned Sparrow
Dark-eyed Junco
Yellow-eyed Junco
McCown's Longspur
Lapland Longspur
Smith's Longspur (AZ)
Chestnut-collared
Longspur
Snow Bunting

**Grosbeaks & Buntings
(Cardinalidae)**
Northern Cardinal
Pyrrhuloxia

Yellow Grosbeak
Rose-breasted Grosbeak
Black-headed Grosbeak
Blue Grosbeak
Lazuli Bunting
Indigo Bunting
Varied Bunting
Painted Bunting
Dickcissel

**Blackbirds & Orioles
(Icteridae)**
Bobolink
Red-winged Blackbird
Eastern Meadowlark
Western Meadowlark
Yellow-headed Blackbird
Rusty Blackbird
Brewer's Blackbird
Common Grackle
Great-tailed Grackle
Bronzed Cowbird
Brown-headed Cowbird
Black-vented Oriole (AZ)
Orchard Oriole
Hooded Oriole

Streak-backed Oriole
Bullock's Oriole
Baltimore Oriole
Scott's Oriole

Finches (Fringillidae)
Gray-crowned Rosy-Finch
Black Rosy-Finch
Brown-capped Rosy-Finch
(NM)
Pine Grosbeak
Purple Finch
Cassin's Finch
House Finch
Red Crossbill
White-winged Crossbill
(NM)
Pine Siskin
Lesser Goldfinch
Lawrence's Goldfinch
American Goldfinch
Evening Grosbeak

**Old World Sparrows
(Passeridae)**
House Sparrow (I)

SELECT REFERENCES

American Ornithologists' Union. 1998. *Check-list of North American Birds.* 7th ed. (and its supplements). American Ornithologists' Union, Washington, D.C.

Corman, T. & C. Wise-Gervais. 2005 *Arizona Breeding Bird Atlas.* University of New Mexico Press, Albuquerque, NM.

Ehrlich, P.R., D.S. Dobkin & D. Wheye. 1988. *The Birder's Handbook: A Field Guide to the Natural History of North American Birds.* Simon & Schuster Inc., New York.

Jones, J.O. 1990. *Where the Birds Are: A Guide to All 50 States and Canada.* William Morrow and Company, Inc., New York.

Kaufman, K. 2000. *Birds of North America.* Houghton Mifflin Co., New York.

Monson, G. & A.R. Phillips. 1981. *Annotated Checklist of the Birds of Arizona.* 2nd ed. University of Arizona Press, Tucson, AZ.

National Geographic Society. 2001. *Complete Birds of North America.* National Geographic Society, Washington, DC.

Parmeter, J., B. Neville & D. Emkalns. 2002. *New Mexico Bird Finding Guide.* 3rd ed. New Mexico Ornithological Society

Rosenberg, K.V., R. D. Ohmart, W. C. Hunter & B. W. Anderson. 1991. *Birds of the Lower Colorado River Valley.* University of Arizona Press, Tucson.

Sibley, D.A. 2000. *National Audubon Society: The Sibley Guide to Birds.* Alfred A. Knopf, New York.

Sibley, D.A. 2001. *National Audubon Society: The Sibley Guide to Bird Life and Behavior.*

INDEX OF SCIENTIFIC NAMES

This index references only the primary species accounts.

INDEX OF COMMON NAMES

Page numbers in **boldface** type refer to the primary, illustrated species accounts.

ABOUT THE AUTHORS

Cindy Radamaker

Raised in a small town in Trinity County, California, Cindy has had a lifelong fascination with birds, mammals and reptiles. As a volunteer bird walk leader for the Arizona State Park System, Cindy enjoys sharing her knowledge and identification skills with beginners and other interested birders. Cindy has co-authored a number of articles for birding journals with her husband, Kurt, and is a published bird photographer. She lives in Fountain Hills, Arizona, with her husband and three Kerry Blue Terriers, Merlin, Ani and Phoebe.

Kurt Radamaker

Kurt Radamaker has been interested in nature and especially birds his entire life. He grew up in Southern California where he began birding at the age of 8. At 15 he completed Cornell Laboratory of Ornithology's Seminars in Ornithology, and he went on his first Audubon Christmas Bird count at 16. His obsession with birding continued through the 1980s, and in the early 1990s he taught ornithology for the University of La Verne in southern California; while at the university he founded the *Euphonia*, a scientific journal of the birds of Mexico. As editor of the Euphonia, Kurt became captivated with Mexico and its birds and has been traveling there regularly ever since. In the mid-1990s he began regular research trips into Baja California, Mexico, and in the early part of the millennium much of his Baja California field notes were published in the ABA Monograph, *Birds of Baja California: Status, Distribution and Taxonomy*. In 2001, Kurt returned to Arizona where he is a founding member of the Arizona Field Ornithologists Society and member of the Arizona Bird Records Committee. Kurt and his wife, Cindy, regularly lead birding trips for Arizona State Parks and the Maricopa Audubon Society.

Gregory Kennedy

Gregory Kennedy has been an active naturalist since he was very young. He is the author of many books on natural history and has produced film and television shows on environmental and indigenous concerns in Southeast Asia, New Guinea, South and Central America, the High Arctic and elsewhere. He has also been involved in countless research projects around the world ranging from studies in the upper-canopy of tropical and temperate rainforests to deepwater marine investigations.